Student Companion to

James Fenimore
COOPER

Recent Titles in
Student Companions to Classic Writers

Student Companion to

James Fenimore COOPER

Craig White

Student Companions to Classic Writers

GREENWOOD PRESS
Westport, Connecticut • London

Library of Congress Cataloging-in-Publication Data

White, Craig, 1951–
   Student companion to James Fenimore Cooper / Craig White.
      p. cm.—(Student companions to classic writers, ISSN 1522–7979)
   Includes bibliographical references and index.
   ISBN 0–313–33413–7
   1. Cooper, James Fenimore, 1789–1851—Criticism and interpretation. 2. Cooper,
James Fenimore, 1789–1851—Examinations—Study guides. I. Title. II. Series.
   PS1438.W48   2006
   813'.2—dc22   2006015694

British Library Cataloguing in Publication Data is available.

Library of Congress Catalog Card Number: 2006015694
ISBN: 0–313–33413–7
ISSN: 1522–7979

First published in 2006

Greenwood Press, 88 Post Road West, Westport, CT 06881
An imprint of Greenwood Publishing Group, Inc.
www.greenwood.com

Printed in the United States of America

The paper used in this book complies with the
Permanent Paper Standard issued by the National
Information Standards Organization (Z39.48–1984).

10 9 8 7 6 5 4 3 2 1

For E. N. Feltskog,
Professor and Editor of Cooper

Contents

Series Foreword

This series has been designed to meet the needs of students and general readers for accessible literary criticism on the American and world writers most frequently studied and read in the secondary school, community college, and four-year college classrooms. Unlike other works of literary criticism that are written for the specialist and graduate student, or that feature a variety of reprinted scholarly essays on sometimes obscure aspects of the writer's work, the Student Companions to Classic Writers series is carefully crafted to examine each writer's major works fully and in a systematic way, at the level of the nonspecialist and general reader. The objective is to enable the reader to gain a deeper understanding of the work and to apply critical thinking skills to the act of reading. The proven format for the volumes in this series was developed by an advisory board of teachers and librarians for a successful series published by Greenwood Press, Critical Companions to Popular Contemporary Writers. Responding to their request for easy-to-use and yet challenging literary criticism for students and adult library patrons, Greenwood Press developed a systematic format that is not intimidating but helps the reader to develop the ability to analyze literature.

How does this work? Each volume in the Student Companions to Classic Writers series is written by a subject specialist, an academic who understands students' needs for basic and yet challenging examination of the writer's canon. Each volume begins with a biographical chapter, drawn from published sources, biographies, and autobiographies, that relates the writer's life to his or her work. The next chapter examines the writer's literary heritage, tracing the literary influences of other writers on that writer and explaining and discussing the literary genres into which the writer's work falls. Each of the following chapters examines a major work by the writer, those works most frequently read and studied by high school and college students. Depending on the writer's canon, generally between four and eight major works are examined, each in an individual chapter. The discussion of each work is organized into separate sections on plot development, character development, and major themes. Literary devices and style, narrative point of view, and historical setting are also discussed in turn if pertinent to the work. Each chapter concludes with an alternate critical perspective from which to read the work, such as a psychological or feminist criticism. The critical theory is defined briefly in easy, comprehensible language for the student. Looking at the literature from the point of view of a particular critical approach will help the reader to understand and apply critical theory to the act of reading and analyzing literature.

Of particular value in each volume is the bibliography, which includes a complete bibliography of the writer's works, a selected bibliography of biographical and critical works suitable for students, and lists of reviews of each work examined in the companion, both from the time the literature was originally published and from contemporary sources, all of which will be helpful to readers, teachers, and librarians who would like to consult additional sources.

As a source of literary criticism for the student or for the general reader, this series will help the reader to gain understanding of the writer's work and skill in critical reading.

Preface

If people today recognize the name of James Fenimore Cooper, most know him as the author of a famous novel, *The Last of the Mohicans*, whose title has graced a number of movies and become a slogan for our ever-changing culture. To call someone "the last of the Mohicans" is to honor him or her as a dying breed from an earlier, more heroic world. Such a changing of the guard is in fact one of Cooper's themes concerning the epic frontier between Native and modern America.

Cooper's frontier, that meeting ground of adventure and ideas, makes his writings a feast of entertainment and education. Cooper, born in the first year of the U.S. Constitution in 1789 and raised on the frontier of New York State, became the nation's first successful professional author and its first novelist to win an international readership. Across his long career he wrote thirty-two novels about people and nations at the crossroads of tradition and change. The images created by these novels continue to thrive in popular culture around the world and in studies of classic American literature.

People who know Cooper wrote *The Last of the Mohicans* might also know this book is one of a series of novels that form a monument in American and world literature known as "The Leather-Stocking Tales." This collective title comes from a remarkable character who appears in all five books. Called by various names, he is identified by his signature leg-wear of "leather stockings." In the first of these tales, *The Pioneers* of 1823, this character is also known by his English name, Natty Bumppo.

Three years later *The Last of the Mohicans* calls him "Hawk-eye," his Indian nickname. As an old man on new territory in *The Prairie* (1827), he is "the trapper." Then, after thirteen years during which Cooper worked on other projects, the Leather-stocking returns as the title character of *The Pathfinder* (1840) and *The Deerslayer* (1841).

This resourceful, sharp-shooting frontiersman became a prototype for other western heroes and a figure of world fiction comparable to Tarzan, Sherlock Holmes, or James Bond. But he is not the only enduring character from the Leather-Stocking Tales. Cooper also forged a persistant image of the American Indian as a "noble savage" by creating Leather-stocking's companion, the Delaware chief named Chingachgook or "Great Serpent."

"If anything from the pen of the writer of these romances is at all to outlive himself," Cooper wrote in a preface to a collection of the tales a year before he died, "it is, unquestionably, the series of *The Leather-Stocking Tales.*" Cooper's prediction has largely come true. A century and a half since his death in 1851, these volumes still stand on classics shelves in America's bookstores or in lists of required readings for high school and college literature courses. Therefore the *Student Companion to James Fenimore Cooper* features a chapter surveying the overall Leather-Stocking saga and a chapter on each tale.

Following this preface, two overview chapters describe the author's life and accomplishments. A subsequent chapter offers tips on reading Cooper. These chapters are followed by an introduction to Cooper's breakthrough book, *The Spy*, the first novel successfully to use American history—in this case, the American Revolution—as a dramatic backdrop for fictional adventures.

This *Companion's* coverage of *The Spy* and the Leather-Stocking Tales amounts to little more than a handful of Cooper's novels and makes little account of his dozen nonfiction books. Since other of Cooper's novels—such as his sea tales, his novels of European intrigue, or his Littlepage trilogy—are seldom assigned for classroom reading, they remain in the domain of specialized or advanced scholarship and so beyond the scope of this introductory study. The texts here selected are those most familiar to the reading public and most commonly assigned in high school and college courses.

NAMES AND DOCUMENTATION

A hallmark of Cooper's style is the many different names by which he refers to characters or peoples. Any comprehensive review must reflect this variety, yet simplify matters for readers who are less familiar with these texts and their conventions. The many names of Cooper's Leather-stocking character are listed above, and another host of nicknames accompanies Chingachgook. All these names are honored in appropriate contexts, but general references are to "Leather-stocking" or "the Leather-stocking" and "Chingachgook." Most critics now spell the first character's name as "Leatherstocking," and Cooper himself occasionally did so. My practice has been to retain the mechanics of hyphenation and capitalization that Cooper himself usually favored. Accordingly, the name of the series' main character is normally spelled as "Leather-stocking," while the collected novels are titled "The Leather-Stocking Tales." Quotations retain their original authors' preferred spelling.

For some brief quotations from Cooper's novels, I have silently simplified the author's punctuation and spelling, but nowhere do these minor changes alter a passage's intended diction or meaning. For instance, the Leather-stocking's dialectal versions of "ra'al" and "natur'" become "real" and "nature" where the original spellings, out of context, might breed confusion. Spellings of characters' names follow those of individual critical editions, which retain Cooper's own inconsistencies—e.g., "Hawk-eye" in *Mohicans*, "Hawkeye" in *Deerslayer*.

This study of Cooper's career, style, and tales does not exhaustively review its subjects' vast critical literature. A concluding bibliography directs students to specialized readings. Textual references to most primary and secondary sources use parenthetical documentation as authorized by the Modern Language Association, with one approved variation. Because so many editions of Cooper's novels are available, references to quotations from novels are made not to pages of a specific edition but instead to chapter, indicated parenthetically by "chap." and the chapter number. Page references are also omitted for brief primary and secondary sources such as Cooper's introductions, papers from the Cooper Society Web page, and widely reprinted texts such as Twain's and Lawrence's essays. This *Companion's* bibliography must substitute for a list of "Works Cited." Such an arrangement may require additional effort by readers in looking up works referenced in the text, but full citations are available to anyone armed with persistence and knowledge of chronological or alphabetical orders.

Acknowledgments

Thank you, dear Doris, Abbey, and Elizabeth White, with love to all our family.

Thanks also to the Literature faculty, the School of Human Sciences and Humanities, and Neumann Library at the University of Houston–Clear Lake, particularly William Boatman.

To my inspiring students in American Renaissance and American Romanticism, whose Web work made a link for my editor, Debra Adams (to whom also, thanks).

To the beautiful brainy baristas and congenial crackpot customers at Diedrich Coffee.

To Sam Hay, who late one night long ago said, "Cooper's worth reading."

And to the seminar in American Romance at the University of Wisconsin–Madison led by E. N. Feltskog, to whose honor this study is dedicated.

1

The Life of James Fenimore Cooper

Every summer, hundreds of thousands of Americans journey to the center of New York State in order to visit a small city known as Cooperstown. These visitors wear ball caps, wave pennants, play catch, and make a pilgrimage to the town's prime tourist destination, the Baseball Hall of Fame. There they celebrate America's national pastime–which, legend has it, was invented in Cooperstown in 1839 by Abner Doubleday.

In fact, the city's association with baseball—or even with Doubleday—is only a legend. But fiction can be as powerful as facts in a nation's culture, for which myths and legends become as real as history. For most Americans, "Cooperstown" means "baseball," one of America's unique contributions to the world.

But baseball isn't Cooperstown's only contribution to America's myths, history, and international image. This small city with its beautiful lake and mountains gave birth to other American heroes who lived on the frontier between fact and fiction—and who shaped the American image far more than sluggers or shortstops.

The key to these legends lies in the name of the city itself. Cooperstown was founded in 1786 by William Cooper, father of the novelist James Fenimore Cooper. The Coopers—elder and younger—became pioneering heroes of the early American nation in and beyond Cooperstown. The young Cooper's Leather-Stocking Tales created classic fictional heroes whose adventures often took place among lakes and mountains like those around Cooperstown. Descendants of these characters—from rugged and resourceful outdoorsmen to noble or savage American Indians—continue to appear in novels and films of early America and to influence Americans' ideas of themselves and the images they project to the world. William Cooper's founding of Cooperstown and his son's creation of a fictional world helped form an America constantly drawn between legend and fact, between past and future.

WILLIAM COOPER OF COOPERSTOWN IN FACT AND FICTION

The historic novels of James Fenimore Cooper constantly present this frontier vision of America. But before Cooper wrote it, he and his father lived it. The novelist's father, William, combined two heroic American myths in one outsized personality. He was a pioneer, and his rise from rags to riches embodied the American dream. Born to a poor farming family near Philadelphia in 1754, the elder Cooper's only advantages were natural qualities his more privileged son would inherit: a powerful physique, a robust personality, and a way with words. William Cooper's first step up the economic ladder was his 1774 marriage to an affluent farmer's daughter, Elizabeth Fenimore, whose maiden name would echo down generations of the Cooper family. Of more immediate financial value, Elizabeth's father bequeathed to the couple a large parcel of land in New Jersey, which his son-in-law used to start a career as a land developer.

After ten years devoted to establishing himself in Pennsylvania and New Jersey, William Cooper combined business success with the adventurousness of a pioneer by acquiring the title to a large tract of frontier land in New York State near Lake Otsego. For centuries this land had belonged to Iroquois Indians, but white traders, soldiers, and settlers decimated these peoples with disease, warfare, and environmental change. By 1786, when the elder Cooper acquired the Otsego patent, several European American communities had tried to settle the land that Cooper surveyed and named Cooperstown. In the 1780s and 1790s Cooper organized the town's stores and industries, financed land deeds for farmers moving west, moved his growing family to his newly built home (Manor House), and rose in wealth and influence, becoming known as "Judge Cooper."

Two classic texts retell the story of Judge Cooper and Cooperstown in greater detail. The first, reviewed in chapter six, is James Fenimore Cooper's first Leather-Stocking Tale, *The Pioneers* of 1823, in which Cooperstown becomes "Templeton." This uproarious, multicultural frontier town is governed—just barely—by "Judge Temple," who is modeled after Judge Cooper, while the novel's heroine, Elizabeth Temple, recalls the Cooper family's oldest daughter, Hannah. Though this historical novel is keyed to the Cooper family's personal history, it also represents the early history of North America. Judge Temple's industrious but wasteful settlers must come to terms with earlier claims to the land by frontiersmen and Indians, who are represented by the characters of the Leather-stocking and his Indian friend Chingachgook or "Indian John."

If *The Pioneers* is the classic historical novel of Cooperstown, its classic history text is *William Cooper's Town* by Alan Taylor, winner of the 1996 Pulitzer Prize. According to Taylor, William Cooper and his novelist son made history but also found themselves caught in its shifting currents. As a self-made man, Judge Cooper seized opportunity from the social upheaval of the American Revolution. Politically, though, he identified not with common people like himself—as Andrew Jackson would in the next generation—but instead with the old ruling order of colonial aristocrats known as Federalists. Such alliances profoundly influenced Judge Cooper's family and his son's literary career and outlook.

JAMES COOPER AND COOPERSTOWN GROW UP TOGETHER

Born as James Cooper on 15 September 1789 in Burlington, New Jersey, the future novelist was brought to Cooperstown as an infant. The youngest of William and Elizabeth Cooper's eleven children and also the longest-lived, James benefited from his father's wealth and power, and after the Cooper family fortune collapsed, he devised ways to adapt and prosper.

As a child, James Cooper—he did not adopt the middle name of Fenimore until he was thirty—enjoyed a life that was privileged in a way that few Americans might ever imagine and history may never reproduce. James and his brothers took pleasure in the outdoor life of a frontier town in one of North America's most scenic landscapes. Hannah, James's eldest sister, wrote of her brothers, "They are very wild and show plainly they have been bred in the woods" (Taylor 339).

Compared to the normal hardships and limits of the frontier, however, the Coopers enjoyed lives of power, leisure, and opportunity. William Cooper served as "first judge" for Otsego County and was elected U.S. Representative to the nation's capital, where he was invited to dine with President George Washington. One of his lawyers was the nation's first treasury secretary, Alexander Hamilton—the face on today's ten-dollar bill. The Coopers' princely income was derived from mortgages the judge arranged with settlers moving westward in the years after the Revolutionary War. As Judge Cooper wrote in 1807, "I have already settled more acres than any man in America. There are forty thousand souls now holding directly or indirectly under me" (Taylor 318).

In Cooperstown the judge planned a library, a fire company, and other civic institutions along the lines laid down by Benjamin Franklin in early Philadelphia. At the center of the settlement he erected a series of grand houses for his family, whose everyday needs were met by servants and slaves. (Slavery was not finally abolished in New York State until 1827.) The Cooper home was visited by traveling Federalist politicians, developers interested in Judge Cooper's practices, and foreign visitors like the French diplomat, the Duc de Talleyrand. Meanwhile, James Cooper and his brothers attended boarding schools with sons of the state's oldest families before attending Yale College.

This environment of fresh air, leisure, and learning provided many backgrounds and experiences from which the young James Cooper would develop his novels. His father's personal library offered access to books, and according to a family tradition he helped set type in Cooperstown's printing office (Taylor 339). Family members recalled Cooper's mother as a devoted reader of novels, a habit continued by her youngest son. Judge Cooper had little formal education, but his verbal gifts were impressive. He told stories, recited poems, wrote letters, checked out books from the public library, and late in life published an account of his settlement of Cooperstown titled *A Guide in the Wilderness* (1807).

The young James Cooper gave no sign, though, that he would grow up to be the United States' first major novelist. Before writing his first novel at the age of thirty, his daughter Susan recalled in her book *Small Family Memories*, he avoided even writing a letter (38). In 1804 he was expelled from Yale for fighting and using gunpowder to blow the door off a dorm room. Two years later he served on a merchant ship to England and joined the U.S. Navy as a midshipman intercepting smugglers on the Great Lakes. When Judge Cooper died in 1809, James resigned his Navy commission and, on New Year's Day 1811, married Susan De Lancey, daughter of a distinguished family in Westchester County, New York. In the 1810s Cooper and his siblings looked forward to raising families of their own in stately homes amid an atmosphere of tea parties, hunting, carriage rides, travel, reading, and good dinners, all financed by Judge Cooper's vast estate.

CHANGES OF FORTUNE: FAMILY DISASTER
AND A FRESH CAREER

But the decade following the death of Judge Cooper battered the Cooper family's dreams. A riding accident had earlier taken the life of Hannah, the judge's most promising and beloved child. By the 1820s, all of William and Elizabeth Cooper's remaining children except James and his sister Ann had died, "worn out," Taylor ventures, "by some combination of high living and financial stress" (393).

The Coopers' financial stress resulted from historical changes that the judge and his children found difficult to manage. The decline of the Federalist Party and the rise of a new party of "common men" deprived Judge Cooper of his offices and involved him in lawsuits. The terms of his will left each of the Cooper children approximately fifty thousand dollars' worth of land and the income it would produce. But prices for agricultural products became depressed, and new lands opened in the Ohio River Valley. As long as Judge Cooper lived, his personality and resourcefulness held his political network and his extended finances together. At his death, though, his children were readier to spend his fortune than to manage it. Their good life continued for a while, but by the 1820s James Cooper was the family's last surviving son, and, instead of high living, he was fleeing Cooperstown in order to dodge creditors for bad loans charged to his father's estate.

The collapse of the judge's personal and financial empire was a tragic outcome for the Cooper family, but without it the development of American literature would be very different, and baseball might be the only reason to remember Cooperstown. The transformation of James Cooper from a pampered young man into a distinguished novelist didn't happen overnight, but it started one night, according to a family story transcribed years later by James's daughter Susan Fenimore Cooper, herself an author:

> My Mother was . . . lying on the sofa, and [Father] was reading this newly imported [English] novel to her; . . . after a chapter or two he threw it aside, exclaiming, "*I could write you a better book than that myself!*" Our mother laughed at the idea, as the height of absurdity—he who disliked writing even a letter, that he should write a book!! He persisted in his declaration, however, and almost immediately wrote the first pages of a tale . . . After a few chapters were written he would have thrown it aside, but our dear Mother encouraged him to persevere; why not finish it, why not print it? (*Small Family Memories* 38)

The result—Cooper's first novel, *Precaution*—was minimally successful. Set in England, the novel is a pale imitation of a British "novel of manners" involving courtesy calls and matchmaking. Such novels were popular among the American leisured classes, who received most of their books from England. In fact, Susan wrote, "*Precaution* . . . was generally supposed to have been written in England, and by a lady." As with many writers, Cooper learned much about the author's craft by writing that first book. When *Precaution* appeared in 1820 he was already at work on his second novel, which would launch his literary career. *The Spy*, published in 1821 but set in the American Revolution, was immediately recognized as something new on the horizon: the first American historical novel.

Later chapters of this *Companion* explore the literary value of Cooper's works, but the practical impact of this second novel on his career and his family fortunes was immediate. As Susan Fenimore Cooper recalled, "*The Spy*, when it appeared, was brilliantly successful. Never before had an American book attained anything like the same success" (*Small Family Memories* 43). Reviews from British and American journals were enthusiastic, copies sold out, and readers looked forward to Cooper's next work. Simultaneous with the collapse of Judge Cooper's estate, James Cooper found a new income: his first royalty checks from *The Spy* arrived as he was on the brink of personal bankruptcy. On a grander scale, Cooper's auspicious start created a new literary scene both for himself and his young nation. In Judge Cooper's time, the founding fathers established the civic and economic institutions of the United States of America. Now James Cooper, born the year the U.S. Constitution was ratified and George Washington was sworn in as the first president, led a new generation that would develop a national literature. Cooper became, in the words of biographer Stephen Railton, "the founding father of American novels" (Railton, "James Fenimore Cooper" 78).

When *The Spy* was published, Cooper—who would die on the eve of his sixty-second birthday—was at his life's midway point in his early thirties. Altogether he would publish thirty-two novels, averaging nearly one a year across his career, in addition to more than a dozen book-length political tracts and travel writings. His output's quality had its ups and downs, as did his relations with the American public, but his industry and his ability to tell exciting stories made him the best-known American author of the 1800s, not only in America but in Europe. As the well-traveled American poet Longfellow recalled, "I was in no country of Europe where the name of Cooper was not familiarly known" (*Memorial* 32). If Judge William Cooper was the archetypal self-made man, James Cooper modeled another kind of American dream: the self-remade man.

A MAN OF LETTERS, AT HOME AND ABROAD

Starting with *The Spy*, the decade of the 1820s marked Cooper's greatest development as an author. In 1823 and 1824 he published two novels that would set the forms for his most lasting contributions to literature. *The Pioneers*, another popular and literary success, was the first of what would become the Leather-Stocking Tales. The next year appeared *The Pilot*, recognized as the world's first true sea novel and the first of several written by Cooper, including *The Red Rover* (1828) and *The Water-Witch* (1830).

The 1820s brought further changes to Cooper's public profile. With creditors to his father's estate continuing to hound him, James Cooper in 1826 tried legally to change his name to James Fenimore, ostensibly to honor his mother but also to evade liability for debts to the name of Cooper. The New York legislature permitted him to add Fenimore as his middle name, creating the composite name by which readers have known him since.

Also in 1826, Cooper moved his family to Europe, published his most famous novel, and began following his father's footsteps into politics. The Coopers spent the next seven years primarily in France but also in England and other countries, where they met European authors like Sir Walter Scott, whose historical novels partly inspired Cooper's work in that genre. He completed two more volumes in the Leather-Stocking series, including the best-known *Last of the Mohicans* (1826), followed by *The Prairie* (1827). He also became involved in French politics through his friendship with the Marquis de Lafayette, who had helped the American Revolution. Such involvement inspired him to write a trilogy of novels concerning European political intrigue, a number of travel books about Europe, and political commentaries on his native country, beginning with *Notions of the Americans* (1828).

His increasing commitment to political writing kept him in the public eye but increasingly distracted him from writing fiction. In 1833, when Cooper and family returned to New York, he wrote *A Letter to His Countrymen*, declaring an end to his career as a novelist. The following year he reacquired the family mansion in Cooperstown. Most of his subsequent writings of the 1830s were travel books, political commentaries, and a *History of the Navy of the United States of America* (1839). These books were generally well received, but Cooper's inability to stay out of public controversies began to cost him readers. Just as Judge Cooper's career was compromised by lawsuits, his son became involved in disputes with the people of Cooperstown over public use of Cooper's private land holdings, which led him to further embroilment in libel trials over journalistic coverage of the dispute.

In the late 1830s, however, Cooper returned to novel-writing and restaked his claim as the foremost American novelist when he resumed the Leather-Stocking Tales with *The Pathfinder* (1840), followed by the series' final volume, *The Deerslayer* (1841). In the last ten years of his life Cooper rarely left Cooperstown but wrote a total of sixteen full-length novels, including more historical novels, frontier romances, and sea tales.

Afflicted by poor circulation but comforted by his wife and children, Cooper died the day before his sixty-second birthday in 1851, followed within a year by Mrs. Cooper. Both are buried in Cooperstown's Christ Church Churchyard. In 1852 the author's friends, admirers, and fellow writers contributed letters and speeches testifying to his character and achievements, which were published as *Memorial of James Fenimore Cooper* (informally known the *Cooper Memorial* and now available on the James Fenimore Cooper Society Web page). In the 1850s the first of many collected editions of his novels began to appear, establishing for future generations the birth of the American novel and a monument to its unpredictable but honorable father.

WHAT SORT OF MAN WAS JAMES FENIMORE COOPER?

Generations of Americans and Europeans may feel as though they know James Fenimore Cooper from reading his books. But whom did people meet when Cooper the living man walked into a room? What sort of person could transform himself from James Cooper, carefree son of a rich politician, to Fenimore Cooper, "founding father of the American novel"? As with many historical figures, various observers saw different faces of a complex and dynamic personality.

The first impression that James Fenimore Cooper made on others was a product of the powerful physique, robust health, and commanding presence he inherited from his father. James made note of his father's "large stature," "fine, manly face," and "expressive, large blue eyes" (Taylor 16). In the *Cooper Memorial*, Washington Irving—author of *The Legend of Sleepy Hollow* and *Rip Van Winkle*—recalled the novelist similarly, as "a castle of a man" (*Memorial* 7). Cooper's physician likewise recalled the son's "manly figure, high, prominent brow, clear and fine gray eye, and royal bearing" as well as his "noble freshness" (*Memorial* 102, 97). A teacher at Yale recalled the future author as "a fine, sparkling, beautiful boy of alluring person and interesting manners" (340).

Blessed with good looks and health as well as by the judge's forthright model, James Cooper projected a bold, high spirit that might turn to insolence or rudeness. As a young man Cooper and his brothers appeared "bright but unreliable, charming but undisciplined," and a Presbyterian minister who instructed Cooper after his expulsion from Yale found that the future author "was rather wayward" and "disliked hard study" (Taylor, *William Cooper's Town* 339, 341).

A Web site publicizing modern-day Cooperstown introduces the man who would someday write the Leather-Stocking Tales as a "class cut-up and party animal" ("Cooperstown . . . America's Village"). Cooper never drank excessively, but this portrait gives a sense of the sociable but tactless personality his contemporaries observed. His personal doctor recollected Cooper's "independence of character" and "natural boldness of temper, which led him to a frank, emphatic, and intrepid utterance of his thoughts and sentiments" (*Memorial* 98). The early American poet William Cullen Bryant would remember "being somewhat startled [by] a certain emphatic frankness in his manner, which, however, I came at last to like and to admire" (*Memorial* 50). Likewise a Cooperstown friend found Cooper "solid, robust, athletic: in voice, manly; in manner, earnest, emphatic, almost dictatorial—with something of self-assertion, bordering on egotism. The first effect was unpleasant, indeed repulsive, but there shone through all this a heartiness, a frankness, which excited confidence, respect, and at last affection" (Taylor, *William Cooper's Town* 411).

These flip sides of Cooper's personality led to positive and negative outcomes. Cooper maintained lasting professional and social relations among people accustomed like himself to give and take with confidence. In New York City in the 1820s, for instance, Cooper formed a "Bread and Cheese" club whose luncheons included, according to his daughter Susan's account, "Officers of the Army and Navy, the prominent Clergy, Lawyers, Physicians, Merchants, etc." (*Small Family Memories* 49–50).

Yet this same bold, frank manner might appear as brusque and prickly. Judge Cooper had raised his sons to take their place among the nation's ruling class. Both father and son were quick to anger at any sign of disrespect, perhaps because of the judge's own humble origins. "If he was at times severe or caustic in his remarks on others, it was when excited by the exhibition of the little arts of little minds," wrote the painter and inventor Samuel F. B. Morse. "His own frank and open nature instinctively recoiled from contact with them" (*Memorial* 36). The poet Bryant remarked "a sensitiveness" on Cooper's part that was "far more acute than he was willing to acknowledge," which brought him "sometimes into friendly collision, and sometimes into graver disagreements and misunderstandings with his fellow-men" (*Memorial* 69). Cooper and his friends in high places kept faith with each other through his ups and downs. But his career would have benefited if his passions and labors had not been distracted by arguments with average people who may have been less interested in attacking Cooper than in protecting their own interests.

Writers, artists, and leaders often display complicated, hard-driving personalities, but few enjoy Cooper's loyal relations with their families. "Cooper, whom any controversy made unreasonable, could not always have been comfortable to live with," Railton writes, "but he was a kind husband, and a devoted father to the four daughters and one son he and Susan raised to adulthood" ("James Fenimore" 77). Few details are available regarding Susan De Lancey Cooper on her own, but she and James Cooper had a marriage of considerable respect and equality. After their marriage ceremony, "the bride and groom played a game of chess!" daughter Susan noted, adding, "From the first months of authorship to the last year of his life, my Father generally read what he wrote to my Mother" (*Small Family Memories* 27, 43).

Susan Fenimore Cooper's *Small Family Memories*, written in 1883, offers many anecdotes and glimpses of Mr. and Mrs. Cooper at home and at ease with their children. One ember of their domestic warmth glows from an anecdote concerning the family's home in Paris, where the "ground floor, and the first story were occupied by a ladies' boarding-school. The second story was our home, pleasant and comfortable, but not so grand. We were to be pupils in the school. . . . Our parents, wishing to be near us, rented the second story" (63–64).

WRITERS IN THE FAMILY

Born in 1813 and living until 1896, Susan Fenimore Cooper herself became a minor writer of merit. She published a novel, *Eleanor Wyllys*, in 1846, and later wrote prefaces for a collection of her father's novels. Her most famous and accomplished text is a book of nature writing on the Cooperstown area titled *Rural Hours*, originally published in 1850 but recently reissued by University of Georgia Press. In addition to writing and editing, Susan Fenimore Cooper directed and raised funds for an orphanage in Cooperstown.

The Cooper family's literary talent also declared itself in the career of another descendant, Constance Fenimore Woolson. The granddaughter of James Fenimore Cooper's surviving sister Ann, Woolson was born in 1840 and grew up primarily in Cleveland. Publishing widely in the literary magazines of the later nineteenth century, Woolson wrote numerous short stories and travel sketches set in the Great Lakes, the Reconstruction South, and Europe, where she died in 1894. Her works have received increasing critical attention from feminist scholars and literary historians, who also record her association with the American novelist Henry James.

COOPER'S RELIGION

One further note on Cooper's character concerns the role that religion played in his life—and, by extension, in his fiction. One major Cooper scholar, Donald Ringe, interprets the author's concern with Christian morality as a unifying theme throughout his career. The diverse voices that form a novel as well as the vast complexity of religion as a subject make it difficult to confirm this view conclusively. Considering, however, that the Romantic period in which Cooper wrote often questioned traditional religious beliefs, Cooper depicted religious characters in his fiction with careful respect. His novels persistently defend traditions of honor, faith, and values even as they honestly encounter and explore an ever-changing world.

Personally, too, religion for Cooper formed a consistent background that became an increasing priority as his life progressed. Both his parents were descended from Quaker stock but never belonged to a church—not an unusual situation for Americans in the period immediately following independence. For years the only established church in Cooperstown was Presbyterian. Cooper appeared indifferent to religion until marrying into the De Lancey family, who were committed Episcopalians. Thereafter Cooper consistently supported that church in various lay roles, and his religious commitment informed his family life. His daughter Susan recalled "no time, from my earliest childhood, when my dear Father did not say grace at table, and also he regularly read family prayers for us every evening" (*Small Family Memories* 66–67). Cooper's friend Charles Ingersoll, a congressman and historian, praised the late author as "unostentatiously devout" (*Memorial* 11). According to Railton, Cooper in 1848 "began actively, searchingly to read the Bible. All his life he had been a nominal Episcopalian. . . . But at the end of his life what had been a merely cultural Christianity was converted to a deeply personal piety" (1979; 90).

Judge Cooper and Cooperstown created a remarkable moment and opportunity in history, which an equally remarkable son met and enlarged in the next generation. Just as the country would find itself constantly looking forward to new possibilities and looking back to past certainties, so James Fenimore Cooper responded to change with the contradictory but compelling mix of optimism, resistance, and faith that is altogether American. His novels likewise depict a steadfast but changing American people on the frontiers of a new land, where the years and generations turn like pages on the binding of history.

2

Cooper's Career and Contributions to American and World Literature

A century and a half after his productive life, James Fenimore Cooper remains a monumental figure in American and world literature, but his reputation has undergone many changes. Cooper's status as the United States' first successful professional novelist, his pioneering development of American subjects, and his extension of literary Romanticism stand as indisputable facts. Beyond such honors, though, critics seldom rank Cooper with preeminent American novelists like Faulkner, Melville, James, Wharton, Hawthorne, and Morrison. American literature courses continue to assign *The Deerslayer* or *The Last of the Mohicans*, and bookstores stock copies of these novels, but coffee shops rarely buzz with chatter on the Leather-Stocking Tales. Cooper's "popular audience," writes biographer Stephen Railton, "has almost completely disappeared" (1979; 74).

Yet for readers who can get past commonplace opinions—or past the first pages of his novels—Cooper offers special rewards. His books combine the appeals of popular and literary fiction. Anyone who writes thirty-two novels produces a few flops, but for most of his career Cooper was a best-selling author who drew men and women readers alike. As in popular fiction of any period, boldly drawn characters follow their passion to exciting adventures in exotic locales. As in serious fiction, Cooper's characters explore complex choices and their consequences.

Cooper's development of the historical novel elevates his stories to profound significance as his characters act on the stage of the New

World's political and natural past. Historical fiction differs in validity from textbooks, travel, or museums. A reader feels how it might be to live and act in another time. The novel's color, conflict, and grandeur excite the emotions and imagination. Cooper manufactures adventures with a disarming honesty that confronts readers with important intellectual and ethical questions.

Cooper's prose has become too old-fashioned and tedious for wide popularity. Yet the substance and beauty of his works will continue to draw serious readers to discover how this novelist, at the beginnings of American fiction, faced urgent issues and forged familiar identities. Such qualities guarantee Cooper lasting status in studies of classic American and Western literature.

To assess Cooper's impact, this chapter surveys the author's career in two phases. An overview of Cooper's career reviews his innovative development of the novel both in America and internationally as well as his influence on other authors. The chapter then traces Cooper's persistence as a subject of criticism, teaching, and scholarship in the generations following his death. A subsequent chapter reviews the challenges and rewards of Cooper's style, offering tips for turning his difficulties to advantage. Here and elsewhere the emphasis will be on how Cooper developed the historical novel as a living text in which the American past models the interest, courage, and understanding necessary for managing the present and future.

BACKGROUNDS OF COOPER'S EMERGENCE AS FIRST MAJOR AMERICAN NOVELIST

A brief history of the novel deepens appreciation of Cooper's achievement as the first major American novelist. The novel's roots trace back to classical epics like *The Iliad* (seventh century B.C.E.). In the Renaissance, romances like Cervantes' *Don Quixote* (1605, 1615) cultivated an audience for picaresque adventures, chivalrous sentiments, and humorous satires. In the 1700s the novel appeared in a recognizably modern form with works like Defoe's *Robinson Crusoe* in England (1719) and Rousseau's *Nouveau Heloise* in France (1761). This new literary genre appeared in many languages and developed from diverse sources. As a phenomenon of popular culture, it rose simultaneously with modern European nations in which urban, literate, middle classes combined self-improvement with entertainment. The novel became a vehicle for depicting and discussing a nation's social character, its environment, and its values. Dickens's London, Austen's parlors, and the Brontës' moors now inform any reader's sense of England. Likewise the fictional picture of France created by Hugo's *Les Miserables*, Dumas's *Three*

Musketeers, and Flaubert's *Madame Bovary* is more enduring than any factual reality.

In light of the novel's significance for national identity, the United
States found itself in a confusing situation in the early 1800s. As today,
the new republic proclaimed itself a model for other nations to imitate, but
in the generation after its Revolutionary War the United States produced
no literary masterpieces to compare with those of Europe—with resulting
damage to the new republic's cultural prestige and international profile.
American "orators and newspaper scribblers endeavor to persuade their
supporters that they are the greatest . . . people upon earth," British critic
Sydney Smith observed in the influential *Edinburgh Review* in 1820. He
deflated such bluster by asking, "In the four quarters of the globe, who reads
an American book?" At this point in literary history, Smith's question was
answered only with embarrassed silence.

In fact, American authors had already written a number of novels, but
these books either failed to win readers or failed to appear distinctively
American. *The Power of Sympathy* by William Hill Brown of Boston,
generally credited as the first American novel, generated little fanfare in
1789, the year of Cooper's birth. Two "seduction novels" published shortly
afterward, Susanna Rowson's *Charlotte Temple* (1791) and Hannah Webster
Foster's *The Coquette* (1797), became bestsellers and are studied today as
examples of American women's early literary voice and status. Fictional
treatments of American cultural and historical scenarios appeared in
the generation before Cooper in *Modern Chivalry* (1792–1815) by Hugh
Henry Brackenridge and *The Algerine Captive* (1797) by Royal Tyler. The
most ambitious efforts were six novels between 1798 and 1801 by Charles
Brockden Brown of Philadelphia. Courses in the American novel may now
read Brown's *Wieland, Edgar Huntly*, or *Arthur Mervyn* for their anticipation of Cooper and Poe, but their meager sales led Brown to forsake literature for business and politics.

Given these mixed efforts, contemporary authors and later historians
surmised the United States was slow to grow a literature because of unique
conditions. Developing nations today disregard international copyrights
so that merchants may bootleg American-produced CDs and DVDs.
Comparably, the early United States flaunted European copyrights, with
the result that American publishers found it cheaper to pirate English
works than to cultivate homegrown talent. Further hindering expressions
of talent were cultural problems of a developing nation, such as unequal
education and the need for work instead of leisure. Nineteenth-century
writers also wondered if the new nation's plainspoken, business-oriented
lifestyle precluded development of literary subject matter. In 1828 Cooper

lamented that, compared to Europe, America offered "no annals for the historian; no follies . . . for the satirist; no manners for the dramatist; no obscure fictions for the writer of romance" (*Notions*). Likewise Hawthorne bemoaned "the difficulty of writing a romance about a country where there is no shadow, no antiquity, no mystery, . . . nor any thing but a common-place prosperity, in broad and simple daylight" (Preface to *Marble Faun*).

AN AMERICAN NOVEL: COOPER'S *THE SPY*

By the time Smith asked, "Who reads an American book?" in 1820, a new generation of authors was prepared to answer his question. In 1819 and 1820 "Rip Van Winkle" and "The Legend of Sleepy Hollow" appeared to great acclaim in the *Sketch Book* of New York writer Washington Irving. These instant classics, which adapted German folktales to the colonies of the Hudson River Valley, made Irving a celebrity in Europe and America. Yet the charm of these "sketches" did not provide the imaginative heft and cultural depth that readers anticipated from a full-length novel depicting large-scale events of American history.

That novel arrived the year after Smith asked his question, with the publication in 1821 of James Fenimore Cooper's *The Spy*, a novel rich in American subject matter that went through three editions in three months and met critical acclaim on both sides of the Atlantic. Cooper had already published *Precaution*, a novel of manners set in England, in 1820, for which he received few sales and reviews. As the following chapter details, *The Spy* retained the novel of manners' concern over proper behavior and expectations among social classes. But *The Spy* balanced mannerly indoor scenes in which moral issues are debated with manly outdoor scenes of military adventure, daring escape, and pursuit. Cooper set *The Spy* during the American Revolution, in whose heroic shadow Cooper's generation had grown up. The book's first thousand copies sold out in a month along with another six thousand copies in the first year. Cooper's royalties of four thousand dollars saved him from bankruptcy and opened the possibilities of an authorial career for him and other Americans.

The Spy launched Cooper's career and opened whole new fields of American literature. The Irish author Maria Edgeworth, whose *Castle Rackrent* (1800) is credited as the first historical novel, wrote that her family "read [*The Spy*] aloud," regarding it as "a work of great genius" and appreciating its "American value": "we found it highly interesting, from describing manners and a state of society that are new to us" ("Letter to 'an American Lady'" 67). *The North American Review* "thank[ed] our author for having demonstrated so entirely . . . that an admirable topic for the romantic historian has grown out of the American Revolution" and for "descriptions of natural scenery" that "contain nothing that is not American" (Gardiner 281, 277).

COOPER AS AMERICAN AND INTERNATIONAL NOVELIST

Forty-five years after the founding of the United States, James Fenimore Cooper founded a distinctly American literature on subjects unique to the New World. According to this scenario, Cooper's novels not only fulfilled the traditional association of the novel with a national image but also expressed a characteristic sense that the American nation has a special destiny. Cooper's novels often examine this attitude of "American exceptionalism," which originated with the early Puritans' idea of themselves as a chosen people and has manifested itself as recently as President Ronald Reagan's description of America as a "blessed land . . . set apart in a very special way." The generation of authors after Cooper—Emerson, Hawthorne, Melville, Whitman, Dickinson, and others—confirmed the arrival of a distinct literature of special American themes, characters, and dilemmas.

Cooper thus stands as a "founding father of American literature," but the facts of his career complicate and enrich this profile. American literature began, like the nation, in a transatlantic world, and Cooper's development and influence took place in an early global economy. European books flooded the American market; in turn, Cooper and other American writers became fixtures and influences for readers in Europe. Cooper's first novel, *Precaution*, imitated the English novel of manners. *The Spy*'s success as a historical novel was inconceivable without the precedent of the British writers Edgeworth or Sir Walter Scott, whose *Ivanhoe* was a bestseller in 1819. As soon as *The Spy* became a sensation, Cooper was referred to as "the American Scott," a nickname that indicates both his instant stature and how American literature was measured by European standards. Yet Cooper and American literature did not merely imitate such standards, but renewed and transformed them. In the decade to come Cooper would remodel the historical novel, and European writers would in turn imitate his success.

Cooper thus remains a founder of American literature, but too exclusive a commitment to this nationalist narrative disregards the larger international network of his career. Among the first facts of this transatlantic milieu is that, for much of the 1820s, Cooper lived in Europe, where he wrote several masterpieces that were immediately translated to European languages. Correspondingly, Cooper's sojourn in Europe saw his first political writings and alienation from his American audience. European audiences remained oblivious to the author's domestic squabbles, while continental critics first discerned his significance.

COOPER AND ROMANTICISM

For students of literature, the single theme that best explains Cooper's international significance is that this author became the foremost American exponent of Romanticism, the dominant literary movement of his era. Romanticism is such a sweeping concept that it eludes simple definition, but it revolutionized the artistic landscape of Cooper's time and continues to influence our time as well. Historically, Romanticism flourished from the late 1700s through the mid-1800s—approximately the span of Cooper's life—but its expressions remain affecting for modern audiences. Romantic art elevated expression of feeling over the classical order and restraint that characterized earlier periods. In Romantic music, the symphonies of Tchaikovsky and Beethoven and the melodies of Schubert and Chopin developed passionate new sensibilities. As a literary movement, Romanticism appeared first in Germany and later in France and England, where the term is associated with British poets such as Wordsworth, Byron, Shelley, and Keats.

Cooper repackaged Romantic themes, characters, and settings in American forms and sold them not only to his fellow Americans but also to Europe, where Romanticism originated. The main features of Romanticism, apart from its emphasis on emotion, included a heightened appreciation for wild nature as a source of feeling. Rousseau, for instance, promoted the idea of the "noble savage": in contrast to the compromises and deceits required by civilized society, a "savage" state permits individuals to live "nobly" according to their natural impulses. Such notions ironically seized the popular imagination just as increasing numbers of Europeans and Americans were moving from the countryside to cities. In these cities growing legions of literate, middle-class citizens became readers of Romantic literature that praised the rural world they or their parents willingly left behind.

The Spy in 1821 established Cooper's ability to write a novel featuring engaging fictional characters participating in familiar events from American history. In his next two novels, Cooper explored natural and historical settings whose Romantic appeal made his works popular and influential in his time and ours. With *The Pioneers* in 1823 and *The Pilot* in 1824, Cooper began two Romantic subgenres of the historical novel—the forest romance and the sea novel.

COOPER'S FOREST ROMANCES

The Pioneers is known today as the first of Cooper's Leather-Stocking Tales, but on a wider scale this novel started Cooper's reputation for writing "romances of the forest." In all, Cooper published eight novels set on the frontier between an ever-expanding western civilization and North America's original Indian inhabitants. Praised by critics for its bold new settings and characters, *The Pioneers* sold out in two days. Cooper's combination of imagination and sales inspired many imitators in the United States and Europe, as his frontier romances became prototypes for later western dime novels, dramas, and films.

The Pioneers developed an American context for Romantic themes and figures that the later Leather-Stocking Tales extended. Set on the New York frontier in a town resembling the author's native Cooperstown in the late 1700s, *Pioneers* traced a central Romantic conflict in the clash between America's settlement by European settlers and prior claims on the land by frontiersmen and Native Americans. Representing the earlier natural state were two Romantic figures who reappeared in other Leather-Stocking novels. The "noble savage" stereotype appears in Indian John, elsewhere identified as the Delaware chieftain Chingachgook, but here an old man torn between Indian traditions, Christian redemption, and alcohol.

A European American variant of the noble savage appears in Chingachgook's companion, who became the title figure of the Leather-Stocking series. An aging hunter struggling to hold his earlier, natural relation to the land, Natty Bumppo finds himself torn, like Chingachgook, between competing historical traditions. European chivalry, Christian religion, and his beloved rifle make claims on his loyalty. Rather than compromise with white civilization and its "wastey ways," the Leatherstocking is constantly drawn away from white settlements to a life closer to nature.

Later chapters of this *Student Companion* review the Leather-Stocking series as well as its individual novels. For American and world literature, these "romances of the forest" created a new historical novel with which Cooper enchanted readers and reshaped fiction. Previous authors had experimented with Romantic themes of untamed nature and heroic individuals in American settings, but Cooper synthesized a perfect bond between North American historical and natural backgrounds and the Romantic yearnings of modern lifestyles and psychology. For American readers the popularity of the Leather-stocking also capitalized on legendary frontiersmen like Daniel Boone, Davy Crockett, and Mike Fink as well as "captivity narratives" about white settlers held hostage by the

Indians. Cooper's forest romances electrified this preexisting audience and spawned a deluge of knockoffs about noble savages—white or red—who found themselves caught between two worlds.

COOPER'S FOREST ROMANCES: INFLUENCES, CRITICISM, AND IMITATORS

Most of the American works inspired by Cooper's forest romances amount only to potboilers from an earlier phase of mass media. The year after the success of *The Pioneers*, a sketch in the *Atlantic Magazine* finds an editor asking about the "pile of rubbish" on his publisher's desk. The publisher replies, "Imitations of Mr. Cooper's novels. . . . [A]ll these writers have thought they might be equally successful, with the help of the backwoods, an Indian, a panther and a squatter" (Dekker and McWilliams 1). Such adventures of white men befriending Indians or rescuing frontier damsels looked back to tales of chivalry from the Renaissance and forward to dime novels and movie westerns.

Other American novelists transplanted or challenged Cooper's character types in order to explore serious issues. As Cooper was nicknamed "the American Scott" after a British novelist, William Gilmore Simms of South Carolina became known as "the Cooper of the South" for *The Yemassee* (1835) and *Woodcraft* (1854), which depicted Indian warfare and frontier life in the Southern colonies. Dr. Robert Montgomery Bird defied Cooper's "noble savage" theme with *Nick of the Woods. . . . A Tale of Kentucky* (1837), which depicted Native Americans as "ignorant, violent, debased, brutal" and frontiersmen as deranged with lust for revenge (Penn Library Exhibitions). Much later, Texas author Larry McMurtry's Pulitzer Prize-winning novel *Lonesome Dove* (1985) offered another version of the vengeful Indian killer in the character of Blue Duck. Popular and critically praised films like *Little Big Man* (1970) and *Dances with Wolves* (1990) continue to explore and indulge the "noble savage" theme in a portrait of Native America that is largely fantasy but meets consumers' imaginative needs.

Given North American peoples' intimate association with such history and legends, the impact of Cooper's forest romances on American literature and popular culture cannot be surprising. Yet American readers may not suspect how deeply Cooper's wilderness adventures affected the homeland of Romantic literature in Europe. Cooper competed with Scott for popularity in England, and his works appeared in scores of translations and collections in Germany and France. Contemporary historian William Prescott observed that Cooper's "merits have been admitted. . . . all over

Europe, as every traveler knows who has seen the translations of Cooper in the different languages of the Continent, holding their place beside those of the great masters of English literature" (*Memorial* 31).

France has frequently been ahead of the times in honoring daring work by American authors like Poe and Faulkner. In 1827 Saint-Beuve described Cooper's Leather-stocking as a "mediator between the Indian and the white race, between the savage life and civilization [, who] possesses everything that is good in them both" (133–34). The novelist Balzac, praising Cooper's resumption of the Leather-Stocking series in 1840, wrote of "the great Cooper. The descriptions of the forest, the waters of the river, and the falls, the wily schemes of the savages. . . . [Y]ou hover, as it were, above that rich vegetation, your heart is all emotion" (197). Anticipating later criticism, George Sand praised Cooper for simultaneously admiring and mourning the European conquest of Native America: "the American let loose from his breast this conscience-stricken cry; 'In order to be what we are, we had to kill a great people and devastate a mighty land.' . . . [A] power acquired at the cost of suffering, murder and fraud, pierced [Cooper's] heart with a deep, philosophical remorse; and . . . floated like a psalm of death over the scattered and mutilated remains of the great families and the great forests of the vanquished land" (267–68).

Novels by French and German authors played surprising variations on Cooper's forest romances. "Cooper's novels," wrote historian Willard Thorp, "inspired a new genre of French fiction, the *roman d'aventure*" (168). Like Cooper drawing on American history to create *The Spy*, Balzac turned recent French history to fiction with the first novel in his Human Comedy series. The title of *Le Dernier Chouan* (1829) or "The Last Chouan" plays on *The Last of the Mohicans*. (Chouans were Royalist peasants during the French Revolution.) The most extraordinary transmutations of Cooper's themes to French life may have been Alexandre Dumas's *Les Mohicans de Paris* (1854) and Eugene Sue's *Mysteres de Paris* (1842–43). The "Mohicans" of the former novel are detectives who can trace footprints through a city as Cooper's Indians did through a forest. Sue's novel likewise transplants Cooper's hunters and savages to the Paris underworld and its ongoing wars between detectives and criminal "Apaches" (Thorp 163–64).

But no country embraced Cooper with greater fervor than Germany, the birthplace of Romanticism, whose artists recognized Cooper's exotic expression of familiar themes. The composer Schubert in his final illness read several of Cooper's works and asked his friends to send new titles. In the 1820s the aging Goethe raced through Cooper's romances. Noting, "I marvelled at the rich materials and his ingenious handling of them," Goethe incorporated materials from *The Pioneers* in his late

Novelle (Thorp 168). Beyond such elite validation, Cooper's novels were popular throughout Germany. The American journalist Charles Leland returned from that country speaking of "Cooper's great popularity among the people. . . . All his works . . . are household words to the German people. . . . Indeed, our Cooper . . . was by the general consent ranked among the greatest masters of romantic fiction produced in any country or age" (*Memorial* 39).

Cooper's prominence in Germany was favored by history, as his great works coincided with a wave of German immigration to the United States. "To those who were leaving Germany, Cooper's novels provided the picture of America which they wanted," wrote Thorp. "For those who remained behind, Cooper offered consolation and escape" (165). Several German immigrants produced their own westerns, but the most enduring German romances of the American frontier were written by an author who, until late in his life, never visited the United States. Karl May (1842–1912) wrote an enduringly popular four-novel series known as "The Winnetou Tetralogy" in which characters resembling Leather-stocking and Chingachgook reappeared as "Old Shatterhand," an American pioneer of German descent, and "Winnetou," an Apache noble savage referred to as the "roten Gentleman" or "Red Gentleman." As recently as the 1960s, six popular films based on May's characters starred an American actor who had played Tarzan, Lex Barker, as Old Shatterhand, and the French actor Pierre Brice as Winnetou. Through the mid-twentieth century German schoolchildren faithfully read May's novels, and every summer the Karl May Festival of the West in the resort town of Bad Segeberg draws tourists dressed as cowboys and Indians. As in a Passion Play based on fantasies of the American West, this festival features a pageant-like drama at the end of which Winnetou—still played by Brice into the 1990s—is betrayed and dies after converting to Christianity.

Later chapters analyze Cooper's Indians in greater depth. Broadly speaking, such blends of fact and fiction shift from the ridiculous to the sublime. In the blissful ignorance of popular culture, dramas of noble savages and scrupulous scouts enact rituals of innocence, guilt, and expiation that otherwise remain repressed. On the more sophisticated level of classic fiction, Cooper's profound expressions of such confrontations and conflicts help people come to terms with modern civilization, in which progress lays waste to preexisting orders whose virtues are recognized only in their passing. In the Golden Age of Russian literature, when that nation, like America, was modernizing and expanding, Cooper was widely read and imitated by authors including Tolstoy, Gogol, Chekhov, and Lermontov.

Repeatedly in their writings a Russian visitor to the outskirts of Asia feels sympathy and admiration for heroic but primitive tribal peoples who maintain traditional values that educated readers and writers feel in danger of losing.

Even now, reincarnations of Cooper's characters and themes continue on new frontiers. Owing to lags in translation, China encountered Cooper a century later than Europe, but this developing nation's expansion and modernization make Cooper increasingly significant not only for university literature courses but for new Chinese literature. Especially "since the mid-1990s," writes Cooper scholar Aiping Zhang, "after China announced its ambitious campaign to explore and develop its remote and mostly uncultivated western region, Cooper's name has been constantly mentioned in reports, essays, and stories related to . . . 'China's Westward Rush.' . . . Some Chinese stories and novels apparently contain many Cooperian characteristics not only in style, but also in perspective."

COOPER'S ROMANCES OF THE SEA

Cooper's forest romances remain his most influential contribution to American and world literature. But Cooper also launched another enduring literary tradition. In 1824, the year after *The Pioneers* initiated the Leather-Stocking Tales, Cooper published *The Pilot*, which fictionalized the exploits of John Paul Jones, the heroic naval commander of the American Revolution. With that novel and *The Red Rover* (1828), James Fenimore Cooper founded the genre of the modern sea novel. In American and world literature this tradition has produced such masterpieces as Herman Melville's *Moby-Dick* (1851) and Joseph Conrad's *Lord Jim* (1900), along with a parade of popular series, most recently the "Master and Commander" novels of Patrick O'Brian.

To claim that Cooper invented the modern sea novel in 1824 may invite disbelief, as seafaring was a motif in world literature since Homer's *Odyssey*, the Bible's Jonah, and the *Arabian Nights*' Sinbad the Sailor. In addition, earlier novels like *Robinson Crusoe* or Tobias Smollett's *Roderick Random* (1748) featured sea journeys, sea-based adventures, and stock characters like the sentimental old sailor. But those journeys, instead of being adventures in and of themselves, usually only moved characters from one land-based adventure to another. Descriptions of the sea resorted to predictable formulas of "mountainous waves" with "clouds rent asunder" (Philbrick, *American Sea Fiction* 40). In fact, Cooper's stated motivation for writing *The Pilot* rose from just such a novel, *The Pirate*, written in 1821 by his old model Sir Walter Scott, which presented itself as a romantic sea novel but betrayed a landlubber's pen.

Creating *The Pilot* and ten other sea novels, Cooper used his romantic imagination, his experience as a youngster in the American Navy, and his knowledge of a glorious period in naval history. This background informed Cooper's authority and boosted the sea novel's popularity in the United States and beyond. His *History of the Navy of the United States* (1839) served for decades as the standard history on this subject. His knowledge of ships and the sea services helped him vary previous formulas, making his "romances of the sea" realistic. Nineteenth-century readers proved enthusiastically receptive. Maritime commerce and exploration then enjoyed the same glamour as flight and aerospace today. The political geography of the United States in the 1820s and 1830s, just before the expansionist decades of manifest destiny, was primarily defined by its Atlantic coastline. American military glory emanated less from the Army than from victories by the Navy in the War of 1812. European readers remembered the climactic nautical battles of the Napoleonic Wars. During his career, Cooper's romances of the sea were as popular as those he set in the American wilderness (Philbrick *American Sea Fiction* 32, 46).

As with the Leather-Stocking Tales, Cooper's strongest contributions to the sea novel were his romantic characters and settings. Instead of minor stock characters, Cooper coined complex individuals who, facing the continual crises of wind and tide, might rise to heroism or fall to dishonor. Cooper's fictional portrait of the historic John Paul Jones in *The Pilot* is complemented by a homespun sailor named Long Tom Coffin— a Leather-stocking of the sea. *The Red Rover* caused a sensation with its dashing title character. The French Romantic composer Berlioz honored Cooper's death by renaming one of his overtures *Le Corsair Rouge*, the French title for *The Red Rover*. Cooper's word-paintings of the sea as a sublime force of romantic nature equaled his forest landscapes. As Conrad later wrote of Cooper's sea tales, "the sea inter-penetrates with life; it is in a subtle way a factor in the problem of existence, and, for all its greatness, it is always in touch with the men, who . . . traverse its immense solitudes" (288).

COOPER'S OTHER WRITINGS AND OVERALL IMPACT

Cooper's range of writings beyond this *Companion*'s purview varies enormously in subject matter and quality. Most of his great innovations appeared in the 1820s. In subsequent decades his political writing and public quarrels broke the congress that existed between his personal ambitions and his audience's desires. Yet he remained a purposeful and inventive writer, ever capable of developing new interests or extending earlier formulas. Various scholars promote the Venetian intrigues of *The Bravo* (1831), Cooper's novels about returning from Europe (*Homeward Bound* and *Home as Found* [1836]), or his historical novels of manners in the Littlepage Trilogy (1845–46). American cultural historians regard his nonfiction *Notions of the Americans* (1828) and *The American Democrat* (1838) as important contemporary analyses. Recent literary studies of travel writing have unearthed Cooper's *Gleanings in Europe*. But any wider readership for Cooper in the twenty-first century will likely maintain the attitude of the contemporary *New-England Magazine*: "We are always sorry to have Mr. Cooper leave the quarter-deck and the forests" (Dekker and McWilliams 18).

Beyond question, however, Cooper's career put American literature on the international stage and opened a way for later writers to succeed. At his death in 1851, his friends and supporters gathered for the "Cooper Memorial." "No public commemoration of an American author by his peers has been more impressive" (Dekker and McWilliams 26). By then the literature of the United States had entered the "American Renaissance." Hawthorne's *Scarlet Letter* appeared the year before; that same year Melville's *Moby-Dick* became a "great American novel" unimaginable without Cooper's sea tales as precedents; and the next year Harriet Beecher Stowe's *Uncle Tom's Cabin* extended Cooper's fusion of fiction and activism. Sentimental romances like Susan Warner's *The Wide, Wide World* (1850) and Susanna Cummins's *The Lamplighter* (1854) became bestsellers in an American market that Cooper initially expanded. Later in that decade, Henry David Thoreau's *Walden* recalled the spirit of nature in Cooper's forest romances, and Walt Whitman introduced innovations in poetry as American and internationally influential as Cooper's experiments in fiction. Like the Leather-stocking, James Fenimore Cooper proved himself a "Pathfinder" for later settlers and rebels of American literature.

THE AFTERLIFE OF COOPER'S CREATIONS: THE NINETEENTH CENTURY

In the century and a half since his death, Cooper's popularity has drifted and languished with the fashions of the day, but his unquestionable achievements endure as foundations. By the 1850s handsome bound collections of Cooper's works had become monuments to American literature and to the taste and prosperity of libraries in which they were shelved.

Soon, though, Cooper was demoted to the status of children's author on account of his outdoor adventures, familiar characters, and unobjectionable morality. Assigning such a status to Cooper may be confusing since his works are notorious for their difficulty, but he likely benefited from parents or nannies reading aloud.

A larger challenge to Cooper's reputation occurred with the change of literary style in the second half of the nineteenth century. In place of the sublime natural settings and larger-than-life characters that flourished in Romantic literature, urban settings and internal psychology began to appear in the writings of a new generation of American authors—Mark Twain, William Dean Howells, Edith Wharton, and Henry James, among others. Broadly classified as "Realism," this new style challenged Cooper's status as a model for American literature with Twain's satirical essay, "Fenimore Cooper's Literary Offenses" (1895).

"Fenimore Cooper's Literary Offenses" displays the skill of America's favorite comic writer. Twain lists selected "rules governing literary art," only to deflate Cooper's pretensions by demonstrating how *The Deerslayer* egregiously violates nearly all of them. Twain's punchy essay has become a standard fixture in American literature anthologies, which cannot indulge the windy Cooper. Consequently, readers who are familiar with Twain's humorous rejection of Cooper now outnumber those who actually read Cooper's novels. This situation poses a prickly problem for those who admire Cooper and promote his indispensability to any history of American literature.

Compounding the problem, many who *have* struggled through a Cooper novel have found in Twain a refreshingly direct, funny, and sympathetic voice, in contrast with Cooper's thick, tedious, and imprecise style. Especially when Twain rants that dialogue should "sound like human talk" and have "a discoverable purpose" and "be interesting to the reader, . . . and stop when the people cannot think of anything more to say," any reader of Cooper can remember wishing that Leather-stocking would shut up and hunt. But not to read Cooper on account of Twain's charges is to sacrifice one great author on the altar of another. The next chapter of this book, "Reading Cooper," reviews Twain's charges in the context of Cooper's trials and rewards. Some readers may find Cooper too much of a challenge, but any serious student of literature must be aware of Cooper's place in American literary history and the near-lethal role of Twain's essay in reducing that position. "Fenimore Cooper's Literary Offenses" may be less a fair indictment of Cooper's Romantic style than skillful literary propaganda for the Realistic style Twain wished to champion. This battle between two styles—the Realistic versus the Romantic—set a stage for debating Cooper's value to American literature.

COOPER'S CRITICAL HERITAGE IN THE TWENTIETH CENTURY

The debate over Cooper's success as a Romantic or his failure as a Realist took new forms in the early twentieth century. A fresh counterpoint to Twain's position was voiced by English novelist and poet D. H. Lawrence (1885–1930), whose own styles ranged from Realism to an adventurous Modernism. In 1923 Lawrence, then living in the southwestern United States, published *Studies in Classic American Literature,* a book of informal essays with a chapter titled "Fenimore Cooper's Leatherstocking Novels." Lawrence freely admits that a novel by Cooper is "not a realistic tale" but "a wish-fulfillment vision, a kind of yearning myth" involving the "most glamorous pictures in all literature" and "lovely half-lies."

Twain's and Lawrence's essays set parameters for twentieth-century studies of Cooper. As American literature grew as an area of scholarship, the novel was studied as a genre that expressed a distinctive American sensibility. Updating "romance," the term that early nineteenth-century writers had used for the novel, Richard Chase in *The American Novel and Its Tradition* (1957) declared that "most of the great American novels are romances" (xii). In contrast with "the English novel," which "renders reality closely and in comprehensive detail," the romance "encounter[s] . . . less resistance from reality" (2, 12, 13). With Brockden Brown, Fenimore Cooper stands as the source of this American tradition, establishing "nostalgia for the simple land and the simple life" and a "poetic quality of the novel we are calling 'romance'" (65). Other major studies in this field, notably Leslie Fiedler's *Love and Death in the American Novel* and Joel Porte's *The American Romance,* intensified focus on masculine outdoor romance as an expression of Freudian psychology and national "myth," for which Cooper was an original and influential exponent.

Such redemption of Cooper as a creator of national myths, identities, and models was opportune. Time eroded his popular audience, and scholarship and teaching influenced by New Criticism deemphasized the historical significance of literature in favor of its formal sophistication—an attitude that found little to celebrate in Cooper's bulky tomes. Cooper as a pioneer of American attitudes and expressions survived in American Studies, an interdisciplinary field in which literature interacts with other media or disciplines including history, art, and architecture. American Studies' early emphasis on myths and symbols, particularly those of western migration and the land, repeatedly drew scholars to examine the Leather-Stocking Tales as a record of national thought and narrative. Founding texts in this tradition include Henry Nash Smith's *Virgin Land: The American West as Symbol and Myth* (1950) and R. W. B. Lewis's *The American Adam* (1955). Revisions such as Richard Slotkin's *Regeneration through Violence: The Mythology of the American Frontier, 1600–1860* (1973) and Annette Kolodny's *The Lay of the Land: Metaphor as Experience and History in American Life and Letters* (1975) confirmed Cooper's Leather-Stocking Tales as durable expressions of the New World's natural and cultural history.

RECENT DEVELOPMENTS AND THE FUTURE OF COOPER STUDIES

Cooper's writings endured through the mid-twentieth century as a classic point of reference for American literature and American studies, but recent movements have again challenged his status. In the 1970s literature curricula began including previously excluded authors and texts representing viewpoints of women and people of color. However praiseworthy, such efforts affected Cooper's reputation negatively. Since a college semester has remained the same length, adding new texts and authors to reading lists often reduced the time available for Cooper's lengthy works. Perhaps more injuriously, the raising of consciousness that attended these changes often led to perceptions of Cooper's portraits of women, Indian, and black characters as stereotypical or patronizing.

Another late twentieth-century movement, New Historicism, balanced these trends in Cooper's favor. Like American Studies, New Historicism examined cultural and historical contexts. Informed by avant-garde studies in "textuality," however, this new movement also questioned the classical notion that literary works imitate reality, suggesting instead that texts both reflect and create history within larger networks of meaning. Such an attitude desensitizes some conflicts over race or gender that are incited by historical novelists like Cooper. In "No Apologies for the Iroquois: A New Way to Read the Leatherstocking Novels" (1985), Jane Tompkins grants that Cooper's novels are "peopled by storybook savages and cardboard heroes, and dotted with scalpings and hairsbreadth escapes" (95). Yet Cooper succeeds in depicting "the cultural categories" of "a social order" (118). "His characters are elements of thought," Tompkins concludes; "captures, rescues, and pursuits of the narrative, are . . . phases in a meditation on the bases of social life" (119).

New Historicism has inspired fresh research and assignments of Cooper's historical novels in courses that study literature as an expression of national ideologies, which Americans continue to express and uphold as a social order. Another historical development that strengthens Cooper's legacy is the ongoing project in the *Writings of James Fenimore Cooper*, begun by James F. Beard, Jr., with the State University of New York Press and continuing with AMS. The "Cooper Edition" has produced scholarly editions of nineteen of the author's fiction and nonfiction works, including all of the Leather-Stocking Tales.

Otherwise the forecast for Cooper's continued prominence is mixed. Cooper's popular stock rose slightly with the 1992 movie *The Last of the Mohicans*, which reduced the novel's action and characters to two hours of grisly violence and heart-throbbing pinups. Earlier Michael Cimino's memorable Vietnam film *The Deer Hunter* (1978) derived its title and its hunting ritual from *The Deerslayer*. The character of Hawkeye Pierce in the 1970s film and TV series M*A*S*H was named for Leather-stocking in *The Last of the Mohicans*—the only book that the later Hawkeye's father ever read.

The recent revival of evangelical Christianity may encourage new attention to the author's religious beliefs, as recommended by Donald Ringe, the dean of Cooper scholars. Given Cooper's eternally fresh vision of the American wilderness, another broad approach for reviving interest may be "ecocriticism," which correlates the "intertextuality" of recent literary theory with the interplay of human and natural ecologies. Following Tompkins's criticism above, Cooper's novels frustrate modern tastes for depth of character, but they construct complex models of cultural representatives interacting with local environments. Robert Daly has proposed that "ecocritical notions of . . . complex adaptive systems may afford us useful ways of reading Cooper."

For Cooper's texts to remain living forces in our own complex and changing culture, we must actually read them. This chapter has reviewed their impact on readers from that time until ours. Such critical and creative experiences begin only when someone opens the books. What nature of text awaits? And how may a reader respond? The next chapter offers an adventurer's guide through the tangled paths of Cooper's prose, across its wilderness of ideas, to its hard-won but sublime heights.

3

Reading Cooper: Problems of Style and Adventures in Ideas

If you've just started reading Cooper and feel like registering a complaint about his laborious style, his flat characters, or his makeshift plots, you'll find yourself at the end of a long line. That line began to form with Cooper's first reviewers, got rowdy with Twain, and has since strung through the halls of many schools. Yet this line for complaints has an inverse corollary. If some of Cooper's readership feels exasperated, some must find his works rewarding, as his books remain in print and on reading lists for new generations to gripe or glow over.

Appreciation of Cooper's unique achievements ultimately demands a less divisive approach than that of classifying his readers as detractors or admirers. From the time of *The Spy*, many of the same critics who scolded Cooper's imperfections also hailed his accomplishments. Even today, Cooper's most dedicated scholars roll their eyes at his excesses or eccentricities. Experience assures them, though, that Cooper's writing is always going somewhere, and that any passage that drags its feet will be offset by others where the action mounts and the meaning soars.

A single author inspires these diverse reactions—Cooper's detractors and admirers may be reacting to the same words. Mark Twain, writing of Cooper's *Deerslayer* in 1895, condemned it for having "the poorest English that exists in our language." A generation later, novelist D. H. Lawrence praised *Deerslayer* as "a gem of a book." Such incompatible responses should not be dismissed as subjective whims but as indexes of great literature's complex reality. In Cooper's case, an uneven style seems inseparable from his visionary achievement—"Lack one lacks both," in Walt Whitman's line. The wrestling between Cooper's language and vision dramatizes creative tensions inherent in his subject matter. The young American nation—much like today—struggled over the ideals and contradictions inherent in being "a nation of many nations."

Given this complexity, the pleasures of Cooper's ponderous novels amount to what sociology calls "deferred gratification." His rewards are not easy or immediate—they are *earned*. In the process they become more valuable and enduring. The downside is that the first impression Cooper's prose leaves on many readers is how hard it is to comprehend and enjoy.

The surest way to overcome Cooper's difficulties is to identify incentives for reading his novels. If readers grow interested in a story, they find ways to circumvent its challenges. Young readers of the Leather-Stocking Tales may rethink the standard emphasis on the series' title character. The aging and garrulous Leather-stocking of the first three tales is the last person young people would ever identify with. Though his significance cannot be underestimated, the earliest tales—*The Pioneers, The Last of the Mohicans*—use him more as a supporting or symbolic character than as a hero. Students might follow more youthful and sympathetic characters like Cora and Uncas in *Mohicans*. If Hawk-eye becomes a commentator rather than the center of attention, his annoyances dwindle to eccentricities. Engaging with non-Leather-stocking aspects of these novels can inspire a young reader to work through their resistant prose in the same spirit that Cooper's characters find their way through the wilderness.

COOPER AS HISTORICAL NOVELIST

Motivated readers will make their way through Cooper's novels, but coming to terms with the author's special challenges may increase the pleasure of the journey. Most of Cooper's works are historical novels in which fictional characters appear in situations or settings drawn from American or world history. Such historical situations may appear obscure, especially since Cooper wrote nearly two centuries ago. At that time the situations were already a part of the past—and are now that much further beyond living memory. Yet Cooper uses history not as a way to exclude the uninformed but as a launching point for enhancing his stories' appeal and significance. His characters share their awareness of the history in which they act and move. But precise details are less important than their sense that the world is shaped by the past, and their actions will similarly affect the future.

For instance, Cooper published the third Leather-Stocking Tale, *The Prairie*, while living in France in 1827, but the novel's action is set twenty-five years earlier in the North American territories recently acquired by the United States through the Louisiana Purchase. Since Cooper never visited the American West, he consulted reports and paintings by expeditions to gain a sense of what *The Prairie*'s characters would witness. Such uses of historical sources lend authenticity to what might otherwise have been a simple but forgettable adventure story.

The Prairie refers to the celebrated Lewis and Clark expedition across North America in the early 1800s, which would have coincided with the novel's fictional odyssey. This parallel between the novel and a familiar event enhances *The Prairie*'s significance as chronicle and prophecy. The values and decisions of the novel's characters resurfaced as the United States entered the expansive period of manifest destiny. Cooper embeds enough historical detail in the texture of his fiction that additional knowledge is not required for comprehending his basic plot or characters.

Students of history may regard Cooper's texts as supplementary sources for studying a period, but most readers find a comfort level simply by following the story on its own terms. Such a comfort level may not be as easily attained, however, with another historical aspect of Cooper's texts—their old-fashioned literary style. Cooper's novels were written prior to several stylistic revolutions that readers now take for granted. His style predates the straightforward realism established by Mark Twain and extended by Ernest Hemingway; the interior mentalities explored by Modernists like Henry James or Virginia Woolf; or the symbolism developed by William Faulkner or Toni Morrison. Complaining about what Cooper doesn't do is normal but accomplishes little. His words remain for new generations to redeem, still offering the same rewards as they did for his original readers— if not greater in the light of their historical validation.

COOPER'S ROMANTIC STYLE, JUDGED UNDER THE HARSH LIGHT OF REALISM

One approach for appreciating Cooper is to see his style as an artifact of the Romantic era in which it was written. As an author of Romantic adventure, Cooper never imagined his style would be judged by Realistic standards established later. Twain's satire, "Fenimore Cooper's Literary Offenses," did not appear until four decades after Cooper's death. This attack on Cooper may be read as a casebook against Romantic style and in favor of the later Twain's down-to-earth Realism. The "nineteen rules governing literary art" cited by Twain against Cooper stress values and principles of the later nineteenth century. For example, Twain insists that "personages in a tale . . . shall exhibit a sufficient excuse for being there" and "confine themselves to possibilities and let miracles alone."

Applied retroactively, Twain's "rules" would severely constrict Cooper's inventiveness and range. *The Last of the Mohicans* begins as the Munro sisters, on a journey to their father's military base, take a detour through the forest under the guidance of a shady Indian. Realism would preclude any such decision and direction. The sisters cannot, in Twain's words, provide "a sufficient excuse for being there." Likewise Hawk-eye, Chingachgook, and Uncas, crossing their paths, need not manufacture a realistic motive for helping them. Honor alone suffices. Under Twain's "rules," Cora and Alice would have stayed on the main road, and Hawk-eye and company would find no practical reason to intervene. Without these initial missteps and reactions, the novel's explorations of the tragic beauty of North American history could never begin.

Twain's condemnation of Cooper's "miracles" would also prohibit much of the action that enlivens the Leather-Stocking Tales. Twain particularly scorns the sharp-shooting feats that, beginning with the turkey shoot in *The Pioneers*, recur throughout the tales. In American action films and police dramas, gunplay serves as a dynamic for distinguishing good guys (who shoot quickly and accurately) from bad guys (who miss—or cheat). Marvelous marksmanship is only one way Cooper's novels stretch the limits of the possible. His characters often assume outlandish disguises, as when Hawk-eye and Chingachgook in *The Last of the Mohicans* disguise themselves as a bear and a beaver, duping friends and hostile Indians alike.

Incredible, yes, but such escapades are part of Cooper's Romantic style. In contrast to everyday reality, Cooper's plots and characters push the envelope of experience. Anything might happen, and part of the reading pleasure is to suspend disbelief and observe how convincingly Cooper contrives scenes that would sound ridiculous if someone told you about them second-hand (especially someone like Twain). If Cooper had anticipated Realistic standards, his fiction might not be remembered today.

Twain's primary justification for the attack was his mission to set Realistic standards for American fiction. "What Twain's critique does not tell us," Wayne Fields notes, "is how the writings of Cooper work on their own terms" (7). Besides, Twain's realism turned out not to be the final word in fiction's evolution. Subsequent generations became as restless with those "rules" as Twain was with the excesses of the Romantics. As Realism receded into history, authors and critics grew less willing to dismiss Cooper.

Reevaluations in the early twentieth century led to a new appreciation for Cooper's contributions to American literature.

COOPER'S CHARACTERS AS EPIC ARCHETYPES

Modernism, the next major literary movement after Realism, exposed new dimensions in Cooper's characters. Readers may miss the inner complexity of a human being, which germinated in Twain's *Huckleberry Finn* and flowered in Modern novelists like James, Woolf, and Hemingway. According to this method, fictional characters are made meaningful by inner conflicts with which readers sympathize or identify. Cooper's villains—Magua in *Mohicans*, Joel Strides in *Wyandotté*, or Old Tom Hutter in *Deerslayer*—sometimes manifest such conflicts. Overall, though, Cooper develops characters from the outside, according to their types or social positions. Carelessly executed, such characterization may appear stereotyped or politically incorrect, especially when applied to women or nonwhite peoples. Within this style's limits and especially within the determinants of history, Cooper usually plays fair by his characters and respects all choices but lust or dishonor.

D. H. Lawrence (1885–1930), author of Modernist masterpieces like *Sons and Lovers* (1913) and *Women in Love* (1920), did much to redeem Cooper's characters for later readers with his essay on the Leather-Stocking Tales in *Studies in Classic American Literature* (1923). Rejecting comparisons between Cooper's characters and everyday people, Lawrence admired their bold simplicity. About characters like Cora and Alice in *Mohicans*, "God knows what the women would really have looked like, for they fled through the wilds without soap, comb, or towel," Lawrence writes. "Yet at every moment they are elegant, perfect ladies." Cooper's characters are conventional, but by the same token they are unburdened by inner doubts or daily needs. Likewise for Lawrence, Cooper's Indians are "gentlemen through and through, though they may take an occasional scalp." The Leather-stocking "is a saint with a gun." This armed avenging angel is familiar in American westerns or war movies featuring John Wayne, Clint Eastwood, or Sylvester Stallone, for whom superior firepower confers moral authority.

Lawrence interprets Cooper's characters as *archetypes*—models or patterns that national myths revisit, repeat, and vary. Rethinking Cooper's characters in this way relieves the expectation they will undergo internal crises and changes like characters in modern novels. In fact, Lawrence locates these types not in the novel but the epic: the Leather-Stocking Tales "form a sort of American Odyssey, with Natty Bumppo for Odysseus."

Novel theorist M. M. Bakhtin explains this association's implications for characterization: "In the epic, characters are bounded, pre-formed, individualized by their various situations and destinies" (35). This approach shifts from regretting what Cooper is not doing to appreciating what he is doing. The Leather-stocking, for instance, always behaves honorably—only rarely does he acknowledge temptation, much less give in. Yet far from monotonous, this character's predictable behavior forces him to clash with the changing society that threatens to overwhelm him with new values.

Cooper's epic style of characterization made his novels a popular resource for twentieth-century literary and cultural criticism. For scholars in American Studies, Cooper's characters exemplified Americans' relations with each other and the land on which they meet. Analysis derived from the archetype theory of Swiss psychologist C. G. Jung informed investigations of myths and symbols in Cooper's novels and other early American art. More recently, the New Historicist critic Jane Tompkins has extended earlier explications of Cooper's characters as national or psychological types. Interpreting his "storybook savages and cardboard heroes" as parts in a complex cultural puzzle, Tompkins saw Cooper anew "as a profound thinker . . . obsessively preoccupied not with the subtle workings of individual consciousness, but with the way the social world is organized" (99).

The general verdict is that Cooper's characters do not invite close identification or sympathy but stand as titanic figures on a grand historical stage in a theater of the collective or national consciousness. For all their fixedness, Cooper's characters show some unique merits that distinguish them in the ranks of literary creation. For starters, his characters are memorable. While many readers may never wish for more of the Leather-stocking, they do not forget him. Students who complain of the Leather-stocking's behavior sometimes act as though he reminds them of a regrettable member of their family. Chingachgook casts such a long and deep shadow as the "noble savage" that it may be difficult to think that this character never actually existed in history.

READING COOPER FOR INTELLECTUAL PLEASURE

Cooper's characters matter, but differently from other famous fictional figures. The inability to identify closely or warmly creates an emotional distance that encourages cooler intellectual pleasures. One such pleasure is to see Cooper's characters as actors in history. What kind of history is created by these characters' interaction? The more one ponders this question, the less Cooper's historical novels resemble anything that ever really happened. Cooper constructs a puzzle or theorem to be acted out in the theater of the mind. The "use of stereotypes" enables Cooper to "move class representatives around as counters"—that is, as checker pieces or chessmen, Kay House writes in *Cooper's Americans* (1963). "The technique is most familiar to us from drama, and it may not be irrelevant that Cooper's lifelong avocations were playing chess and reading Shakespeare" (12). For Tompkins too Cooper's characters become "elements of thought, things to think with" that fulfill "the requirements of an abstract design" (119, 113).

Little wonder that Cooper's novels now survive in academic communities. Instead of becoming absorbed with characters who more or less resemble oneself, a reader meets characters who *cannot* be like him or her—and are thereby *more* interesting. Such a taste approximates the postmodern aesthetic of "defamiliarization," in which frustration challenges the imagination. While everyone else is undergoing some extreme makeover, Cooper's characters retain some original quality. As further incentive, Cooper's historical novels give a picture of an earlier social system centered around virtues like honor, responsibility, and social expectations. However eccentric or contrary his characters may appear, Cooper involves them in a world of larger forces and purposes.

Such rarefied admiration does not preclude a reader from regarding Cooper's characters as creatures worthy of compassion. Cooper rarely descends to crude or mean-spirited stereotypes. More positively, his fixed characters' moments of vulnerability grow more poignant. In *The Deerslayer,* Judith, a powerful beauty compromised by earlier sexual adventures, invites the young Leather-stocking to propose marriage to her. Destiny or honor condemns these intense misfits to lonely and dangerous lives. Yet Judith's brief humility, and Deerslayer's discreet denial, fill this moment with pathos far outweighing any willfully happy ending. These titans become momentarily human. Their feeling appears more authentic by its strange modesty, as when men almost (but do not) cry, or when women strain to withhold pity.

COOPER'S WOMEN CHARACTERS AND READERS

Judith's doom marks a simmering issue in Cooper studies: the status of women characters and, in turn, the author's status among women. Then as now, American literature depended on a market dominated by women readers. At his peak of popularity, Cooper may have been read by as many women as men. Readers of Cooper's anonymous first novel, *Precaution,* assumed it was written by a woman because it conformed to the novel of manners exemplified in works by Jane Austen. In Cooper's second novel, *The Spy*, attitudes toward the American Revolution are largely determined by the Wharton sisters, one of whom favors the British, the other "the Continentals." Other novels by Cooper feature strong young women. Elizabeth Temple in *The Pioneers*, Cora Munro in *Mohicans*, and Ellen Wade in *The Prairie* may have benefited from models in Cooper's life, including his sister Hannah, his wife Susan, and his daughter Susan Fenimore Cooper.

Two centuries later, though, Cooper's writings present as many deterrents as attractions to a woman reader. Women are "generally his poorest characters," House writes. "Cooper's world is definitely a man's world, and ... women are almost completely outside it" (14). By the end of Cooper's career this gap in his appeal was commonplace: "It has been said by some critics ... that he had no skill in drawing female characters," observed Cooper's contemporary, William Cullen Bryant (*Memorial* 56). James Russell Lowell rhymed in *A Fable for Critics* (1848) that "the women he draws from one model don't vary, / All sappy as maples and flat as a prairie." Cooper's interest in the manly frontiers of wilderness and ocean along with his various political causes may also have weakened feminine interest in his fiction.

Cooper's diminishing appeal to women readers may account for much of his decline in popular readership. Similar issues may affect his status in classrooms and scholarship. Women authors—in his time Maria Edgeworth and George Sand, in our time House and Tompkins—stand among Cooper's best critics. But men's names dominate bibliographies in Cooper scholarship and American Studies. The Cooper Society Web page features articles by women who defend the author's characterizations and promote the teaching of Cooper in introductory and advanced literature courses (Bower; Gaul; House, "Cooper's Females"). But feminist research first recovers neglected women authors before it redeems works by difficult men. Like Cooper's fiction in Leslie Fiedler's description, Cooper studies generally remain "an anti-Eden from which Eve has been banished."

COOPER'S SURFACE STYLE: IF HE WAS SO POPULAR, WHY ISN'T HE EASIER TO READ?

Cooper's writing is strongly marked by peculiarities of surface style. Few authors of Cooper's rank have attracted as much derision for clumsiness and carelessness, but equally few have succeeded in painting such large and indelible canvases. How are we to reconcile the two sides of James Fenimore Cooper, whom Fiedler calls "the Good Bad Writer?" (1979).

Cooper's prose, in balance with its immediate rewards, requires more labor than most readers are used to expending when turning pages and following a story. Many critics have glanced at the particular obstacles Cooper presents, but Twain alone attempted an exhaustive list. Cooper's failure to "employ a simple and straightforward style" conforms to Twain's "large rules" for literary realism. But Twain also echoes earlier criticisms of Cooper, especially his "slovenliness of form" and "surplusage" or wordiness. As far as "slovenliness," Twain targets Cooper's diction or word choice: Cooper should "use the right word, not its second cousin" and "say what he is proposing to say, not merely come near it." Edgar Allan Poe in an 1843 review of Cooper's *Wyandotté* likewise complained that Cooper's word choice was "*remarkably* and *especially* inaccurate" (215). As to wordiness, Twain wished Cooper's characters would "stop when [they] cannot think of anything more to say," and Poe laments that Cooper indulges "too much mere talk for talk's sake" (211). A similar complaint was registered in the 1840s by the novelist William Gilmore Simms, who credited Cooper with scenes of "great beauty and boldness" but questioned whether the rewards compensated for the work involved in reaching them: "We are astonished when we see them,—we wonder and admire,—but our feet have grown weary in the search for them,—we have had a long journey" (219).

No magic wand or pep talk can dispel the toil required to read Cooper. Poe wrote that Cooper's "sentences . . . are arranged with an awkwardness so remarkable as to be matter of absolute astonishment" (214). Yet another "astonishment" or puzzle remains: given the consensus against Cooper's style, how was he so popular? Biographical and historical backgrounds partly explain his foibles. Cooper's old-fashioned diction and wordiness may be attributed to Romanticism and other aspects of early nineteenth-century history. Nostalgia for earlier times encouraged archaic words and syntax. Cooper's language was already old-fashioned in its own time but valued for this very quality. Cooper's expansive descriptions may have found a model in the dramatic, spacious landscapes of the Hudson River School that then dominated North American painting. In fact, the master of the Hudson River School, Thomas Cole, painted a series of enormous canvases based on *The Last of the Mohicans*. Photography, which is now widely accepted as a direct and exact representation of the real world, was still mostly unknown. Romantic art did not seek the precision of a snapshot but the large impressions of a panorama. Like a large-scale painter, Cooper developed his subjects gradually, by dabs and degrees.

Earlier reading habits may have indulged Cooper's leisurely and inexact style. The fast-paced, clock-driven lifestyle of industrial cities was still new. Memories of country life may have bred patience with Cooper's slowly ripening plots and his careful observation of everyday details. The actual practice of reading may also have differed. Evidence suggests that readers in Cooper's time did not exclusively follow our model of reading silently by ourselves. A Cooper novel was frequently read aloud while others listened in a family or group setting. Such a situation might turn Cooper's faults to advantage. "Cooper writes in long, balanced, carefully constructed sentences, intended to be listened to, not just scanned in a hurry with the eye," writes Hugh McDougall, director of the Cooper Society ("Reading Cooper for Enjoyment"). When puzzling over one of Cooper's difficult sentences, one can resolve its meaning by reading it aloud. In families or groups, listeners might have asked the reader to retrace or paraphrase a passage that otherwise got by. Listeners could also simply wait for things to clear up, as Cooper repeats himself, and what is missed in one place often turns up later—or sometimes doesn't matter!

Cooper's work habits may also have contributed to his novels' "longeurs and ineptitudes" (Fiedler, "Good Bad Writer," par. 11). Thirty-two novels in thirty-two years testify to great productivity. Cooper's physician remarked on his "habits of methodical industry" and "astonishing readiness and skill in literary execution" (*Memorial* 95–96). The downside of this high rate of production is that Cooper rarely paused to edit or refine. E. N. Feltskog, editor of critical editions of Cooper's novels, once remarked how manuscripts Cooper sent his publishers generally appeared as initially drafted, with only an occasional word crossed out and replaced. Cooper's confidence and swiftness in composition might account for the sense in his large scenes of relentless forces of nature and the sweep of history, but such precipitance might also lead to careless errors and ill-considered improvisations. An early reviewer who praised *The Spy* for having "laid the foundations of American romance" concluded on a cautionary note. "We protest most seriously against modern rapidity of production"; Cooper's writing would meet "no harm if he were to read it over once" (Gardiner 66).

COOPER'S ROUGH GREATNESS: THE ADVENTURE OF IDEAS

Paying little attention to critics, Cooper plunged forward to new projects through which his faithful readers agreeably plowed. The historical outcomes are a heroic but uneven body of work and an author whose profile is an American archetype. Mary McCarthy classified this type in a 1947 review of a Eugene O'Neill play: "O'Neill belongs to that group of American authors, which includes [novelists James T.] Farrell and

[Theodore] Dreiser . . . ; none of these men possessed the slightest ear for the word, the sentence, the speech, the paragraph" (31). Cooper, Whitman, John Steinbeck, and Jose Antonio Villareal might be included in this class of authors, whose raw style delivers powerful ideas or innovations. "[T]hey drive an idea or a theme step by step to its brutal conclusion," McCarthy adds. "Their logical graceless works can find no reason for stopping, but go on and on, like elephants pacing in a zoo" (32).

A brilliant stylist like McCarthy has little patience for such plodding, but classing Cooper with these tedious fellow authors helps reconcile his unpolished style with his exemplary achievements. Authors like Cooper and those named by McCarthy do not evoke the fine harmonies of individual consciousness. Instead they orchestrate stormy symphonies that strike universal chords. One unexpected bonus is that these authors' work translates well. Ask non-English, nonexpert readers from overseas which American authors they have read. Rarely do they mention subtle crafters of language and consciousness like Emily Dickinson, Nathaniel Hawthorne, or Henry James, whose nuances may be lost in translation. Instead foreign readers often express familiarity with authors who write ungainly English but whose broad visions and candid feelings survive the journey to a new language intact. "All his excellences are translatable," Bryan wrote of Cooper's popularity in Europe. "[Those excellences] pass readily into languages the least allied . . . to that in which he wrote, and in them he touches the heart and kindles the imagination with the same power as in the original English" (71). Might some translations have improved on the original?

Considered in context with these other writers, Cooper's clumsiness signifies the scale of his ambition. His "graceless logical" style provided a vehicle for his young nation's conflicted idealism. Readers overcame its difficulties because, embodying America's heroic struggles, it satisfied their ideas about the past and the future that had grown from it. But readers also liked Cooper's books for a simpler reason: the universal pleasure in a story of adventure. Critics belittle Cooper's plotting for telegraphing intentions, for appearing improvised, for setting up a few great scenes with many dull ones, and for repetition. Most readers don't wince at such finer points but keep turning pages to see what happens next.

"[S]ome of the very defects of Cooper's novels [may] add . . . to their power over the mind," wrote Bryant. Their uneven quality, their monotony, even their unintelligibility are at some level more consistent with life's complexity and strangeness than the most exacting realism. Unlike a well-told story, an adventure happens always beyond one's expectations, at odd angles, with sudden action punctuated by long pauses, during which someone like the Leather-stocking talks too much. An appropriate metaphor, given Cooper's frequent subject of warfare, may be a military campaign, which soldiers have described as being "ninety percent boredom, ten percent terror." Bryant finds Cooper "long in getting at the interest of his narrative" but draws another metaphor from Cooper's invention of the sea novel. "The progress of the plot, at first, is like that of one of his own vessels of war, slowly, heavily, and even awkwardly working out of a harbour. We are impatient and weary, but when the vessel is once in the open sea, and feels the free breath of heaven in her full sheets, our delight and admiration is all the greater at the grace, the majesty and power with which she divides and bears down the waves, and pursues her course, at will, over the great waste of waters" (71–72).

For all their faults, Cooper's novels made a transition from popular bestsellers to critical masterpieces by combining the adventures that appeal to one sort of reader with the intellectual interests that appeal to another. A vital immediacy leads us to follow his characters through ambushes and obstacles to their destinies. These novels "interest us" Fiedler writes, as "'escapist trash' interests us. Like all such trash, they are, not accidentally but essentially, violent, melodramatic, sentimental" (Fiedler, *Good Bad Writer*, par. 2). Yet for all this instinctive delight, these adventures resonate memorably and morally. "For Cooper at his best," critic Marius Bewley observed, "an action is the intensified motion of life in which the spiritual and moral faculties of men are no less engaged than their physical selves" (73). Forthright characters and captivating narratives animate the pages of a best-selling author who is no longer popular. Historical and moral significance spring from a style that offends critics with its recklessness. The writing of James Fenimore Cooper cannot meet all demands at once, but it uniquely combines a zest for adventure with a love of ideas.

4

The Spy: A Tale of the Neutral Ground (1821)

James Fenimore Cooper is remembered for his five Leather-Stocking Tales, but he wrote twenty-seven other novels that also influenced American and world literature. His numerous romances of the sea, for instance—*The Pilot* (1823), *The Red Rover* (1827), and others—were once as popular as his romances of the forest, and founded the literary genre of the sea novel.

Cooper's works claimed many firsts in literary and cultural history, but none more than his second novel, *The Spy* of 1821.

- As the first bestseller and critical success by an American author on an American subject, *The Spy* proved that the United States offered compelling material for fiction and launched the American novel as an international phenomenon.
- *The Spy* was the first American historical novel in a period when such fiction, blending actual and imaginary characters in real historical contexts, served as a popular expression of national politics and identity.
- Coincidentally, *The Spy* is the first novel about the American Revolution.
- Cooper's *Spy* is also the first spy novel, founding a genre developed by later authors including Tom Clancy, John LeCarré, and Ian Fleming, creator of James Bond.
- Finally, *The Spy* was also the first American novel to be dramatized. As with contemporary bestsellers that quickly turn into movies, *The Spy* debuted on a New York City stage only weeks after the book's publication,

and American and French theaters staged adaptations throughout the nineteenth century.

Thanks to these firsts, Cooper's second book holds a special place in American literature. Yet Cooper's successful experiments in this novel set the stage for greater works to appear.

INSIDE *THE SPY*: ATTRACTIONS OF ITS OWN

These historic firsts make *The Spy* an automatic if underappreciated classic of American literature. Even better, the novel remains appealing on its own terms. Historical novels may not sound glamorous, but *The Spy* goes right to the top by ingeniously involving in its plot the "father of our country," General George Washington—later our first president. The plot involves Washington crossing British lines during the Revolutionary War to meet with the novel's dashingly deceptive title character. The genteel inhabitants of the home where Washington and his spy meet soon find themselves in the middle of Revolutionary War intrigues and battles that test this family's allegiances to nation, king, and each other.

In addition to this tense plot, readers of *The Spy* will find as many sources of pleasure as its original audience did two centuries ago, including:

- Characters galore—a houseful of spirited ladies and dashing officers, a countryside rife with outlaws and comic riffraff, and the towering figure of George Washington made human.

- The mysterious figure of the spy himself, a prototype of Leather-stocking who moves between the upper classes and the riffraff, and between civilization and the wild.

- A fascinating mix between the action of a historical novel and the family and courtship issues of the novel of manners.

- A stark but fascinating setting—only a generation after the American Revolution, Cooper draws a realistic, compelling portrait of the American land in time of war.

- For devoted readers of the Leather-Stocking Tales, a fresh, early take on those books' dependable themes and values of patriotism, class, honor, authority, tradition, and change, as well as their shifting appearances.

Altogether *The Spy* announces a young writer coming into his powers and anticipates the glories of Cooper's coming masterpieces.

High school and undergraduate college courses assign *The Spy* only occasionally. The book more often appears in courses on special subjects like

"History of Spy Fiction," in surveys of early American fiction, or seminars devoted to Cooper's writings in addition to the Leather-Stocking Tales. Because of the advanced nature of such courses, this chapter does not use the standard chapter headings for settings, themes, and characters used elsewhere in this *Companion* but instead highlights *The Spy*'s unique features for American literary history, Cooper's career, and studies of genre.

THE SPY AS FOUNDING TEXT AND LIFESAVER FOR COOPER'S CAREER

The Spy's success came at a critical time for Cooper—and for American literature. Hard-pressed by the collapse of his father's fortune, Cooper was straining to maintain the style of a country gentleman while living on his wife's family's estate in New York State. Testing authorship as a source of income, he wrote *Precaution*, a novel of manners set in England and involving a society of inherited wealth, genteel parties, and engineered marriages like the one in which he grew up. Published anonymously in 1820, *Precaution* received respectful notices and, in England, a number of reprints, but its formal atmosphere and conventional plot limited the historical depth, innovative characters, and impassioned landscapes that distinguish Cooper's best work. *Precaution* did nothing to prevent a British critic from asking the next year, "Who reads an American book?"

The Spy soon refuted that question by selling prodigiously and receiving enthusiastic reviews in the American and English press. But how did Cooper's second novel achieve its breakthrough status as the first major American novel? And what is its interest for students of literature today? One broad answer is that *The Spy*, early in the development of the novel, fuses the historical novel, the novel of manners, and the spy novel with intensely American subject matter. This fusion achieves a surprising union of historical subject and literary achievement. Telling a story of the American nation's birth, *The Spy* gives birth to the American novel—and to the career of the United States' first major professional novelist.

Remarkable coincidences behind *The Spy*'s composition magnify its historical resonance. Cooper wrote *The Spy* while living in the area where it is set and where his wife's uncles and cousins had participated in Revolutionary War battles. Cooper received the idea for the novel's central character through an anecdote told him firsthand by one of the nation's Founding Fathers. The resulting work marks an early yet fruitful stage in Cooper's career-long exploration of ideas in action. *The Spy* has all the qualities that made Cooper's Leather-Stocking Tales popular as adventure stories: wilderness journeys, dangerous pursuits, hairbreadth escapes. Yet

The Spy also contains serious dialogues on family duty, military honor, and civic responsibility in a Revolutionary society.

Accounting for *The Spy*'s runaway success, Cooper in 1831 gave credit to his American audience's "love of country" and his book's expression of a "real patriotism" that "has the beauty of self-elevation, without the alloy of personal interest" (preface). Such attributes appear splendidly in the characters of the spy, Harvey Birch, and his "control," General George Washington, and in other characters like Frances Wharton the ingenue and Captain Lawton, an American officer from the South. According to Cooper scholar George Dekker, reviewers praised Cooper's novel for depicting "a unified front of New York and Virginian military forces against the common British enemy" and "how the historical romance could help overcome regional misunderstandings and jealousies" (24).

AN AMERICAN HISTORICAL NOVEL: MORE THAN PATRIOTISM

Patriotism alone cannot account for *The Spy*'s interest. Cooper shows Americans working out the claims of patriotism relative to "personal interest[s]" of reputation, family duty, or material wealth. "If Cooper intended his 'patriotic' novel to justify the American Revolution," John P. McWilliams observes, "*The Spy* can only be considered a fascinating contradiction." Instead of "oppressive redcoats" versus "simple, decent republicans," the "British troops [are] never villainized," while "native forces" commit "nearly every act of violence" (1972; 49). The worst of these are the pro-American "Skinners," who maintain a "semblance of patriotism" but are in fact "gangs of marauders" (chap. 10). *The Spy,* in contrast to Hollywood revenge-fests like Mel Gibson's *The Patriot* (2000), shows individuals and families not just choosing the right side but remaining open to the possibilities of history, learning something about themselves and the nation they form.

Rather than simplifying the past, Cooper conveys an energetic sense of history in motion. *The Spy* opens in the style of historical novels then popular in Europe, adapted to the new American nation. In "the year 1780"—a critical moment in "the war of the Revolution"—a man of noble bearing rides his horse through the same Westchester County where Cooper was living as he wrote *The Spy* (chap. 1). The novel's subtitle, *A Tale of the Neutral Ground*, refers to this historical setting. Now a fashionable residential area, Westchester County in the Revolution was a "neutral ground" or "no-man's-land" between New York City—held by "Tories" faithful to England—and the Highlands of the Hudson River Valley, which were the stronghold of Independence forces. The horseman calls himself "Mr. Harper" but is gradually revealed to be the Continental Army's General George Washington, traveling incognito. Whatever his larger purpose, he seeks shelter from an impending storm that appears to symbolize the Revolution itself.

To this point *The Spy* fulfills the standard attributes of a historical novel as developed by Sir Walter Scott and other British writers of the early 1800s. Scott often set novels like *Rob Roy* (1817) and *Ivanhoe* (1819) in areas between two armies or peoples. Another convention appears when Cooper's horseback rider seeks cover at the roadside home of the novel's title character. A historical figure (Washington) speaks and interacts with an entirely fictional figure, in this case a fretful housekeeper who points Mr. Harper to a larger house nearby, The Locusts, home of the well-to-do Wharton family. Whereas a novel of manners like *Precaution* confined itself to purely fictional characters in a private realm of personal sentiments, *The Spy* gives a sense that larger issues are afoot.

FROM HISTORICAL NOVEL TO NOVEL OF MANNERS

For Cooper, though, the political is always personal. With Washington's entrance to The Locusts (named for locust trees), Cooper shifts from the outdoor historical novel to the indoor novel of manners. An African American servant shows "Harper" into an "extremely neat parlor" that might have appeared in *Precaution* (chap. 1). Harper-Washington meets Mr. Wharton and three "women of the higher order of life": Wharton's daughters Sarah and Frances and their maiden aunt, who speak of dashing officers and gentlemen. According to James D. Wallace, "a brilliant Americanization of the setting and characters of *Precaution*" turns that earlier novel's family into the Wharton family (1985; 40).

Since readers know Cooper best as a novelist of manly outdoor adventure, they may be surprised how much of *The Spy* resembles novels of manners by Jane Austen, Henry James, or Edith Wharton. Much of *The Spy*'s action takes place not in battles in "the neutral ground," that is, but in well-appointed interiors where officers and gentlemen discuss honor, marriage, and affection with ladies. In *James Fenimore Cooper: Novelist of Manners*, Donald Darnell writes that "Cooper complements [*The Spy*'s] announced theme" of patriotism "by incorporating characters, plots, and themes appropriate to the novel of manners" (23). This genre typically shows refined people speaking careful, witty dialogue in intensely social situations. However frivolous such "manners" may appear, they serve the serious business of courtship and marriage among well-connected people and form an index to morals and motives.

Why does Cooper's first historical novel revert to the novel of manners with which he began his career? One reason is the author's comfort and familiarity with this genre, which formed much of his literary background. But *The Spy*'s merging of genres also made sense as a marketing strategy. Like today's categorization of films as "chick flicks" or "guy movies," different novel styles appealed to men or women readers. The only best-selling American fictions had been sentimental novels like *Charlotte Temple* and *The Coquette*, which appealed primarily to women. The historical novel might develop a reading audience among men. *The Spy*'s "crossover" status created a unified American reading public, much as the American Revolution had created a unified American nation. Transplanting the British novel of manners into an American historical novel, Wallace writes, "Cooper at once retained his original audience and transformed it, inventing simultaneously the American novel and the American reader" (1985; 43–44).

The Spy's blend of historical novel and novel of manners exposes a complex profile for Cooper on gender and family issues. The Leather-Stocking Tales frequently symbolize masculine themes like the American frontier or manifest destiny, while the novel of manners elevates women's character and concerns. Cooper writes in *The Spy* that "good treatment of their women is the surest evidence that a people can give of their civilization," and feminist critic Nina Baym affirms that "women are central characters" in Cooper's novels, forming a "nexus of social interaction" that "establish[es] an American civilization" (*The Spy*, chap. 30; Baym 696–97).

This mix of genres shows the early United States struggling with issues similar to today's "culture wars" over gender, marriage, and family. Cooper champions the values of the upper class in which he was born—and from which he was threatening to fall. In his nonfiction *American Democrat* (1838) Cooper wrote, "[T]he educated and affluent classes of a country are more capable of coming to wise and intelligent decisions in the affairs of state than the mass of a population." *The Spy* shows well-bred women and officers exemplifying "the values, manners, and morality necessary for a civilization" (Darnell 22). Like a British novel of manners, it matches high-class characters to lead the nation. "The inherent superiority and ultimate ascendancy of the gentry," writes W. M. Verhoeven, is "confirmed by intermarriage, inheritance, and . . . genealogy" (89).

Yet the Revolution threatens—or promises—change. *The Spy* alternates between rational talk and radical action, matching the mixed feelings of

Americans torn between order and independence. The "storm . . . rag[ing] with great violence" outside also seethes within, as the novel's action toggles between military battles and family conflicts: "At the time of which we write, we were a divided people" (chap. 12). Mr. Wharton's daughters "differ in their opinions" over the war. Sarah, the elder, endorses "the rights . . . of a sovereign" and is engaged to a British colonel who has a wife in England. Frances prefers the "rights of my countrymen" and an American major (chap. 4). According to Donald Ringe in "The American Revolution in American Romance," Cooper thus began a tradition in Revolutionary War fiction: the "disrupted social order" is "expressed . . . through the device of the divided family" in which "the young . . . side with the colonies" (358, 359). This tradition of families divided by war has continued in American fiction, film, and drama about conflicts from the Civil War to Vietnam.

Such conflict may be normal, as the American Revolution gives birth to a modern society in which different agendas coexist and old privileges give way to new realities. This storm of change intrudes again on the Whartons' parlor with the entrance of another visitor in disguise who drags the family from "differ[ences] in opinion" to the battlefield of history. When Harper-Washington retires for the night, the new visitor takes off his wig, eye patch, and cloak to reveal himself as Mr. Wharton's only son Henry, a British captain who has crossed enemy lines to visit the family. Henry's sentimental but rash deed produces the major complications of the novel's plot, as he is captured by American "Regulars," rescued, and recaptured—a familiar story-pattern in Cooper's fiction.

THEMES: WHY THE FIRST GREAT AMERICAN NOVEL WAS A SPY NOVEL

For new readers, Captain Wharton's disguise exposes another of Cooper's standard plot devices. "Great numbers wore . . . masks," Cooper writes of the Neutral Ground's rivals. Comparably, in *The Last of the Mohicans*, Leather-stocking disguises himself with a bearskin, and Chingachgook deceives onlookers by swimming like a beaver. Readers may flinch in disbelief, but Romantic authors like Cooper routinely tested everyday limits. Far-fetched disguises were a well-established literary convention from Shakespeare to Scott. For a veteran reader of Cooper, one of *The Spy*'s delights is that, despite the absurdity of some of its masquerades, the subject of espionage partly redeems this gimmick. In a book entitled *The Spy*, deception assembles the puzzle of the first major American novel. "*The Spy* positively abounds in self-inventions, masquerades, actings-out," writes A. Robert Lee (37).

Creating the first spy novel helped Cooper resolve formal and thematic challenges to the first great American novel. Formally, the spy novel bridges gaps between the novel of manners and the historical novel. The morning after Harper and Henry arrive, the title character of *The Spy* brings the war into the Whartons' home. By means of a ruse, Harvey Birch—at whose house Harper-Washington knocked in the novel's opening scene—gains entry to the parlor. Birch, the spy, is one of Cooper's most original creations, and his appearance at The Locusts is one of the author's most inventive and absorbing scenes. The country folk know Birch as a peddler, a type of merchant who hikes between towns and farms with goods for sale. Peddlers also served as walking newspapers, sharing knowledge and gossip picked up on their travels.

Appearing before the assembled family, guests, and servants for the ostensible purpose of displaying his merchandise, Birch stretches the upper-class novel of manners to cross into new relations. Birch's "common manners" vary the parlor's upper-class style. A peddler like Birch was an essential part of the early American economy, but his social class placed him midway between the Whartons and their servants. This in-between status provides a perfect cover for Birch or any spy to move between characters and groups that might not normally communicate.

The resulting relationships change Cooper's novel of manners into a historical novel. America's revolution operates not by aristocracy and exclusion but equality and diversity. The "itinerant trader" pulls "varied articles" from his pack while answering requests for news. His report of war in the Southern colonies stimulates new identities and relations for the novel's major African American character, the Whartons' manservant Caesar. At this point in American history—indeed, until a few years before Cooper wrote *The Spy*—slavery was legal in New York State. So far Caesar has been a stereotypical figure, partly minstrel-show and partly the crafty slave of ancient theater. However, when Birch speaks of a Continental general who "lives somewhere among the Negroes" in South Carolina, Caesar retorts, "No more neger than be yourself, Mister Birch" (chap. 3).

To this point, little has been heard from Caesar, but now he finds his voice—an important step for a multicultural nation. "A black man [is] as good as white," Caesar declares, to which Sarah replies, "And frequently much better." The peddler corrects himself by referring to "colored people," but Caesar won't drop the issue and brings his wife from the kitchen to the parlor to receive her share of Birch's "silks, crepes, [and] gloves." Later a British colonel challenges the Americans, "Why not set your slaves at liberty?" (chap. 13). These issues rise afresh when a pious sergeant cites "the good Mr. Whitfield that there was no distinction of color in heaven" (chap. 21). His reference is to George Whitefield (pronounced Whitfield, 1714–70), an evangelist who stimulated the eighteenth century's Great Awakening and supported slavery as a means of bringing Africans into the church, which contributed in some areas to the abolition of slavery.

Birch's visit to the parlor thus raises important issues for the nation being born, and his actions stir other critical issues. As with Whitefield's attitudes toward Africans, *The Spy*'s depictions of African Americans resemble Cooper's depictions of women and Indians, which mix stereotypes with a sense that any person may transcend them. Such ambiguous portraits discomfit modern readers but make a historical novel in which "real patriotism" has to merge personal and national identities.

Cooper's spy novel develops mechanisms for joining diverse people in a new nation. Birch's public business as a peddler covers his function as "the spy"—a role that adds mystery to the question of American identity. Birch secretly works for Washington but is "distrusted and greatly harassed by the American officers" (chap. 5). Accustomed to deception, he sees the deceptions of others. With a glance and a casual remark to Washington in the Whartons' parlor, he confirms that the disguised Henry is a British officer. Such interactions heighten characters' awareness of each other—and their potential disguises. The younger Wharton sister Frances observes Harper attending to Birch's seemingly casual words on the war and begins to cooperate with the peddler's actions on her family's behalf. Such developments help her grow to maturity, even heroism.

Such perceptions enrich *The Spy*'s patriotic theme. For a nation devoted to democratic capitalism, the American Revolution demands that individuals seek their own interests. But how does a community rise from self-seeking? Characters who act too exclusively on "self-interest" are, like the British colonel who proposes to Sarah, "too apt to judge from externals" (chap. 7). Characters committed to "self-elevation" look beyond "externals" and act in the interests of all—an enlightened self-interest that stabilizes society. As negative examples, Cooper portrays real estate swindlers capitalizing on the desperate people of the Neutral Ground, only to be exploited in turn by "the Skinners." These pro-American outlaws blur the difference between "a patriot and a robber," creating a Darwinian jungle where, their leader proclaims, "the law of the Neutral Ground is the law of the strongest" (chap. 14).

In contrast, *The Spy*'s virtuous characters—Frances, Birch, Washington— see beyond self-interest to the community. Following the peddler's visit to the parlor, the novel returns outdoors to military history and intrigue. As the storm clears and the house party gathers on an outdoor plaza overlooking a serene coastline, Washington exclaims, "May such a quiet speedily await the struggle in which my country is engaged . . . !" (chap. 4). But Birch's extraordinary eyesight—an aptitude shared by the Leather-stocking—spies "whaleboats" bearing patriotic troops. If *The Spy* only banged the drums of American nationalism, such a sight would be good news. The Whartons, however, fear that Henry will be captured. Before slipping away, Birch says "there will soon be fighting near us" and briefs Captain Wharton on how to evade capture (chap. 4).

EXPERIMENTS IN CHARACTER: A NEW PEOPLE AND THEIR SPY

This point marks an important stage in Cooper's composition of *The Spy*. Cooper wrote the opening chapters quickly and felt "partial" to them. But "making American Manners and American scenes interesting to an American reader is . . . arduous," he wrote to his publisher, and his efforts to complete the novel were uneven. The rest of *The Spy* only intermittently rises to the level of its opening chapters. As in many Cooper novels, the action is exciting but often seems improvised rather than carefully planned. But as in all Cooper novels the patient reader is rewarded with brilliant scenes and trenchant ideas. American cavalry meet "the royal horse" in sight of The Locusts, "[bringing] home" the "horrors of war" (chap. 7). Dashing scenes of military maneuvers, standard in many of Cooper's later novels, are balanced with realism as The Locusts becomes a hospital for wounded soldiers. Henry is captured by the Americans, escapes, and is recaptured again, only to be freed by Birch's machinations and disguises.

Yet the novel admirably focuses on an evolving sense of justice among a people who are uprooting themselves from tradition. As with later novels featuring Leather-stocking, Cooper coordinates such themes and action through the central character of Birch. At times the spy is the only glue holding together the book's tangled comings, goings, and masquerades— much as Leather-stocking anchors the sprawling tales that bear his name.

For instance, Birch's role as spy develops the personal and political connections necessary for the novel's plot and themes. According to John Cawelti and Bruce Rosenberg in *The Spy Story*, fascination with spies derives partly from their "secret identities" but also from their free-wheeling nature, which expresses "the way many people feel about the basic patterns of their lives," particularly their "alienation" from "corporations, bureaucracies, professions" (32). At a desperate moment Birch cries, "all places are now alike, and all faces equally strange" (chap. 14). R.W.B. Lewis observes, "The mission of poor Harvey Birch . . . at once forces him into dealing with the affairs of the Wharton family and prohibits him from forming bonds with them or anyone else" (100). Yet this same rootlessness enables the spy to connect with diverse characters of the emerging American nation. Thus Cooper became the first major American novelist by becoming "the writer of the first spy novel" (Cawelti and Rosenberg 36).

Cooper also invests his hero with the dashing style that became a staple of later spy fiction. Cooper's *Spy*, Cawelti and Rosenberg write, "combines the theme of espionage with . . . romantic adventure" (39). Darnell notes the "romantic qualities" of "timely arrivals, . . . disguises, cunning and bravery" with which Harvey Birch rescues the Whartons (30). Potentially unattractive deceptions are offset by remarkable competence. Birch, though less glamorous and high-tech than James Bond, "[runs] with incredible speed," walks with "enormous strides," and proves "a dexterous pilot" of the wilderness (chaps. 9, 32, 29).

Birch also anticipates modern fictional spies by appearing less as a realistic conniver and more as a romantic hero. Cooper increasingly omits references to Birch's "country manners" and invests him with the phantom-like powers of later romantic heroes like *The Count of Monte Cristo* or *The Scarlet Pimpernel*. Upper-class characters glimpse a "mysterious being," while lower-class characters regard him as "a mystified body . . . like the winds in the Good Book—no one could tell whence he came, or whither he went" (chaps. 19, 25). As the novel labors to its conclusion, Cooper increasingly uses melodramatic plot devices including secret messages on slips of paper that are variously revealed, eaten, or attached to rocks and thrown through windows.

THE REAL HISTORY BEHIND THE FIRST AMERICAN HISTORICAL NOVEL

Yet as in many novels to come, Cooper rewards a reader with heroic scenes set against stirring natural backdrops. Frances journeys alone by night through wooded mountains to plead with Birch and Washington to rescue Henry from hanging. Nighttime raids by Skinners burn first Birch's home, then The Locusts. These upheavals bring Birch's loyalties and motives under constant question, but he repeatedly acts heroically to resolve plot and theme. In a climactic scene, Washington offers his spy a financial reward, but Birch rejects payment on the grounds that he performed his patriotic acts not, in the words of Cooper's preface, for "personal interest" but rather for "self-elevation." Finally, in a scene of disturbingly violent justice, Birch manipulates British troops to arrest and hang the vicious leader of the Skinners.

This summary omits consideration of much of the novel's earthy texture. Like Cooper's next novel—*The Pioneers*, first of the Leather-Stocking Tales—*The Spy* features realistic settings and characters as well as capable comic relief. *The Spy* teems with details of frontier life in time of war. Crops and fields are abandoned, fences overturned. Military camps, temporary "hotels," and service wagons are staffed by motley army surgeons, herbalists, and a rowdy woman "sutler" who provides food and shelter to the troops. Alternately aiding and exploiting each other, these camp-followers nurse wounds, make toasts, roar songs, and recite odes. Readers up to translating these characters' colloquial language gain a glimpse of common American life during the Revolution.

The history of *The Spy* ends in a more privileged realm—the remarkable coincidences that helped Cooper write realistically of the birth of the nation while founding great traditions in the American novel. The collapse of his inheritance, as noted, led Cooper and his young family to move to his wife's family's estate in the former "Neutral Ground" of Westchester County. That relocation aligned with historical events that inspired Cooper to write a patriotic novel set in the area. The first of these events, the victorious War of 1812 with Great Britain, renewed pride in national identity and appreciation for the Revolution a generation earlier.

In addition, a diplomatic event contemporary with Cooper's composition of *The Spy* reminded him and his readers of the Revolution's most notorious case of espionage. In 1821 improving British-American relations resulted in the remains of British Major John Andre being removed from his grave in Tappan, New York, to England's Westminster Abbey, the resting-place for English royalty and heroes. This event recalled how Benedict Arnold, an American general during the Revolution, had conspired to give the British control of the West Point military academy and its strategic position on the Hudson River. Arnold's contact was Major Andre, who in September 1780 entered the Neutral Ground disguised for a rendezvous but was captured by Skinners and hanged by Washington's forces. The English as well as some Americans questioned Andre's execution, comparing the British major's honorable composure to Arnold's undignified flight.

Andre's fate was an essential background for Cooper's novel. A play entitled *Andre: A Tragedy in Five Acts* was staged in New York in the late 1700s. In 1819, Washington Irving in his *Legend of Sleepy Hollow* referred to "the great tree where the unfortunate Major Andre was taken." Memory of the Andre affair persisted in Cooper's landscape as well. "Cooper's Westchester environs were redolent with Andre's complicity in Arnold's treason," Bruce Rosenberg reports in *The Neutral Ground: The Andre Affair* and the Background of Cooper's The Spy (1994). "Nearby was the modest house of . . . one of Andre's captors" (63). On a tour after The Spy's publication, Cooper "knowledgeably pointed out various parts of the topography relevant to Andre's last days" (73). The Andre affair contributed much to The Spy's military and ethical scenario. "Cooper places the first days of the novel at the end of October 1780, only days after the real Andre had been captured and hanged" (Rosenberg 111). Henry Wharton's crossing of enemy lines in disguise and his sentence of hanging lead several characters to compare his situation directly to Andre's and to question justice in the emerging American nation commanded by General Washington.

Susan Cooper remembered her father interviewing their neighbors concerning local history, but family stories may also have informed Cooper's composition of The Spy. One cousin of Mrs. Cooper's had been "Colonel of the Cow-Boys" (the Skinners' rival gang), while another replaced Andre as intelligence officer after the latter's execution (Elliott xxi). Knowledge of American spy craft may also have derived from family connections to a director of George Washington's secret service (Rosenberg 76). James Cooper never met Washington, but the first president must have been a living fact of his youth, as his father was a U.S. Representative during Washington's administration.

But the most essential historical source for The Spy was another of the nation's founding fathers who was also a Cooper family friend. John Jay (1745–1829) was retired to Westchester County at the time of The Spy's composition. The nation honored him as an author of The Federalist Papers that molded the Constitution, as the first chief justice of the U.S. Supreme Court, and as governor of New York State. Cooper referred to Jay in his 1831 preface to The Spy, which recalls a conversation heard "at the residence of an illustrious man" who told "an anecdote, the truth of which he could attest as a personal actor" ("Preface to the Second Edition" 12, 13). As chairman of a committee on intelligence for the Continental Congress, Jay had contracted the services of a spy much like Harvey Birch: "He was poor, ignorant, so far as usual instruction was concerned; but cool, shrewd, and fearless by nature" (13). Jay later "met him in a wood at midnight" and "tendered . . . money" for his services. This historical spy—like the fictional Birch with the fictional Washington—"drew back, and declined receiving it," for "patriotism was uppermost in the heart of this remarkable individual" (14).

Cooper never learned "the name of [Jay's] agent," though Susan Cooper recalled how "various individuals, twenty years later, claimed to have been the original Harvey Birch" (Small Family Memories 15; 41). Making a direct match between the fictional Harvey Birch and a real person gains a reader less, though, than observing how Cooper combined stray facts from neighborhood, family, and friends into a compelling historical novel. A similar process would synthesize his next novel, *The Pioneers,* and initiate the Leather-stocking saga. For the moment *The Spy* jump-started Cooper's career as well as the American novel.

THE SPY CREATES A FUTURE FOR COOPER AND AMERICAN LITERATURE

The primary sign that *The Spy* was a special event in American literature was its immediate success among readers and critics. "The Spy, when it appeared, was brilliantly successful," Susan wrote. "Never before had an American book attained anything like the same success" (*Small Family Memories* 43). The original printing of one thousand copies sold out in the first month, and in a year at least six thousand copies were sold, earning Cooper royalties of four thousand dollars (Taylor, "Fenimore Cooper's America"). *The Spy* also remained popular, with forty-eight reimpressions of the book appearing in Cooper's lifetime (Verhoeven 185). The novel succeeded in staking Cooper to the international renown on which his Leather-Stocking and maritime tales would later capitalize. *The Spy,* Cooper wrote, "was early translated into most of the languages of Christendom, including those of Russia, Poland, Denmark, Sweden, &c and I got credit, in my own country, for being translated into French and German!" (Elliott xxv). Of comparable importance was the encouragement *The Spy* provided to American authors. The novelist William Gilmore Simms recalled that Cooper's novel "at once opened the eyes of our people to their own resources" (Elliott xxx). Thirty years later Richard Henry Dana wrote, "Many of us can remember how we were stirred on the first appearance of the 'Spy'" (*Memorial* 32).

The Spy introduces character and setting types that later Cooper novels develop and vary. Women characters divide to competing sides of history: Frances and Sarah Wharton anticipate Cora and Alice in *Last of the Mohicans* or Ellen and Inez in *The Prairie*. The weak-willed Mr. Wharton resembles Judge Temple of *The Pioneers* and other of Cooper's patriarchs in their wish to have history both ways. Above all Harvey Birch forms a prototype for Leather-stocking, not only in his physical appearance—"a man of middle height, spare, but full of bone and muscle"—but as a talented man of humble background who maintains his integrity while choosing which master to serve. Beyond characterization, the threateningly seductive "Neutral Ground" of *The Spy* anticipates Cooper's archetypal setting: "It may be a battlefield . . . More commonly, it is either the sea or the forest, each of them conceived as a frontier" (McWilliams 1979; 8).

As the Declaration of Independence and the Constitution set a foundation for American politics, *The Spy* formed a starting point for Cooper and American literature by virtue of its straightforward honesty and vibrant complexity. This single text displays Cooper's talents at their freshest— particularly his generosity of spirit, which appears to wish the best for any honorable participant in the American scene. *The Spy* succeeds in telling two stories. In fiction, Harvey Birch spies a young nation into being. In history, James Fenimore Cooper writes the first major American novel.

5

The Leather-Stocking Tales: An Overview

Cooper's next book after *The Spy*—titled, aptly enough, *The Pioneers*—became the first in a series of novels whose eventual status as classics was anticipated by no one, including Cooper. Like other major artists who appear at the births of national cultures, however, this author developed characters and scenarios that frame critical questions. What does it mean to be an American? How is this identity expressed? *The Pioneers* became the first of five novels known as the Leather-Stocking Tales that have shaped the image and imagination of all Americans, even those who never learn Cooper's name.

The Leather-Stocking Tales—"the nearest approach yet made to an American epic"—take their name from a single character who appears in each novel at a different stage of his career, which unfolds across the early periods of American history (Nevins Preface and Introduction 5). In each novel this character has a different name, but his distinctive footwear consistently identifies him as "the Leather-stocking."

The Leather-stocking's personality, values, actions, and conflicts endow the tales with much of their epic quality. Yet the acid test for these works' stature is their persistent claim on the attention of readers in the United States and elsewhere. "If anything from the pen of the writer of these romances is at all to outlive himself," Cooper wrote in his "Preface to the Leather-Stocking Tales," published a year before his death, "it is, unquestionably, the series of *The Leather-Stocking Tales*" (vi).

As usual with Cooper, though, some static disrupts the pleasure of the tales. "The five Leather-Stocking romances," writes George Dekker, "undoubtedly constitute not only Cooper's greatest achievement but also a cultural monument that deserves all, or nearly all, it has received in the way of ridicule, execration, love, rapt readership, and interpretive overload" (26). To help a reader manage that overload, this chapter first offers basic facts about the tales.

BASIC INFORMATION ABOUT THE LEATHER-STOCKING TALES

Scholars debate what the Leather-Stocking Tales mean individually and together, as well as the order in which they should be read. Such questions lead to rewarding discussions but are difficult to manage without some standard information about the novels, which the table below provides in the order of the novels' publication.

Brief Title	Year Published	Name of Leather-stocking	Age	Setting	Time of action
The Pioneers	1823	Natty Bumppo	70	"Templeton," fictional counterpart to Cooperstown, New York State	1793, America's early national period
Last of the Mohicans	1826	Hawk-eye	38	New York-Canadian border near Lakes Champlain and George	1757, during French and Indian War
The Prairie	1827	the trapper	82	western plains of Louisiana Purchase near Missouri River	early 1800s, time of Lewis and Clark Expedition
The Pathfinder	1840	Pathfinder	42	Fort Oswego on Lake Ontario; "Station Island" in "Thousand Island" area	French and Indian War, subsequent to action in *Mohicans*

The Deerslayer	1841	Deerslayer > Hawkeye	21	Lake Otsego or "Glimmerglass" near future Cooperstown	1740–1745; prehistoric: North America as pioneers found it

Full titles for the Leather-Stocking Tales

The Pioneers: or The Sources of the Susquehanna: A Descriptive Tale (1823)

The Last of the Mohicans: A Narrative of 1757 (1826)

The Prairie: A Tale (1827)

The Pathfinder: or, The Inland Sea (1840)

The Deerslayer: or The First War-Path (1841)

Details appear below and in chapters devoted to individual novels. For now, note that Cooper did not write these novels in a systematic order. The Leather-Stocking character is youngest in the final novel, *Deerslayer*, while in the first of the series, *The Pioneers*, he is already an old man, who dies in the middle installment. "This series of Stories," Cooper reflected in his 1850 "Preface to the Leather-Stocking Tales," "has been written in a very desultory and inartificial manner. . . . The order in which the several books appeared was essentially different from that in which they would have been presented to the world had the regular course of their incidents been consulted" (v).

Given this random or "desultory" order, in what sequence should the Leather-Stocking Tales be read? If you want to read all five, do you start with *The Pioneers* and the other two tales published in the 1820s, or with the last two from the 1840s, where Leather-Stocking is a younger man? What is the proper point of entry into the series? Or if a reader wants to try only one or two of the tales, which should be read first? Each novel has unique strengths, and the order in which the tales unfold can influence the series' overall meaning.

IF YOU'RE ONLY READING ONE . . .

Few people will immediately commit to reading all of the Leather-Stocking Tales at once. If a student wants to test the waters by reading one of the tales, or if a teacher wants to assign one, which one should it be? "Good critics have differed widely in their choice of favorite," writes critic

Allan Nevins (Preface and Introduction 6). Later chapters review the individual novels in detail. This chapter now offers an overview of each novel's recommendations as a stand-alone text.

Nearly two centuries after the series began, a combination of historical influences and intrinsic qualities has made two of the Leather-Stocking novels the most prominent: *The Last of the Mohicans* and *Deerslayer*.

The Last of the Mohicans has several incidental features that recommend it to a reader. First, it's Cooper's most famous title—many people who could never identify James Fenimore Cooper or the Mohicans recognize the phrase "the last of the Mohicans." In addition, this Cooper novel enjoys the prestige of being made into a popular movie in the relatively recent past. If you want to read a novel by Cooper and have other people be prepared to talk about it with you, *The Last of the Mohicans* is a good place to start.

More important than these historical conditions, however, are the attractions *Mohicans* offers on its own. Cooper's most remarkable and romantic cast of characters appears in the title character of Uncas, a splendid Indian prince; the beautiful and tragic Cora, a young woman of mixed race; and the daring villain Magua, a chief fallen to dishonor through contact with the whites. These titanic figures race through unrelenting action across spectacular natural landscapes. Cooper scholar Allan Nevins concludes that if someone reads only *"one* Leather-Stocking tale," it is "usually *the Last of the Mohicans*" (Preface and Introduction 6, ii). An additional advantage to this novel is that *Mohicans* includes Cooper's most detailed look at Indian tribal life, in contrast to his usual portraiture of isolated Indian survivors.

Other Leather-Stocking Tales may stake their own claim as foremost in the series. Cooper's next most famous novel after *Mohicans* may be the final installment, *The Deerslayer*—though maybe not for the best of reasons. Many well-read people who never opened the book know *Deerslayer* as the target of Mark Twain's "Fenimore Cooper's Literary Offenses," which describes *The Deerslayer* as a "literary delirium tremens" whose "English . . . is the very worst that even Cooper ever wrote." Yet British author D. H. Lawrence called *Deerslayer* "the most fascinating Leather-Stocking book" and "a gem." Indeed, the last Leather-stocking novel embodies all of Cooper's foibles to excess but is wondrously luminous and tender, combining its author's mature practice with the deepest romantic fantasy.

If *Mohicans* and *Deerslayer* are the most recognizable Leather-Stocking Tales for readers today, they also have appeal as the best examples of literary romanticism. Set deep in the American wilderness, their plots pulsate with

Cooper's stock-in-trade action of pursuit, capture, and escape. Their characters appear larger than life yet reveal deep yearnings. The settings are mysterious and breathtaking, from gothic enclosures to Edenic landscapes and devastating scenes of war.

In contrast, Cooper's first Leather-Stocking Tale to be written and published, *The Pioneers*, is by far the series' most realistic novel. Its setting is Templeton, a fictional version of Cooperstown that Lawrence describes as "a village of crude, wild frontiersmen." Its motley characters—by turns ambitious, greedy, virtuous, impulsive, and conniving—are generally less than heroic, but this downscale scenario features Cooper's best comedy, which mocks social pretensions among the settlement's rambunctious rabble. The Leather-stocking himself in his first fictional appearance is an old man who mourns the vanishing world of the forest and disdains the clear-cut farms and muddy streets that take its place. Rich with characters, detailed in setting, and searching in its historical themes, *The Pioneers* is Cooper's most intelligent and socially responsible novel.

The third Leather-stocking novel to appear, *The Prairie*, stakes its own claim to greatness. Set on the vast prairie of the western states in the earliest days of European American exploration, the novel finds an extraordinary cast of characters in a spectacular setting that Cooper never visited, but which he drew from travelers' reports. The result is a strange cross between an early western and a science fiction novel, in which nomadic white families and noble Indian tribes meet on alien landscapes alive with spirit and meaning. Cooper noted that many readers of his time regarded *The Prairie* as his finest novel, but it may not be the best novel to start with. Appearing a few years after the events of *The Pioneers*, the Leather-stocking meets his death on the western plains. Therefore the novel hardly serves as a starting point for the series.

Cooper's fourth Leather-Stocking Tale, *The Pathfinder*, was also popular in its time, but most scholars seem now to regard it as the series' least successful installment. *Pathfinder* appeared in 1840, thirteen years after *The Prairie* concluded with the Leather-stocking's death. Restarting the series, Cooper did what Arthur Conan Doyle would later do for Sherlock Holmes or Ian Fleming did for James Bond. Like them, Cooper creates a fictional time before the hero's death. *The Pathfinder's* action takes place a few years after *The Last of the Mohicans*. Its settings on and around Lake Ontario (where Cooper served in the U.S. Navy) combine the subjects of Cooper's forest and sea romances as well as a novel of manners on the frontier outposts, as Leather-stocking courts a younger woman. Overall, *The Pathfinder* seems better for reserving than for starting with.

If *The Prairie* is withheld from a reader's initial foray on account of its conclusion of Leather-stocking's life, and *The Pathfinder* is only a minor classic, the choice of which single Leather-Stocking Tale to read comes down to three. Readers may select the series' most famous adventure (*Mohicans*), its most lyrical fantasy (*Deerslayer*), or its most realistic novel (*Pioneers*). Among further recommendations, *Deerslayer* is the first Leather-Stocking Tale in terms of the hero's life, while *Pioneers* is first in publication and reader reception. This issue of "firsts" leads to a larger question: If you intend to read all the Leather-Stocking Tales, what order should you choose?

READING THE LEATHER-STOCKING TALES AS A SERIES

If you decide to march through all five Leather-Stocking Tales, what books should you start and finish with? How does one novel lead to another? Like the novels in *The Lord of the Rings* trilogy or the films of *Star Wars*, the various Leather-Stocking Tales can be experienced on their own or as part of a larger epic saga. Like *Star Wars*, the Leather-Stocking Tales were not originally planned as a series, and their order of appearance does not match the order of the fictional events they relate.

In the long run, no one should worry overmuch about getting the order right or wrong. Memory and imagination can shuffle and recombine sequences, regardless of the actual order of reading. But if you wish to be systematic, scholars and critics discern two major paths through Cooper's tales. The dominant approach is to read the Leather-Stocking Tales in the order in which they were written and published. The next most common approach aligns the novels with the order of the Leather-stocking's age, so that the last tale written—*Deerslayer*—becomes the first to be read. The following table lists the outcomes of these two approaches:

The Leather-Stocking Tales in Order of Years of Publication	The Tales in Order of the Leather-Stocking Character's Age
The Pioneers 1823	*The Deerslayer*: 21
The Last of the Mohicans 1826	*The Last of the Mohicans*: 38
The Prairie 1827	*The Pathfinder*: 42
The Pathfinder 1840	*The Pioneers*: 70
The Deerslayer 1841	*The Prairie*: 82

These orders substantially differ, but with only five novels to consider, any student can comprehend the attractions of either.

The order of publication prevails for two reasons. First, historicism—interpretation of literature in its historical context—dominates American literary and cultural studies. Historical studies default to chronology as a common objective order. Thus the most reliable fact about the Leather-stocking series is that Cooper produced them one after the other in the first sequence listed above. "For Cooper's readers today I believe the order of publication to be the best one," Geoffrey Rans asserts, on the grounds that Cooper created—and most of his contemporary readers experienced—each novel with reference to previous installments (xvii).

D. H. Lawrence's brilliant interpretation of the Leather-Stocking Tales reinforced this historical approach. Noting how the tales' central character appears first as an old man in *The Pioneers*, only to end as the young Deerslayer, Lawrence observed that the tales "go backwards, from old age to golden youth. That is the true myth of America." This rendition of the saga as a redemptive myth had a strong influence on the "myth and symbol" school of American Studies. As exemplified by R.W.B. Lewis's analysis in *The American Adam*, the Leather-Stocking Tales in their order of publication emphasize a perpetually reborn Adamic hero on the American frontier, where the old world is perpetually replaced by the new. The "myth of America," Lawrence wrote, is the "sloughing of the old skin, towards a new youth."

This progression offers a redemptive vision. The tales end not with an aging, dying Leather-stocking but a figure whom Lawrence describes as "a young man of the woods" who is "silent, simple, philosophic, moralistic, and an unerring shot." This symbolic figure may be recognized as an American masculine fantasy, whether in real-life hunting season, in the movie *The Deer Hunter*, in nostalgia for unspoiled nature, or in the hills of Afghanistan or plains of Iraq. The symbol of an eternally youthful and virtuous armed man ignores complications of age and failure, but fantastic escapes are a staple of literature. Robert H. Zoellner, citing Lawrence's observation that the tales progress from "a decrescendo of reality" to "a crescendo of beauty," writes that "most students of the *Leather-Stocking Tales* have commented on the fact that there is a progressively increasing idealization from novel to novel" (406).

Despite the dominance of the historical progression, a counter-tradition persists in which the tales align with the life of the Leather-stocking. Cooper himself insisted that the volumes be arranged in order of the title character's career. As he wrote in his "Preface to the Leather-Stocking Tales," "Taking the life of the Leather-stocking as a guide, *The Deerslayer* should have been the opening book, . . . succeeded by *the Last of the Mohicans*, *The Pathfinder*, *The Pioneers*, and *The Prairie*" ("Preface to the

Leather-Stocking Tales"). Cooper affirmed this order in letters to publishers and acquaintances concerning the arrangement in collections or reading lists. Among modern critics, David W. Noble, Terence Martin, and Allen M. Axelrad affirm Cooper's intentions "that the five novels should be read in the chronological order of Leather-Stocking's life" (Axelrad, "Wish Fulfillment" 190). This approach, they argue, gives Cooper credit for having planned the Leather-stocking saga, despite their "desultory" production. As circumstantial evidence, if the tales' titles are arranged in Cooper's preferred sequence, they fall into perfect alphabetical order: *Deerslayer, Last of the Mohicans, Pathfinder, Pioneers, Prairie* (Axelrad, "Wish Fulfillment" 192–93).

Yet a reader's career may be as desultory as that of authors and their works. The first Leather-Stocking Tale I read was *The Prairie*—third in order of production, last in the hero's life. My motivation was a colloquium on cowboy literature, which listed that novel by Cooper among the first westerns. Breaking both preferred sequences did not prevent me from picking up the other four novels as opportunity presented and thinking of them in whatever order met the needs of the moment. In the long run the best advice for any student of literature is always to keep reading.

THE LEATHER-STOCKING TALES AS AMERICAN EPIC

The Leather-Stocking Tales' status as required reading has grown less definite as a multitude of new texts competes for attention from our diversifying society. Yet the Tales continue to attract readers, partly because of their traditional eminence in American literature. Compared to other literary traditions—where, for instance, students of modern British poetry may know little of Old English literature—Americanist scholars pride themselves on comprehensive knowledge of their national literature (a stance aided by the United States' shorter history). As long as the tradition of "reading everything" persists, experts in American literature will expect each other to know the Leather-Stocking Tales—though some, as always, will know only Twain's condemnation of them.

The Leather-Stocking Tales endure primarily because of the seriousness of their contents and their influence on later texts and traditions. The Tales' depiction of realities facing Americans at the dawn of our culture repeatedly gain the attention of readers and other writers, who extend Cooper's models and magnify their meanings. As a result, the experience of the Leather-Stocking Tales may go beyond the novels themselves. The characters, relations, and settings spawned by these texts replicate in later literature and media, here and overseas. Earlier chapters summarize Cooper's critical reception and name writers who directly imitated his characters and scenarios. This chapter focuses more exclusively on the essence and impact of the Leather-Stocking Tales as a special body of work.

Literary criticism on the Leather-Stocking Tales offers an intellectual experience of surprising depth and range. Since Cooper's labored style and character types inevitably repel some readers, his fans make a select club. Accepting their cast-off status with knowing humor, these readers find rewards in the fountainhead of characters, settings, events, and ideas that flow from these novels. With so much material to choose from, each reader seems to discover his or her own Leather-Stocking Tales. Consequently, a foray into the Tales' criticism becomes an opportunity to discover new glories in a territory that is shared and familiar but never completely mapped or controlled.

The diverse readings of the Leather-Stocking Tales benefit from varied trends in literary criticism and theory. Rans lists "formalistic, generic, psychological, biographical, symbolic, historical, phenomenological" readings of the tales. Scholarly disciplines including American Studies, American literature, Romanticism, and the history of the novel find indispensable expressions of their subject matter. "This range testifies to the intrinsic interest of Cooper's Tales," Rans asserts, which draw these diverse interests to common ground (xii).

But what is the nature of Cooper's achievement with the Leather-Stocking Tales, and how may we speak systematically of the series? The most inclusive category for describing the whole series' literary impact may be Allan Nevins's assessment that the Leather-Stocking Tales constitute "the nearest approach yet made to an American epic" (Preface and Introduction 5). The concept of "epic" remains so sweeping and indefinite that few analyses of its application to Cooper's tales have appeared. One important exception, Joel Porte's *The Romance in America* (1969), cited *The Last of the Mohicans* and *The Prairie* as "the two most epic-like of the Leather-Stocking books," in which "Cooper wrote, in the broadest sense, his *Iliad* and *Odyssey*" (39).

The Leather-Stocking Tales' resemblance to the epic genre sets a foundation for unifying the various interpretations of Cooper's signature novels. Formally, epics and novels conform in appearance. The novel, developing later in Western history, reflects modern variety by being more diverse in content than the epic—for instance, the detective novel, the novel of manners, and the spy novel. Cooper's other novels explore such a range of subjects, but as a group of historical novels the Leather-Stocking Tales share the history, substance, and style of the epic. Historically, the tales cover a sixty-year sweep from pre-nationhood to the early national period. Their emergence early in the American republic matches the profile of epics like Homer's *Iliad* and *Odyssey*. All such epics—from Homer and *Beowulf* to Dante's *Divine Comedy* and Milton's *Paradise Lost*—represent a founding past and its makers. Epics are classic literature not simply because they're old but because they embody essential structures and values. Like the *Iliad*, Porte writes, *The Last of the Mohicans* "celebrates the heroic virtues of individuals," while the frontier "world of *The Prairie*, as in that of the epic normally, . . . [recalls] the age of the gods" (41, 42).

Reading the Leather-Stocking Tales as an original epic of the United States provides a broad framework for accommodating these novels' diverse critical reception. The "reigning tendencies," Rans writes of research on the tales, "have been first the sociopolitical and then the mythological" (xii). The sociopolitical trend primarily concerns historical currents of the early 1800s, whether in party politics or in Cooper's depictions of distinct races, classes, and genders. Lawrence, as noted in chapter 2, essentially founded the "mythological" approach to Cooper extended by the myth and symbol school. Like an epic, the Leather-Stocking Tales construct an imagined past in which our American forebears represent values and act out conflicts involving our nation's identity against the contested backdrop of the New World.

SETTING: THE LEATHER-STOCKING TALES AS THE FIRST WESTERNS

Aside from the heroic figures of Leather-Stocking and Chingachgook, the tales' most epic feature is their perennial setting on the frontier, where the American land and identity are vitally connected. "We cannot correctly speak of landscape in Cooper as a mere background for his action," Nevins writes; "it is a participant—just as it was a participant in the events of our national history" (Preface and Introduction 9). If the United States is a nation of many peoples, then any group's or individual's claim to being American—from the Native American to the new immigrant—is their presence on the land. Yet this identification is rarely static or secure; instead, it undergoes perpetual transformation. What draws people to the land is a force that changes both. The magnetic appeal to immigrate is inseparable from a way of life instituted by European conquest and settlement. A continent rich with natural capital becomes home to a lifestyle of mobility and consumption.

This transformational history inspires mixed feelings, which the Leather-Stocking Tales evoke by staging their action on the frontier—the dividing line between America's Edenic garden and the modern development that comes next. Any American feels properly torn between desire for economic betterment and regrets for the changes such desires wreak on nature and communities. Part of Cooper's greatness is that he doesn't offer cheap or sentimental resolutions to such quandaries. Instead, he dramatizes the dynamic and conflicted quality of Americans' relationship with their land and with each other.

Numerous critics stress this dynamic quality in Cooper's settings. Lewis in *The American Adam* wrote that Cooper's "most memorable creatures come into moral being in the environmental influence" of an "area of possibility" poised "upon the very brink of time" (99). Likewise for Roy Harvey Pearce, "The Leather-Stocking Tales focus on the area between the civilized and the primitive," and Henry Nash Smith found *The Pioneers'* conflict to be "the old forest freedom versus the new needs of a community which must establish the sovereignty of law over the individual" (Pearce, "Civilization and Savagism" 108; Nash 68). This conflict finds a personal expression, we shall see, in the character and conflicts of Leather-stocking himself.

Cooper's provocative settings testify anew to his expression of currents and cross-currents in Western civilization, especially the changes Americans make on the land—and the land, in turn, makes on them. Such scenarios recur in later literature and culture. "In his exploration of the dialectic between advancing civilization and the free and natural life of the wilderness," writes John G. Cawelti, "Cooper invented the western" (195).

The Leather-Stocking Tales as the first westerns extend their impact to audiences who never heard of James Fenimore Cooper. The western genre has proven a persistent favorite, whether in classic cowboy movies like *Stagecoach* or in science-fiction films like *Star Wars* where the genre's conventions are relocated to outer space. In this light, the setting of the Leather-Stocking Tales may be regarded as the model for thousands of other westerns. The first condition of this genre's existence is the land itself: "The element that most clearly defines the western is the symbolic landscape in which it takes place," writes Cawelti, justifying "why this particular form has come to be known by a geographical term, the western . . . " (193).

The frontier setting of the Leather-Stocking Tales keys their action and that of all westerns. "The symbolic landscape of the western formula is a field of action that centers upon the point of encounter between civilization and wilderness, East and West, settled society and lawless openness," Cawelti concludes. "Historically, the western represents a moment when the forces of civilization and wilderness life are in balance, the epic moment at which the old life and the new confront each other and individual actions may tip the balance one way or another, thus shaping the future history of the whole settlement" (195).

THE LEATHER-STOCKING HERO

Fans of the Leather-Stocking Tales who feel defensive over disrespect for Cooper's accomplishments sometimes insist on the importance of the Leather-stocking hero. According to this argument, the Leather-stocking enjoys a status comparable to archetypal figures of fiction like Sherlock Holmes, Tarzan, and James Bond. Like the Leather-stocking, these characters appear in numerous texts and media, many not written by their creators. These characters also thrive under different names in popular knock-offs. In the century since Tarzan debuted in 1912, the forests and valleys of pulp novels, comics, television, and movies have teemed with jungle lords like Ka-Zar, Turok, Ki-Gor, Kaanga, and Beastmaster, as well as satires like George of the Jungle and spin-offs like Sheena and Bomba. Such figures gain a greater popular reality than the average fictional character, who lives only in a single book.

Claiming equivalence for Leather-stocking with Tarzan, Holmes, and James Bond reflects some glitz on Cooper's creation. However, any minimally literate person knows who Tarzan is or what to expect in a James Bond movie, but average people draw a blank if you refer to "the Leather-stocking." Aside from reluctance to plow through big novels like the Leather-Stocking Tales, this ignorance grows from several issues concerning this character's identity.

The most immediate problem is the Leather-stocking's name. Since it changes in each novel—from Natty Bumppo to Hawk-eye, the trapper, Pathfinder, Deerslayer—even fans aren't sure how to refer to him. The 1992 movie *Last of the Mohicans* simplified the rewritten hero's name to Natty Poe. This chapter uses the standard name of convenience, "Leather-stocking" or "the Leather-stocking," from the leggings that often mark the character's appearance. Cooper himself spelled this name as Leather-stocking. As with many English compound words, the hyphenated spelling has increasingly disappeared in standard usage over time to become Leatherstocking.

Comparisons with other larger-than-life characters suffer also from the fact that Leather-stocking is not an easy figure to identify with. Except in *The Deerslayer*, the series' last novel, this character couldn't be more different from the dashing James Bond or the hunky Tarzan; he is rather, in Lawrence's phrase, "a grizzled, uncouth old renegade, with gaps in his old teeth." Detached from domestic interests, he resembles the eccentric Sherlock Holmes, another character defined more by relations with other men than by his occasional flirtations with women.

As a result, the Leather-stocking's offspring and imitators may be more famous than the original. Many people who never heard of Natty Bumppo would recognize the Lone Ranger, Shane, Clint Eastwood's Man with No Name from the 1960s Spaghetti Westerns (so named because most were directed by Italian movie makers such as Sergio Leone), or legendary mountain men like Kit Carson and Jeremiah Johnson. These figures might have made their mark anyway, but Cooper cast the mold when he created the Leather-stocking.

These figures also show that this fictional character was never completely original but instead grew from the culture Cooper shared with his audience. The images and exploits of frontiersmen like Daniel Boone, Davy Crockett, and Mike Fink contributed to Cooper's creation and his audience's reception of the Leather-stocking. Closer to home, Cooper partly based his original portrait of Natty Bumppo in *The Pioneers* on a real woodsman living near Cooperstown named David Shipman. According to Susan Fenimore Cooper, Shipman "dressed in tanned deerskin, and with his dogs roamed the forest, hunting deer, bears, and foxes." As with genetic code, authors select and recombine materials from diverse sources to make a new creation. In his *Chronicles of Cooperstown* Cooper called Shipman "the Leather-stocking of the region" (Taylor, *William Cooper's Town* 53). Yet his 1850 "Preface to the Leather-Stocking Tales" he warned, "In a physical sense, different individuals known to the writer in early life, certainly presented themselves as models, through his recollections: but in a moral sense this man of the forest is purely a creation."

Thus Cooper's Leather-stocking cut a figure for other characters in American literature and culture, yet the success of these figures depended on their reflection of the national character. People today might grudgingly accept the Leather-stocking's importance because teachers say he's important, but in his time his appeal was manifest. Early in the first book in which he appears, *The Pioneers* of 1823, Cooper seems to regard him as one of many secondary characters who populate Templeton: "a standard lower-class comic character" (Fiedler, *Love and Death* 181). By the end of the novel Cooper has discovered this character's potential, and Natty's exile makes a statement about the community growing on the frontier.

How could so much American history and character be bound up in the singular figure of the Leather-stocking? Most critics start with the tales' historical settings, which elevate the title character to mythic dimensions. As cited earlier, Lawrence's 1923 essay inspired mythic interpretations of the Leather-stocking, but this idea's most systematic expression appeared in Lewis's *American Adam*. Setting early America as an Edenic garden in which human innocence is reborn to be tested anew, Lewis defines the hero as "an Adamic person, . . . at home only in the presence of nature and God" yet "thrust by circumstance into an actual world and an actual age" (89). This "noble but illusory myth," Lewis continues, "begins rightly with Natty Bumppo" (89, 91), an insight supported by Cooper's description of his title character as a "type of what Adam might have been supposed to be before the fall" (*Pathfinder* chap. 9).

This American Adam is tested morally by the perverse creativity of history. Since the United States imagines itself as a classless society and the American Adam would supposedly transcend such considerations, it is ironical that one of Cooper's intractable problems with the Leather-stocking's development was the character's inferior social standing. Cooper was defensive over his own status as a would-be aristocrat, but in *The Pioneers* Natty Bumppo is an illiterate squatter. Cooper had faced a similar paradox in *The Spy*, where the tobacco-chewing title character was ineligible to partici-pate in that novel's marriage-go-round. In the case of the Leather-Stocking Tales, writes Robert Zoellner, "The result is a constant tension, a constant fumbling toward an idealization of Natty in which Cooper cannot bring him-self, aristocrat as he is, to believe wholeheartedly" (405).

Yet paradox may add to a character's profundity. Incapable of being domesticated through marriage, the Leather-stocking always finds him-self on the frontier between the wilderness and civilization. These conditions lead to contrary actions: he rescues the representatives of civi-lization, then retreats to the vanishing wilderness. Cawelti redeems this paradoxical quality as "stereotype vitalization," in which a "stereotypical character . . . embodies qualities that seem contrary to the stereotypical traits" (11). Readers remember Sherlock Holmes as a "supreme man of reason" for instance, but forget how his mind is haunted by depression and dependency. Similarly Leather-stocking fuses the conflicted ambi-tions of American culture by combining "contrary" stereotypes. Through his "double gifts of civilization and savagery," he becomes "the prototype for the western hero and thus the progenitor of countless stories, novels, films, and television programs" (Cawelti 199, 194).

One way the Leather-stocking combines "contrary" elements is his mix of European and Indian lifestyles. But the most striking description of Leather-stocking's "double" nature is Lawrence's characterization of "Natty" as "a saint with a gun." Leather-stocking as a "saint" may appear far-fetched, but like a hermit priest he remains celibate, scornful of worldly vanity, and devoted to service. Furthermore, as "the American Adam" the

Leather-stocking enacts the born-again narrative that accompanied the Puritans and other Christian missions to North America.

If he is a saint, though, the Leather-stocking is also "a man with a gun," a "killer" (Lawrence). Americans, accustomed to an armed society, have little trouble processing a hero with lethal weaponry, but how does it comport with the same character's sainthood? Beyond logic or hypocrisy, the answer lies in a historical conquest rationalized by Christian mission but enabled by firepower. The "myth of the essential white America," according to Lawrence, finds expression in Leather-stocking as "the stoic American killer of the old great life" who "kills, as he says, only to live."

Expressions of this myth abound. As a brief example, one of my favorite childhood TV shows was *The Rifleman*, a violent half-hour western drama whose title character often declared at the outset of episodes that he was "a peace-loving man." Before a half-hour was up, though, the show earned its title when the peace-loving man was forced to become the Rifleman. Characters played by film idols like John Wayne, Clint Eastwood, and Mel Gibson conform to Leather-stocking's model of a good man who seeks peace but resolves conflict with violence: "a saint with a gun." Also like the Leather-stocking, such heroes then ride off into the sunset, always further west, into the good old world where the violent purity of America will be reborn yet again.

CHINGACHGOOK: GREAT SERPENT AND NOBLE SAVAGE

Cooper's tales are named for the Leather-stocking, but the title character's Indian companion enhances their stature and significance. Like the Leather-stocking, this principal Indian character first appeared in *The Pioneers* as a vagabond on the margins of Templeton. Indian John, a.k.a. Mohegan, teeters from Natty's cabin in the woods to the town's church or tavern, torn between Indian traditions, Christian redemption, and alcoholism. Dying in a forest fire at the end of *The Pioneers*, this ancient soul is only a memory in *The Prairie*.

But this Indian character's appearances in the other Leather-stocking novels—especially *Last of the Mohicans*—earn him a mythical status comparable to that of his white friend. Elsewhere in the series "Indian John" is better known as Chingachgook, venerable chief of the vanquished Delawares, father to Uncas, the last of the Mohicans, and to his enemies a figure of sudden, silent bloody death. Just as the Leather-stocking crystallized the image of the white hero as a frontiersman, Chingachgook shaped European and American perceptions of the Indian.

Cooper's triumphs never go down easy, though. As with Leather-stocking, what to call him? The Indian's tags also change: Indian John, John Mohegan, Big Snake, Great Snake, Big Serpent, the French "Gros Serpent," plus variations and family and tribal names to boot. His most consistent name in the novels and criticism is Chingachgook. In the language of the Unami Delaware, "ching" or "big" combines with "achgook" or "snake" to make "Chingachgook" or "Big Snake" (Starna). Such authenticity is gratifying, but it's hard to imagine a name that more baffles the eyes or twists the tongue. A reviewer of a *Mohicans* series in *TV Guide* referred to the chief as "He-whose-name-is-hard-to-pronounce" (Starna, par. 17). Mark Twain in "Fenimore Cooper's Literary Offenses" suggests the Indian's name be "pronounced Chicago," which offers a way out but no way forward. One clue occurs at the end of *The Pioneers* when Indian John dies and Oliver Effingham, the novel's leading man, prepares a headstone that misspells the name as "Chingagook." Natty corrects the inscription by sounding out, "'Gach, boy;—'gach-gook." The name may be pronounced not with the distinct emphases of an English name but, as the Indian himself instructs the feeble-minded Hetty in *Deerslayer*, as "'Chin-gach-gook,' pronouncing the name slowly and dwelling on each syllable" (chap. 13).

After chewing that jawbreaker, one may proceed to judge Chingachgook as a fictional portrait of a Native American. A practical approach is not to regard Cooper's Indians in absolute terms—as either totally accurate or utterly bogus. Cooper was as conscientious in his treatment of Indians as could be expected from a white author at his time in history, but he was writing neither anthropological reports nor factual history. As an author of historical novels, Cooper simplified and dramatized an Indian reality that can never be rendered in all its complexity. Within these limits, Chingachgook and Cooper's other Indians are not realistic but imaginary figures who represent ideas that developed in the conquest of America. However unfair or incomplete, this scheme for thinking of Indians has thrived for centuries. No author is more crucial to this tradition than James Fenimore Cooper in the Leather-Stocking Tales.

Cooper's attitudes and knowledge of American Indians resembled those of other educated Americans in the early nineteenth century. Except in the unsettled West, perceptions of Indians as threats had faded, replaced by a new interest in Native Americans. The "irony in American cultural history" was that "it was not until the Indian was in fact disappearing that Americans wanted—perhaps *could* want—to study his nature and his way of life" (Pearce, "Civilization and Savages" 96). Growing up in a frontier town, Cooper may have glimpsed a few Indians in Cooperstown's backwoods, but he left no records of any encounters. "I never was among the Indians," Cooper later wrote. "All I know of them is from reading, and from hearing my father speak of them." Cooper read missionaries' and explorers' accounts of Indian life, though he once visited Washington "to see . . . a large deputation of Indian chiefs, from the Western tribes," which informed his portraits of the Pawnee and Sioux in *The Prairie* (Susan Fenimore Cooper, *Small Family Memories* 58–59).

VANISHING INDIANS: NOBLE OR SAVAGE?

Cooper's images of Indians in the Leather-Stocking Tales crystallized a number of persistent traditions in Western literature. The most important of these concepts was that of the noble savage. This notion from the eighteenth-century philosopher Rousseau romanticizes the Indian as one who lives a simple, heroic existence in a state of nature, separate from the compromises and corruptions of civilization. Thus Chingachgook and his son Uncas speak honestly, move gracefully, and act decisively in their native forests. Their elemental elegance lights up a reader's imagination, and Cooper, to his credit, knows better than to overexpose them. These passages are spare and brief but live long in the imagination and memory.

The evanescence of these Indians' appearances reinforces another truism that Cooper dramatizes. As "the last of the Mohicans," Chingachgook and Uncas exemplify the myth of the vanishing Indian. Popular American art from Hollywood movies to CD covers, decorative plates, and truck decals glorifies the image of a single Indian riding alone into the sunset (sometimes raising his arms in mournful worship of nature or the Great Spirit). Such an image expresses not so much Indian culture as a fanciful projection of Romanticism with its themes of heroic individualism, lyrical nature, and the twilight of the gods. In this tradition, Cooper's noble savages appear (or disappear) as princes without a people, imparting a sense of nostalgic melancholy to a pure American nature that existed before the white man changed everything. These objects are less about actual Indians than screens on which readers project fantasies of an alternative to modern life.

However conflicted in origin, such images push the emotional buttons of white readers—but as such they represent, at most, only facets or strands of actual Indian existence. Perhaps no voices other than those of Indians themselves can express Native American experience. What is certain is that Cooper's Indian portraits extend long-established traditions in European American literature. For instance, the noble savage myth sounds like an overdue tribute to peoples who have suffered much wrong, but this myth may also be just another stereotype that dehumanizes Indians.

This stereotypical scheme is evident at those moments in the Leather-Stocking Tales when Cooper's noble savages face a negative image of themselves. In *Last of the Mohicans*, Uncas's youthful purity and his friendship with Leather-stocking are countered by Magua, a Huron leader corrupted by the white man's liquor who shifts among different tribes like a politician, gathering support for his vengeful plots. In *The Prairie* the chivalrous Sioux chieftain Hard-Heart faces a dark and devious version of himself in the Pawnee chief Mah-to-ree. Thus Cooper, writes Nevins, "naturally romanticized the Indian as either hero or villain" (33). Such oppositions duplicate a pattern identified by the prominent European scholar Tzvetan Todorov in *The Conquest of America* (1982). Todorov writes that, from the earliest explorations, Europeans "characterize the Indians only by adjectives of the *good / wicked* type," leading to "two apparently contradictory myths, one whereby the [Indian] is a 'noble savage' . . . and one whereby he is a 'dirty dog'" (38, 49).

In brief, Europeans and their descendents chronically imagine the Indian as either better or worse than normal humanity. Indians appear either god-like in goodness or demonic in evil, rather than the mixture of good and evil that makes up Leather-stocking or other white characters. "Cooper never combines a good Indian and a bad in a single skin," Leslie Fiedler writes, "for this would make him human" (196). Like most other European American authors, Cooper fails "to recognize the Indians" as human beings who have "the same rights as oneself" but operate from a different cultural perspective (Todorov 49). Not until American Indians made their own written contributions to American literature would this system of myth begin to correct itself. Cooper is not to be blamed for inventing this system, and his Indian characters often extend or complicate these stereotypes. Overall, though, his Indians, for all their literary power, inhabit an imaginative structure that denies them complete humanity. Cooper wrote better of the Indians than other authors of his time, but his descriptions operate primarily in a framework of European American history.

The pervasive power of this scheme for thinking about American Indians is evident in its durability and adaptability. In most western novels, dramas, and films after Cooper, Indians appear as either noble savages or bloodthirsty killers. In American pop media this bipolar stereotype has a stature comparable to black men's depiction as either excitable thugs or gentle martyrs. In western epics like *Little Big Man* (1970) and *Dances with Wolves* (1990), Indians adopt whites as children or brothers—or menace them irrationally. This underlying pattern survives regardless of shifts in the ratio of good to wicked Indians. "The western," Cawelti writes, "has undergone almost a reversal in values . . . with respect to the presentation of Indians and pioneers" (36). Before the 1960s, movies depicted Indians almost exclusively as savages; subsequently the same figures became almost uniformly noble. Meanwhile, white pioneers and soldiers, formerly shown as noble, now appeared as savages. Such familiar dramatizations make for exciting stories that sell tickets, but they maintain a pattern of violent conflict that offers little knowledge of the peoples portrayed. Development of a real Indian (or African American) character is subordinated to the figure's supportive or threatening relation to whites.

Cooper adapts the scheme to classify entire Indian peoples. Most of the "good" or "bad" Indians in the tales line up with two historic groups of Native Americans. Allies like Chingachgook and Uncas are associated with Algonquian peoples, who primarily populated the Atlantic Coast from Maine to Virginia—from the New England tribes met by the Puritans to the Powhatans, including Pocahontas, near Jamestown. Cooper's numerous names for these Indians are tangled as usual. Chingachgook and Uncas are "Mohicans," a variant spelling and pronunciation for "Mohegans," the New England Algonquian tribe that formed under the historic chieftain Uncas after splitting off from the Pequot tribe in the 1600s. The appeal of the Mohegans as an ancestral source for Leather-stocking's friends may have risen from the historic Uncas's alliance with the New England colonies, whereby the Mohegans maintained peace as long as the English didn't send missions to convert them to Christianity. By the time of Cooper's fictional settings in the 1700s, these original Mohegans had dispersed. Chingachgook, a fictional descendant of Uncas's royal family, now associates with another Algonquian people, the Delawares or Lenni Lenape, themselves scattering under pressure from white settlement.

Most of Cooper's "bad" Indians (at least as judged by Leather-stocking) are associated with the Iroquois, the Algonquians' longtime enemy from the Great Lakes region. The Iroquois or "Six Nations," who call themselves the Haudenosaunee or "people of the longhouse," were several peoples—Mohawk, Onondaga, Cayuga, Seneca, Oneida, and Tuscarora—joined by language, culture, and a political confederation that some claim influenced the U.S. Constitution. Leather-stocking calls these people by many names: Iroquois, Mengwe, Maqua, or Mingo. Far from being inherently evil, the Iroquois count as bad Indians partly because two of the Leather-Stocking Tales—*Mohicans* and *Pathfinder*—take place during the French and Indian War (1754–63). The Iroquois, Delawares, and other Indian groups often changed their allegiances in response to European fortunes, but Cooper simplifies history by associating the Iroquois with the French and the Delawares with Englishmen. Antagonism between devious

Iroquois and noble Algonquians is the norm in the tales, but when *The Prairie* goes west the author relocates this paradigm to the Pawnee and Sioux as good and bad stand-ins.

The other main idea associated with Cooper's Indians—that they are "vanishing" from the American scene—remains equally resonant but just as problematic. The persistence of the Vanishing Indian as an icon of American popular art helps explain why people who never heard of Cooper recognize the phrase "last of the Mohicans." Cooper constructs this motif by depicting Indians, Nevins notes, "as individuals, not as tribes or communities" (Preface and Introduction 27). Fiedler similarly observes that Cooper feels "not sympathy for the Indian people in general but for the Indian chief, the aristocrat at the end of the line" (*Love and Death* 177). Putting Cooper's chronic class-consciousness aside, his depiction of one or two lonely but noble savages makes a tragic myth that offsets the frontier as a place for the white man's rebirth. "The idea of civilized mission," Pearce writes, generated a "tragic role" for the "Indian whose sacred destiny was to be destroyed" (1969; 118, 121). Like the Noble Savage, the Vanishing Indian is less an objective fact concerning the Indian than an assumption about his relation to white civilization.

The myth of the Vanishing Indian underlies much of the romantic nostalgia of the Leather-Stocking Tales as well as their enduring popularity with European and American audiences. Facts support the Vanishing Indian myth, but it nonetheless remains more an expression of white imagination than objective truth. As far as such facts go, the Mohegans, like many Indian peoples, suffered catastrophic population declines from European diseases against which Indian immune systems were defenseless. European settlement shattered native ecology and economies.

But Mohegan history disputes any notion that Chingachgook or Uncas could ever be "the last of the Mohegans," for this people in fact survive. Following federal recognition of the tribe in 1994, more than one thousand Americans count themselves as Mohegans ("Mohegan History"). The majority live around Uncasville, Connecticut, where many work at the Mohegan Sun Casino, a popular gaming, entertainment, lodging, and sports center whose decor includes symbols of "the sacred turtle"—the same emblem tattooed on the chests of Chingachgook and Uncas. With such information, a new story of Native America begins to emerge: the American Indian has not vanished but adapted and survived.

Cooper may be forgiven for failing to imagine blackjack dealers among Uncas's descendants. What later readers can now see that Cooper couldn't is that the Mohegans, like many other Indian peoples, adapted to the new America created by the white man—and they're selling tickets. Yet the gamblers at Mohegan Sun Casino would recognize the idea of the Vanishing Indian and the meaning of "the last of the Mohicans" (though maybe not the literary reference).

What accounts for this cognitive dissonance? How can the Vanishing Indian and Indian casinos be part of the same American culture? As we shall see, another myth developed by Cooper in his tales has created a powerful and lasting distraction: an idea of racial and sexual relations that is embodied in the friendship of Leather-stocking and Chingachgook.

LEATHER-STOCKING PLUS CHINGACHGOOK: IS THERE AN ISSUE?

Leather-stocking and Chingachgook share company with other famous all-male couples in literary and cultural history: Sherlock Holmes and Dr. Watson, Batman and Robin, Kirk and Spock, and cop teams in "buddy movies" like *Rush Hour* and *Lethal Weapon*. But Cooper's companions, with their implications for race, class, and gender at the birth of the American Republic, carry a special significance that ripples across countless later manifestations. Fiedler writes, "Two mythic figures have detached themselves from the texts of Cooper's books and have entered the free domain of our dreams: Natty Bumppo, the hunter and enemy of cities; and Chingachgook, nature's nobleman and Vanishing American" (*Love and Death* 187). However imposing these individual components, their relationship may better connect the puzzle of their appeal. As more Americans in every generation live in cities, why do we imagine ourselves on the frontier? And even as we gamble at Indian casinos, why do we cherish the myth of the Vanishing Noble Savage?

The companionship of Leather-stocking and Chingachgook did not begin the tradition of the hero and his best friend in literature, but Cooper developed it in uniquely American ways. Honors for the original literary "buddies" may go to Achilles and Patroclus in Homer's *Iliad*. Like them, Roland and Oliver of the medieval French epic *Song of Roland* were also companion warriors. In the early Spanish novel *Don Quixote* (1604, 1615) Cervantes paired his title character with the comic sidekick Sancho Panza. The New World changed this paradigm's racial dynamics. Achilles and Patroclus were cousins and lovers, Oliver the sensible advisor to the tempestuous Roland, while Quixote was master to Sancho's trusty servant. In Daniel DeFoe's novel *Robinson Crusoe*, however, Crusoe and his "man Friday" diversified the master-servant relationship into different races—Crusoe the white Englishman, Friday the darker Native American.

Like Crusoe and Friday, Leather-stocking and Chingachgook put human faces on the historical encounter that, since Columbus, has revolutionized life on our planet. The frontier becomes human—in Todorov's phrase, "the discovery *self* makes of the *other*" (3). The meeting of modern First World culture and traditional Third World cultures expresses itself in many forms. Together, Leather-stocking and Chingachgook are the consummate expression of a fictional relationship that reappears from the early novel to the multiplex cinema. Lawrence first isolated this relationship's quality: "in his immortal friendship of Chingachgook and Natty Bumppo . . . [Cooper] dreamed the nucleus of a new society. . . . [H]e dreamed a new human relationship." This bonding clones itself in *Huckleberry Finn*'s Huck and Jim, in *Moby-Dick*'s Ishmael and Queequeg, in the Lone Ranger and Tonto, in *Lethal Weapon*'s Riggs and Murtaugh, and in Kirk and Spock on *Star Trek*'s "final frontier." In contrast to the master-servant relationship of *Don Quixote* or *Robinson Crusoe*, these "new human relationship[s]" are a prototype of an egalitarian society. "Natty and the Great Serpent are neither equals nor un-equals," Lawrence writes. "Each obeys the other when the moment arrives."

This "new human relationship" is so familiar as to escape comment, much less analysis. But why, apart from the gestures toward equality, does this relationship form so persistent and agreeable a pattern for imagining frontier society? Perhaps we do not ask questions because the model is, in Lawrence's phrase, "an evasion of actuality." But the Vanishing Indian myth provides a clue and an answer to the actuality that interracial buddies evade.

In a word, sex is what interracial buddies like Leather-stocking and Chingachgook evade—sex and its possibility of procreation, in this case mixed-race offspring. "Beyond all this heart-beating stand the figures of Natty and Chingachgook: two childless, womanless men, of opposite races," wrote Lawrence. "Each of them is alone, and final in his race." Limiting mixed-race to same-sex prohibits interracial procreation. Just mentioning this concept sets off alarms for earlier generations of Americans or those raised in traditionalist households today, so student readers must set their own goals and proceed at their own pace. This companion's chapter on *Last of the Mohicans* relates such issues to the mixed-race heroine Cora. Feminist readers may ponder the sexual politics of the frontier, starting with Annette Kolodny's *The Lay of the Land* (1973). Students interested in a careful early discussion of homosocial or homosexual content in classic American literature should start with Fiedler's *Love and Death in the American Novel* (1960).

For present purposes we limit ourselves to the myth of the Vanishing Indian—the myth, that is, in opposition to Indians' actual survival. When

Americans think of the Vanishing Indian, they think of a noble savage inhabiting long-ago forests or prairies. They do not imagine people who work on construction lots or in offices, or who invite their conquerors' descendents to drink and gamble. But above all, white Americans do not think of Indians as being part-white or part-black. Chingachgook and Uncas are "the last of the Mohicans" for Cooper because they are the last *pure* specimens of their people. "The Vanishing [Indian is] shown to have vanished because (so Cooper at least believed) the color-line is eternal and God-given," Fiedler notes, but, he adds, this "is a fantastically ahistorical note" (*Love and Death* 205). Americans tend to think of races as pure, permanent, and separate, but most pureblooded Indians—like most pureblooded English, German, or Irish people in America—have vanished primarily through intermarriage or other interracial opportunities for procreation. Many people at work on the new economic frontiers of casinos and proudly claiming Native American heritage may have at least as much European, African, or Asian lineage.

Such an observation does not impute hypocrisy to Cooper or Indians. It only suggests the issues of American identity that Cooper's Leather-Stocking Tales expose for readers nearly two centuries after the novels were written—and even longer after their fictional action. Race remains always in play, but Cooper's conservatism is not simple racism. A son of privilege who lost nearly everything, Cooper tried to keep people and things in their place, to conserve a world in which natural aristocrats like Chingachgook and himself receive due respect. But Cooper was honest and creative enough to acknowledge how the qualities of that world shine forth only as it slips away. Never entirely real to begin with, such an order becomes more beautiful for being lost—as a new world order looms over the frontier's horizon to declare a fresh change of laws and values. In the chapters that follow, this *Companion* journeys to the frontier of each individual novel in the Leather-Stocking epic to witness the rebirth of another lost world that never was, whose heroes continue to define the American imagination.

6

The Pioneers: or The Sources of the Susquehanna: A Descriptive Tale (1823)

Two years after his breakthrough success with *The Spy,* Cooper scored another hit with *The Pioneers* (1823). *The Pioneers* was another historical novel, but different in both the kind of history it told, and the kind of people who were making that history. Where *The Spy* depicted great historical events like the American Revolution and figures like George Washington, *The Pioneers* painted a teeming, colorful portrait of change on the North American frontier. In a grubby little town like many others, a rowdy gang of "pioneers" was transforming formerly Indian country into a nation of cleared land, increased productivity, and settled laws. Cooper's *Pioneers* became the first of many American novels to tell this wrenching, triumphal story of a distinctively American community rising on lands that once belonged to others. Later classics of this genre include Frank Norris's *The Octopus* (1901), Willa Cather's *O Pioneers!* and *My Ántonia* (1913, 1918), and William Faulkner's *Absalom, Absalom!* (1936).

The Pioneers was also historical in starting the series of novels that would place Cooper's name among the United States' most important authors. *The Pioneers* is the first of the five books collectively called the Leather-Stocking Tales. These novels remain the foremost reason Cooper is read and remembered today. *The Pioneers* set the foundation for this extraordinary series by introducing "the Leather-stocking," a character also known in this novel by the name Natty Bumppo.

Little in the Leather-stocking's debut predicted this character's significance, or suggested that *The Pioneers* would spawn an epic series of tales. As the novel opens, Natty appears as a grumpy old man, one of many quaint characters populating the frontier town of Templeton. His friend Indian John or Mohegan—later identified as Chingachgook—veers from Christianity to alcoholism to memories of Indian life. As the story unfolds, though, these characters assume the titanic stature of the later tales.

If you've read other Leather-Stocking Tales, you may be surprised at the difference in *The Pioneers*. In place of the other Tales' wilderness settings and their mounting action of captivity, escape, and pursuit, *The Pioneers* takes place mostly in a small town and proceeds at a deliberate pace from one carefully composed social scene to another. The first two hundred pages cover a mere two days—from Christmas Eve to the day after Christmas—in which the townspeople are introduced and their social relations established. As its subtitle indicates, this *Descriptive Tale* is a portrait of a time and place. Altogether the first Leather-Stocking Tale is a disarmingly realistic novel, not a "romance" of high adventure. Instead of larger-than-life heroes who settle social concerns through violence in extreme conditions, *The Pioneers* features earthy characters who join the early American melting pot with its implicit social contracts of buying in or moving on.

A cheerful side effect to this social realism is that *The Pioneers* is Cooper's most comical tale. The novel swarms with conniving lawyers, uncivilized squatters, greedy land-grabbers, headstrong housekeepers, impractical innkeepers, willful servants, and disguised heirs, all thrown together on rough terms of frontier equality. This motley crew schemes, sings, dances, and argues on muddy roads, in rowdy barrooms, in makeshift courtrooms, at Christmas services, or at outdoor hunts and harvests.

As a sign of its success, *The Pioneers* surpassed *The Spy*'s early sales records. Many readers who grew up in the early United States must have felt that they were looking in a mirror of their own experiences. Three decades later, the *Memorial* for Cooper's death received a letter from Ralph Waldo Emerson. This giant of American literature, born fourteen years after Cooper, recalled "an old debt . . . of happy days on the first appearance of the Pioneers" and "the unanimity with which that national novel was greeted" (*Memorial* 32–33).

POINT OF VIEW: THE PLEASURES OF OMNISCIENCE

Cooper uses an old-fashioned third-person omniscient point of view in all his major fiction. *The Pioneers* is no exception. As in his other works, though, Cooper adapts this style to serve his subject matter.

Today's tastes in literary fiction discount third-person omniscient viewpoint in favor of more limited perspectives such as first person and third-person limited. With their internal views, these limited styles expose deeper psychological identities and conflicts. In contrast, the omniscient or all-seeing view may appear old-fashioned and shallow. Along with first-person style, omniscient perspective dominated the early novel, with third-person limited perspective developing later. Yet third-person omniscient viewpoint remains standard for mass-market fiction—note, for example, *The Da Vinci Code* or *The Hunt for Red October*—which rapidly shifts perspective from one character or scene to another like a movie camera. For later readers this resemblance between Cooper's viewpoint and cinema remains one of the author's greatest appeals.

Cooper's "omniscience" respects zones of privacy, however, such as "the sanctuary of parental love" between a father and his rescued daughter, or Natty's home: "What more was uttered by the Leather-stocking . . . was rendered inaudible by the closing of the door of the cabin" (chaps. 30, 27). Modesty may partly account for complaints that Cooper's characters are shallow and stereotyped. Third-person omniscient again resembles a movie camera by penetrating surface appearances only briefly and occasionally. As film characters depend on words or actors' expressions to suggest depth, Cooper's novel reveals character through outward signs. For example, *The Pioneers* describes Oliver Edwards, its male romantic lead, by external rather than internal signs: "the strong emotion exhibited in the countenance of the youth gradually passed away" (chap. 18).

Though frustrating to modern readers, this touch-and-go style offers rewards. For instance, it can reveal two minds working simultaneously. On returning to the home where Mrs. Temple has died during Elizabeth's absence, "Elizabeth and her father . . . both experienced the same sensation . . . [T]he figure of [the house's] lamented mistress was missed by both husband and child" (chap. 5). Similarly, when Elizabeth meets her minister's daughter, Louisa Grant, "the two young women [felt], instantly, that they were necessary to the comfort of each other" (chap. 12).

Cooper's camera style creates exquisite angles of sight. Under a brilliant moon, a party including Louisa and Chingachgook (called Mohegan) walks through the snow after Christmas services. Oliver Edwards, also in the group, is "led to consider the difference in the human form, as the face of Mohegan, and the gentle countenance of Miss Grant . . . met his view, at the instant that each turned, to throw a glance at the splendid orb which lighted their path" (chap. 12). In *The Pioneers* Cooper's omniscient point of view gains both grand and elegant perspectives on a diverse community in a beautiful natural environment.

SETTING: COOPERSTOWN REINVENTED

"Templeton," the village setting of *The Pioneers*, is unmistakably based on Cooperstown, which was founded in the late 1700s by Cooper's father. Both the real Cooperstown and the fictional Templeton have a lake and county named Otsego. Cooper's 1832 introduction to *The Pioneers* confirms the match. "The author was brought an infant into this valley and all his first impressions were here obtained," Cooper writes; "there can be no mistake as to the site of the Tale."

Authors who base fiction on their actual world face a hazard of piling up details of personal interest instead of creating a setting compelling to others. "In commencing to describe scenes . . . that were so familiar to [my] own youth," Cooper acknowledges "a constant temptation to delineate that which [I] had known rather than that which [I] might have imagined" (1832 Introduction).

Cooper fictionalized his historical world partly by framing familiar situations as "genre scenes." A style of art that began in seventeenth-century Europe, "genre paintings" featured scenes of everyday life: people hunting, eating, drinking, dancing, or making music at outdoor festivals, or in taverns or homes. "Genre scenes" also appeared in literature. Washington Irving's "Legend of Sleepy Hollow" (1820), published three years before *The Pioneers*, features genre scenes of Ichabod's singing circle, fireside ghost-stories, and the Van Tassels' farm. Such pictures of a disappearing past anticipated the later literary movement of regionalism, which portrayed vanishing ways of life after the Civil War.

"Some of the loveliest, most glamorous pictures in all literature," D. H. Lawrence wrote of *The Pioneers*. Besides inspiring nostalgia, this novel's genre scenes serve Cooper's thematic purposes. *The Pioneers'* Christmas chapters are a pageant of genre scenes: the landscapes Elizabeth beholds on her sleigh-ride, her homecoming, the Christmas Eve service, the tavern, and, on Christmas day, the turkey shoot. Later genre scenes include the making of maple sugar, a pigeon shoot, and a nighttime fishing expedition. Such scenes evoke cooperative traditions but end by revealing budding conflict, as characters raise "a spirit of angry contention, with resentment and boasting, with competition and the jealous assertion of rival claims" (Philbrick, "Cooper's" 588).

Later in the novel, the villagers' rancor finds a focal point in other fictional settings whose exploration climaxes *The Pioneers'* plot. Their locus of interest is Leather-stocking's hut, which becomes an early example of a key contribution by Cooper to American literature: the wilderness as a gothic setting. Gothic literature—now associated with mysteries, thrillers, and horror—was originally developed in Europe, where the gothic gestalt rose from ancient spaces full of secrets and intrigue such as a dark castle, a manor house, or a deserted abbey. Edgar Allan Poe became the supreme American practitioner of this European gothic style.

The gothic genre was problematic, though, for novelists of the frontier: the United States had few old buildings where mystery might gather, and even those were rapidly replaced. In *The Pioneers* Natty's cabin serves as a gothic space. The novel's point of view never directly enters the cabin, and "idle tales . . . circulated through the village" (chap. 24). The excitable villagers' greed spawns a gothic fantasy: that the cabin hides a cache of gold from a secret mine. The cabin's actual secret concerning the title to the land is not revealed until the introduction of another gothic space—a cave or cavern on the other side of Mount Vision. Cooper mutes the wilderness gothic in order to coordinate it with *The Pioneers*' general realism, but his next Leather-Stocking Tale, *The Last of the Mohicans*, would take these gothic elements to new extremes.

PLOT AND STRUCTURE: SEASONS OF HISTORY

Descriptive overload makes *The Pioneers*' plot points hard to discern. Cooper noted the novel's challenge to a conventional plot: "I would advise any one, who may take up this book, with the expectation . . . of feeling that strong excitement that is produced by battles and murders, to throw it aside at once" (1823 Introduction). Instead, *The Pioneers* carefully coordinates its descriptive passages with narrative conflicts and themes.

The speeches and dialogues that stretch many chapters in *The Pioneers* present special problems. Some characters speak in dialect and allude to names and places far beyond current reference. But simple attitude adjustments can help one appreciate the roles of these voices in the story. The characters' French, Irish, German, and African American dialects reflect the frontier's ethnic and linguistic diversity. As far as their extravagant range of reference, most of these ethnic speakers are minor characters. Thus their speech is usually comical and incidental to plot development. Ben Pump, for instance, translates every situation into his past experience as a sailor in the English Navy. After laboring through yet another explosion of the old salt's bewildering verbiage, a reader may take comfort that people in the book don't seem to know what he's talking about either.

Sensitivity to the novel's major themes and characters also helps a reader distinguish the comic from the consequential. Conflicts in *The Pioneers* repeatedly raise disturbing questions for a new nation. Who owns the land and its products, and by what title, authority, or law? With such questions in mind, the plot gains purpose. The scenic sleigh ride of the first chapter is interrupted when Elizabeth's father, the area's chief landowner, stops to shoot a deer that is simultaneously struck by bullets from other hunters, including Leather-stocking. The deer was running on Judge Temple's land, but who owns the slain deer? The landowner, or the hunter whose bullet killed it? This contest over "determination of right" is heightened by the hostility expressed toward Judge Temple by a handsome young stranger—partly identified as "Oliver Edwards"—who accompanies Leather-stocking.

Thus Cooper coordinates description, plot, and theme from the outset. As that first chapter ends, the reader must remain alert to the brief second chapter, which withdraws from the immediate action to provide a back-story regarding Judge Templeton and his settlement. This sudden exposi-tion on the land's title or "patent" has its own challenges: Cooper wants to tell just enough without telling too much. Pay attention to the name and claim of Major Effingham, his family, and their relationships with Judge Temple. These relations ultimately explain Oliver's antagonism, the Leather-stocking's presence, and the mystery inside his cabin.

Otherwise, two conceptual schemes structure the novel's events. The novel's final chapter summarizes that "events of our tale . . . [make] nearly the circle of the year" (chap. 41). Arranging literature to reflect the passage of a year was a convention of descriptive literature like James Thomson's *The Seasons* (1730), which provides the epigraph for *The Pioneers'* first chapter. Later American literature would similarly organize itself on the cycle of the year: Thoreau's *Walden* (1854), Whitman's *Song of Myself* (1855), and *Rural Hours* (1850) by Cooper's daughter, Susan Fenimore Cooper.

Seasonal change inherited from nature gains dramatic significance from a more disturbing order of change. The other conceptual scheme that structures *The Pioneers* is human history—specifically, modern economic expansion, which transforms nature through capital "improvements." This competing pattern of change appears early in the novel as the sleigh bear-ing the Judge and his daughter nears Templeton: "time was given Elizabeth to dwell on a scene which was so rapidly altering under the hands of man" (chap. 3). The competition between natural and cultural change determines the conflicts of major characters as well major themes in *The Pioneers*.

MAJOR CHARACTERS: HEROES OF THE PEOPLE

Enough characters appear in Cooper's *Pioneers* to justify a census. At least twenty named figures have speaking roles, and many scenes swell with anony-mous servants, urchins, and vigilantes. Classifying these numerous figures as major and minor characters makes order of the novel's social scene and distinguishes prevailing themes. With the exception of Chingachgook, its major characters are less distinct as ethnic types than the minor characters. Descending from early English settlers, the major characters control the community's property and debate what kind of community Templeton will be.

These central characters are divided into elder and younger generations. The major characters of the elder generation—Major Templeton on one side, and Leather-stocking and Chingachgook on the other—divide primarily by whether they live in or out of town and, as an extension, by their attitude toward the economic and environmental changes sweeping across North America.

Marmaduke Temple, the founder and namesake of Templeton, is modeled partly on the author's father, William Cooper, who founded and named Cooperstown. Like Judge Cooper, who died in 1809 as the region's leading developer and politician, Judge Temple appears as a warm, complex, and enterprising man of Quaker descent. Of "unconquerable good nature," Judge Temple shows "a fine manly face, and particularly a pair of expressive, large blue eyes, that promised extraordinary intellect, covert humour, and great benevolence" (chap. 1). Events and opposition test these qualities, but the judge's behavior justifies this "promise." Consolidating his own wealth and power, he helps the town's settlers realize the American dream of owning property and increasing their wealth.

But the relentless changes that accompany the American dream raise resistance from earlier ways of life and claims to the land, positions for which Chingachgook and Leather-stocking are the chief representatives. As an Indian, Chingachgook is one of "the original owners of the soil" (chap. 8). As a white frontiersman, Leather-stocking embodies the self-governing lifestyle of a previous European American generation on the frontier.

Cooper disclaimed any model for Natty Bumppo, but his *Chronicles of Cooperstown* (1838) mentions an area hunter named David Shipman, who was "the 'Leather Stocking' of the region" (chap. 2). Cooper's daughter Susan wrote that Shipman "dressed in tanned deerskin, and with his dogs roamed the forest, hunting deer, bears, and foxes" (Taylor, 53). Likewise in *The Pioneers* Natty typically appears accompanied by his dogs Hector and "the slut." (That last, regrettable reference corresponds to the dictionary definition of "bitch" as a female dog.)

Leather-stocking does not debut as a conventional romantic hero. Except for his "robust and enduring health," most readers today might think he resembles an old homeless person, given his oddly layered clothes, his unkempt hair, his face "thin almost to emaciation," and his one tooth—a "single tusk

STUDENT COMPANION TO JAMES FENIMORE COOPER

of yellow bone"—for chewing (chap. 1). His "leggings of the same [deerskin] material as his mocassins" gain him "the nick name of Leather-stocking" (chap. 1). Mrs. Hollister, the Irish innkeeper, describes him as "a poor hunter, who is but a little better in his ways than the wild savages themselves" (chap. 8). Far from being homeless, though, the Leather-stocking has a cabin whose existence predates Judge Temple's acquisition of the land. In addition, all Templeton knows Natty as the town's best marksman and trapper.

Thus, even though Leather-stocking is socially inferior to Judge Temple, his peculiar stature gives him authority as a voice of resistance to the expansive civilization transforming the land. Other characters like Elizabeth notice the changes afoot, but Leather-stocking openly criticizes: "the game is becoming hard to find, indeed, Judge, with your clearings and betterments" (chap. 1). Throughout the novel the settlers carelessly ravage one natural treasure after another—trees, fish, birds. At these moments the Leather-stocking chastises their "wastey ways" and urges conservation: "use, but don't waste" (chap. 22). The settlers resent the old man's scolding, but his reputation as an outdoorsman lends him moral authority.

These differences between Leather-stocking and common humanity mark qualities that made him a more romantic figure in Cooper's later tales. As Europeans and Americans moved to towns and cities, fictional heroes connected instead to rural nature. "In *The Pioneers*," the poet William Cullen Bryant recalled at the Cooper Memorial, "Leatherstocking is first introduced—a philosopher of the woods . . . whose life has been passed under the open sky" (*Memorial* 47–48).

Leather-stocking would continue to develop as a character, but Chingachgook speaks and acts more prominently in *The Pioneers* than in any other Leather-Stocking Tale. "Generally known as John Mohegan, or, more familiarly, as Indian John," his presence invests any scene with a special gravity, yet his personality and gestures are remarkably varied (chap. 8). Extended scenes find him conversing with Louisa's father, the local minister who encourages Chingachgook's interests in Christianity. In the Bold Dragoon tavern, however, "cider and whisky" seduce him to stagger and sing war songs in Delaware. Thus he fulfills the stereotype of the Vanishing Indian lamenting past glories, but he also reveals tragic depth and complexity by ashamedly referring to himself as "a Christian beast" (chap. 16). Humane and realistic touches detail this portrait. In several tense conversations Chingachgook intervenes intelligently; he uses Indian craft as a skilled healer; and Elizabeth and others refer to his business as a maker of baskets and brooms. Altogether Cooper creates an impressively sophisticated characterization of the aging chief of the Delaware and Mohicans.

As the elder generation, Judge Temple, Leather-stocking, and Chingachgook all carry the burdens of past obligations and present duties. The two major characters of the younger generation—Elizabeth Temple and Oliver Edwards Effingham—must inherit and resolve the previous generation's conflicts. Elizabeth's profile, energy, and resilience make her one of Cooper's better woman characters.

But overall Elizabeth and Oliver resemble most romantic couples from Shakespeare to Hollywood. They glow with youth and potential; they have good hair and straight features; they speak in elevated tones and rounded sentences; if only they could somehow be real, everyone would want to meet them. But in contrast to the conflicted or comical realism of the other characters in *The Pioneers*, they are only silhouettes where, with the pain and passage of time, characters might grow.

ROLE OF MINOR CHARACTERS: A SPECTRUM OF ETHNICITY

An acid test of great literature is its creation of characters who seem invested with lives of their own. Homer, Shakespeare, Dickens, Faulkner, Toni Morrison—these titanic authors are inseparable from their equally titanic characters: Odysseus and Achilles; Romeo, Juliet, Hamlet, and Falstaff; David Copperfield and Miss Havisham; Caddie, Dilsey, and the Snopes family; Macon Dead and Baby Suggs. These characters stand on their own fictional feet, speak with their own unique passion, intellect, and language, and look and act like no one else.

James Fenimore Cooper is widely acknowledged to have created one great character in the Leather-stocking, and perhaps another in Chingachgook. Only Judge Temple attains a comparable magnitude in *The Pioneers*, yet the novel proves its greatness by portraying a host of highly individualized minor characters who bounce and bluster with a comic eccentricity comparable to Dickens's novels of London. Such exuberance appears only occasionally in American literature: Harriet Beecher Stowe's *Uncle Tom's Cabin* (1852), Twain's *Huckleberry Finn* (1885), and Faulkner's *The Hamlet* (1940). Like these other novelists, Cooper is most fertile in creating minor and lower-class characters. These figures function as types, but formulaic characters may leap from the page with flair and energy.

In *The Pioneers* Cooper draws Templeton's inhabitants from streams that met in historical Cooperstown. That frontier town was a crossroads for immigrants from other countries. At the Christmas Eve service in Templeton's church, "half the nations in the north of Europe had their representatives in this assembly" (chap. 11). Major Hartmann ("Old Fritz") from Germany,

Monsier Le Quoi ("the Gaul") from the French colonies, Benjamin Penguillan ("Ben Pump") from the English Navy, and Mrs. Hollister from Ireland have limited roles in the novel's plot but season its dialogue with accents from their native lands.

Immigration from elsewhere in North America contributes Templeton's other major source of settlers, as it had for Cooperstown. The community's native English-speakers play more direct roles in *The Pioneers'* action. Lacking distinctive accents, Cooper casts them as familiar types of American fiction and folklore. Major Temple's cousin Richard "Dickon" Jones and the woodsman Billy Kirby swagger and boast about their powers and accomplishments. This tradition of bragging and bullying has roots in literature as deep as *Beowulf* and appears later in sources as diverse as Twain's *Life on the Mississippi* (1883) and today's professional wrestling. Billy, with his "great stature," "good-natured" spirits, and woodcutting power, anticipates other corn-fed hunks including Midwestern legends like Paul Bunyan; Hurry Harry in Cooper's *Deerslayer*; and Tom Bombadillo in J.R.R. Tolkien's *The Hobbit* (1937).

Another Anglo-American tradition contributes familiar figures from the "old states" of New England (chap. 19). For Cooper, "the moral states of Connecticut and Massachusetts" combine Puritan religiosity with deceitful haggling to produce shiftless jobbers and conniving lawyers (chap. 8). These characters are often identifiable by biblical or pious names—Jotham Riddle, Hiram Doolittle, and Remarkable Pettibone. The town's Yankee doctor, Elnathan Todd, resembles Ichabod Crane in "Sleepy Hollow" with his "rare personal proportions" ("six feet and four inches" and "a small bullet-head"), his addled bookishness, and even a father named Ichabod (chap. 6). Such stock figures were common in early American literature, and Cooper's next Leather-Stocking Tale, *The Last of the Mohicans*, would produce another Ichabod in David Gamut.

African American slaves and servants generally appear only fleetingly in *The Pioneers*, and white characters casually refer to them with embarrassing slurs—"them Guineas down in the kitchen"; "the lazy, black baste [beast]" (chaps. 30, 13). However, Cooper briefly develops two African American characters whose status and speech reveal historical conditions on the northeastern frontier two generations before the Civil War. The very first character to appear in the novel is Aggy or Agamemnon, Judge Temple's sleigh driver. As a Quaker the Judge is prohibited from slave-dealing, so Dickon Jones owns Aggy's "services for a *time*." The inevitable ugliness of slavery is exposed in chapter 4 when Dickon extorts information from Aggy by withholding "Santaclaus" and threatening him with a whip, yet the two men negotiate and conclude in "most perfect cordiality."

To that chapter Cooper later added a footnote explaining New York state's "gradual manumission" of slaves. In addition, the turkey shoot scene in chapter 17 shows a "freeborn" African American character. "The owner of the birds was a free black" named Abraham or Brom Freeborn. This character's dialect and antics make him a crude if good-natured stereotype. Yet Freeborn has freedom to operate within the "principles of public justice that prevailed in the country": "the negro affixed his own price to every bird," and he demands "fair play" from the contestants. Cooper's mortifying portraits of African Americans are forgivable on account of the time in which he writes, but already those times are changing.

SYMBOLS AND ALLUSIONS: WHICH SIDE IS CIVILIZED?

A novel rich in historical description like *The Pioneers* runs thick with allusions. The characters' speech refers frequently to the diverse historical backgrounds from which American pioneers like themselves converged on the frontier.

Like all the Leather-Stocking Tales, *The Pioneers* fabricates an elaborate back-story for Indian-white relations. Native American uprisings such as King Philip's War, and individuals and leaders like Pocahontas and Corn-Planter, are mentioned (chap. 19). The French and Indian War of 1754–63, when the Leather-stocking served under Oliver's grandfather, Major Effingham, also creates a common context. Chingachgook uses his Indian experience to introduce a related historical background. The Temples' Quaker descent leads Indian John to allude to the Quaker founder of Pennsylvania, William Penn (1644–1718), by his Indian name of "Miquon" and to the Judge and Elizabeth as "children of Miquon." Penn's peaceful negotiations with the Delawares provides the background by which Major Effingham—called Fire-Eater by the Delawares—inherited the Indian title to the land.

Trees, wildlife, and other natural bounty become symbols for the land's proper use. Symbolic human portrayals also raise the question of the frontier's effect on "pioneers." To which culture—Indian or white—do characters like Leather-stocking and Oliver belong? Early in the novel at the Judge's manor house, Elizabeth "stares . . . in wonder" as one of Oliver's hands "rested lightly on [her] ivory-mounted piano": "A single finger touched the instrument as if accustomed to dwell on such places. His other . . . hand grasped the barrel of his long rifle" (chap. 5). Which hand—that of civilization on the piano, or that of savagery holding the rifle—determines the real Oliver?

THEMES: CREATIVE DESTRUCTION

The Pioneers tells an American creation story. In a pristine natural world once inhabited by others, a first generation of settlers founds a growing but stable community of laws. For anyone who doesn't like those laws, a fresher frontier beckons farther west. With its title, action, and introduction of the Leather-stocking hero, this "national novel" serves a purpose similar to that of Genesis, the Declaration of Independence, Darwinian evolution, and other "origin stories" that define American culture. It tells of beginnings, conflicts of authority, and a reconciliation of roles and values for all the inhabitants of the New World.

As in all creation stories, conflict threatens apparent stability or unity. Judge Temple appears as a god-like master and provider, but Oliver and Leather-stocking—like the serpent in Eden—emerge from the forest to question his authority. Through the Effingham family, Oliver has a competing claim on the land. Like Christ in Revelation, the King in Tolkien's *Rings* Trilogy, or other mythic figures who return to dispense final justice, the ancient Major Effingham—the Fire-Eater who was given the land by the Indians—at last comes out of hiding to deliver prophetic justice. (In *The Last of the Mohicans*, the ancient Indian Tamenund plays a similar climactic role.) Oliver's and Elizabeth's marriage resolves any remaining questions by uniting the Effingham, Temple, and Indian claims once and for all.

In a parallel creation story, *The Pioneers* resolves competing attitudes toward the law, represented by two opposing but conscientious men—Judge Temple and the Leather-stocking. As judge over the town's unruly inhabitants, Temple must impartially uphold and enforce systematic laws. As a woodsman used to watching out for himself, Leather-stocking asks, "[W]hat has a man who lives in the wilderness to do with the ways of the law?" (chap. 28). Matters come to a head when Leather-stocking slays another deer out of season. Though Natty has saved Elizabeth from a panther, the judge must sentence him to humiliating punishment.

Like the founding fathers for the early United States, the judge establishes, in John Adams's words, "a government of laws and not of men"—a system of laws that operates without regard for personal considerations or connections. "*The Pioneers* is one of those rare works," writes John McWilliams, "in which an author has fully understood and successfully dramatized all the ramifications of a conflict that is crucial to his civilization's development" (1972; 129). Among those ramifications or impacts, Natty in the end declares to Elizabeth and Oliver, "your ways isn't my ways," and abandons Templeton's regulated community to journey to a new frontier where he can "eat when hungry and drink when a-dry, [while] ye keep stated hours and rules" (chap. 41).

These characters' division between the town's civil law and frontier ethics reflects a lasting division in American art and society. Most Americans obey the rule of law and accept the restraints necessary to uphold a diverse and complex civilization. But American fiction puts a spotlight on individualistic heroes who follow not what Natty calls "the troubles and [deviltries] of the law" (chap. 32) but a personal code of justice and honor. Examples abound in which vigilantes move beyond the normal compromises of society and circumvent the courts with righteous violence: Rambo, Dirty Harry, the heroes of *Death Wish* or *Lethal Weapon*. Judge Temple's law must prevail for Templeton, as it would for North America's growing cities and settlements in the early 1800s. Hereafter, however, Cooper's later and more famous novels in the Leather-Stocking series will not concern the civic harmony established by the judge. Instead they follow the path of the Leather-stocking, who quits the settlements and their laws. As a result, people who live in cities or suburbs governed by complex and impersonal rules constitute the audience for American fiction. But fiction's subject typically concerns an individual or family living out their personal codes of honor on some frontier, whether the inner city, the West, or outer space.

Creation stories also concern relations between humans and nature. In Genesis, for instance, God commands man, "Be fruitful, and multiply, and replenish the earth, and subdue it: and have dominion over . . . every living thing that moveth upon the earth" (1.28). Describing an outpost of a civilization shaped by this command, *The Pioneers* explores the conflict between nature's limited resources and modern humanity's desire to have more of everything as soon as possible. Early in the novel Elizabeth marvels at "the alterations that a few short years were making in the aspect of the country"; "Five years had wrought greater changes, than a century would produce in [older] countries" (chap. 3).

The most striking sign of such change is deforestation. In Cooper's time as in ours, this intensive process continues to provide employment and products for growing populations while radically transforming huge portions of the natural and developing worlds. The character in *The Pioneers* who most represents this hallmark of modern economic development is the woodcutter Billy Kirby. His occupation proves "ominous of the fall of the forest, which had flourished there for centuries"; upon finishing his clear-cutting, he "march[es] away, under the blaze of the prostrate forest, like the conqueror of some city" (chap. 17). For better or worse, the destruction of the great North American forests has been one of the indisputable accomplishments of European settlement—the same activity for which the

United States now criticizes development in the Amazon rainforest and other tropical woodlands. A consistent motif in all the Leather-Stocking Tales is that, as soon as the new people arrive, the forest begins to fall.

The moral and material consequences of such activity may be more profound than we can yet perceive. *The Pioneers*, as with its comprehension of the competing claims of personal and civil law, depicts the complexity of modern America's relation to nature. As an educated and far-seeing developer, Judge Temple expresses conservationist attitudes by deploring the "wastefulness of the settlers" in cutting down the "jewels of the forest" (chap. 9). But Natty reminds the judge that, for all his expressions of conscience, he enables such devastation by attracting the settlers with loans and improvements. Such quandaries continue today as increasing numbers of twenty-first-century citizens feel alarm over climate change, but few can imagine foregoing the fossil fuels that contribute to global warming.

In one major scene after another, the settlers of *The Pioneers* decimate not only the trees of the forest but the bass and pigeons that have filled the lakes and skies. Most modern readers will take the Leather-stocking's side as he scolds them for their "wastey ways" (chap. 22). But Cooper never sacrifices the art of the larger picture for simplistic preaching. Other voices in the novel counter Natty's call to conserve; Billy Kirby defends the slaughter of the pigeons, for instance, by citing the birds' destruction of his wheat crop, and Dickon Jones notes that all the hungry people in the village will eat that night. *The Pioneers* again constitutes our "national novel" by depicting an America of heroic, tragic complexity: much as Americans love freedom but need laws, so we love nature but cannot live without destroying it.

ALTERNATIVE READING: *THE PIONEERS* AS A NOVEL FOR WOMEN

Gender roles also feature in origin or creation stories. *The Pioneers* shows women operating in a formative society whose ethics still influence American culture. The gender dynamics in the novel are those of a frontier. Today in Alaska or at other outposts of resource extraction, for instance, men far outnumber women, whose identities tend to be defined by male models, authority, or protection. If you factor in Cooper's reputation for male-oriented adventure, few would consider *The Pioneers* as a text for feminist interpretation. But Cooper started as a novelist of manners, and his leading woman, Elizabeth Temple, appears in more of the novel's scenes than any other character. As always, Cooper offers so many materials rich with potential significance that a reader can find support for a wide range of interpretations. As seen above, however, contradiction, irony, and ambivalence are part of the modern American life that starts in scenarios like that of *The Pioneers*.

Admittedly, some of what Cooper writes may justify dismissing this author as a sexist, a racist, or any other –ist available. Two late chapters concerning the sacrifice of the Temples' dog Brave in the fight against the panther first praise Brave by comparing its intelligence with Elizabeth's, and subsequently by comparing its appearance with the slave Aggy. As usual, Cooper's coarse playfulness displays his threatened sense of privilege. But such flaws should not blind us to his more sober descriptions of the village's social dynamics, which give a fair representation of the restrictions and occasional liberties of women in a frontier community.

Feminist methods can help readers appreciate the conflicting and cooperating voices in this complex novel. An accessible and enjoyable source is Anne L. Bower's description of cooperative discussion techniques she used to teach *The Pioneers* to a class of women college students—an essay that is posted on the Cooper Society Web page. Titled "Resisting Women," Bower's paper relates how her class's attention to historical roles for women and Cooper's treatment of the subject overcame the class's resistance to Cooper's obnoxious style and attitudes. The class's "students decided" that Elizabeth Temple "is set up as the 'perfect' female—submissive to the strong men in her life and yet showing considerable spirit, initiative, physical bravery, and independence of ideas." Under scrutiny, Elizabeth's apparent "perfection" reveals her dependence on "heroic males." Further, Cooper's development of her character was "trapped" by contemporary requirements for depicting women. Some students began to see Cooper as a "crypto-feminist." Others extended discussion of gender into economic class, finding that Elizabeth's relative "freedoms" result from "the status conferred by her father," without which "Elizabeth would be driven to . . . either the sappiness of Louisa or the harshness of Betty and Remarkable," two minor characters who work for their livelihood.

An alternative feminist tradition that can enhance the muffled voices of women in early American literature helps today's readers appreciate Elizabeth's role on Cooper's frontier. In comparison with familiar styles of feminism that emphasize gender equality, "difference feminism" highlights women's potential not merely to take on men's roles but to provide distinct social perspectives and functions. This school of feminism takes a number of forms and has been criticized for reinforcing traditional stereotypes, but a careful application can illuminate how a woman's voice develops and varies *The Pioneers'* major themes.

Such a theme, identified earlier, is the conflict between the community's law as represented by Judge Temple and the more individualistic frontier justice articulated by the Leather-stocking. As an alternative to such theoretical oppositions between men, the psychologist Carol Gilligan proposes a conciliatory approach to issues of justice. According to Gilligan's 1982 study, *In a Different Voice: Psychological Theory and Women's Development,* men consider moral and social issues through a "justice orientation" or an "ethics of justice," while women work from a "responsibility orientation" or an "ethics of care." As a result, men think in terms of rules and justice that take the form of hierarchy and opposition, while women think more in terms of caring and maintaining relationships with others.

One of Elizabeth's and Louisa's outings provides a brief example of how this difference-based feminist ethic can redeem traditional womanhood's intentions and actions. As the two approach Leather-stocking's cabin, Elizabeth reflects on Oliver's mysterious aloofness toward her father. The "abstraction" of Judge Temple enables him to rationalize the young man's behavior, but "women are always more alive to such subjects than men" (chap. 28). Elizabeth does not choose sides but seeks to understand and improve the relationships between her father, Oliver, and herself. Such behavior may simultaneously acknowledge the entrapment of Cooper's women characters in a sexist framework and explore women's management of such situations.

A larger demonstration of Elizabeth's "ethics of care" occurs after her father sentences Natty to the stocks and prison for poaching a deer. Elizabeth directs Oliver to "tell the Leather-stocking he has friends as well as judges in us" (chap. 31). When Judge Temple reviews the case with his daughter, though, he imposes a "justice orientation" that Elizabeth cannot overcome. The "sanctity of the laws must be respected," Judge Temple asserts. Elizabeth counters that "those laws, that condemn a man like the Leather-stocking to so severe a punishment, for an offence that even I must think very venial [i.e., minor], cannot be perfect in themselves." The narrator intones that Elizabeth's "logic . . . contained more feeling than reason" while the Judge retorts, "There thou talkest as a woman, child," and asks if Elizabeth is taking sides against him. Faced with an argument that threatens to divide rather than maintain relationships, she withdraws: "nay, do not put such questions to me" (chap. 35).

The novel's remaining action is too grand and complex to be the design of a single character, but its concluding chapter suggests that Elizabeth's maintenance of relationships, while less public and pronounced than the judge's campaign for civil law, has partly succeeded. Her marriage to Oliver reconciles the competing land claims, and, at her urging, the judge arranges a pardon for Leather-stocking. Judge Temple does not otherwise appear at the end, but Elizabeth presides over a brief reunion of herself, Oliver, and Leather-stocking at Chingachgook's and Major Effingham's graves. Elizabeth reveals that, also upon her directive, Judge Temple has found Mr. Grant a ministerial position in a more established town where Louisa might meet a partner "proper for one of her years and character" (chap. 41).

"Bess! You amaze me! I did not think you had been such a manager," Oliver marvels, to which Elizabeth answers, "Oh! I manage more deeply than you can imagine, sir." One might make too much of a moment that is familiar from romantic comedy. Yet woman's "different voice" demonstrates that, however much Cooper may mash or lift a given voice at any time, the creation story of *The Pioneers* is like the nation whose birth it describes. Many voices clash and cooperate to make a new country and its "national novel."

7

The Last of the Mohicans: A Narrative of 1757 (1826)

In 1826 James Fenimore Cooper's second Leather-Stocking Tale became an immediate international bestseller. Two centuries later, the book maintains a niche in the publishing marketplace, and its title echoes in the mind like a trumpet or a drum. *The Last of the Mohicans* is by many estimates Cooper's greatest book and a monument of American literature. Yet this proud reputation arrives with baggage. Most people who recognize the title have never read the novel, and those required to read this or another Cooper novel in literature courses may recall the experience with rolling eyes and heavy sighs. How to reconcile these diverse responses?

A positive start is to acknowledge the novel's popular impact. People who never heard of Cooper can process the phrase "the last of the Mohicans" to describe the passing of a heroic generation. That title must already have meant something in the 1820s when the novel made a sensation in the United States and Europe. In contrast to most bestsellers, *The Last of the Mohicans* never fell out of print. Today more than a dozen editions are available for bookstores to display on their classics shelves. As a further sign of vitality, the novel's title, characters, and story have crossed over to diverse media including paintings, comics, and movies. The grand scale, bold adventure, and bittersweet nostalgia of *The Last of the Mohicans* met or set the standards of American popular fiction.

But Cooper's popular audience has moved on to simpler, newer fare. Today *The Last of the Mohicans* sells primarily because teachers require students to read it. In their defense, the novel incomparably dramatizes early America, particularly the tragedy of the Indian nations' devastation as a result of western progress. Such claims may appear beside the point, though, for first-time readers who struggle to track the novel's action or identify with its characters. For such readers, this chapter offers working attitudes and techniques for making the most of a powerful but demanding work of art.

For starters, the qualities that make *Last of the Mohicans* a great novel are inseparable from those that make it a hard novel to read. Cooper attempts so much that his style is constantly under strain. Titanic characters, life-and-death conditions, and exotic data crowd every page—but, as critic John McWilliams writes, "At times we feel that . . . *The Last of the Mohicans* contains too many characters, too much description, too involved a plot" (1995, 39). Besides being "too involved," that plot can turn at so rapid and violent a pace that events and locations blur. Those "too many characters" are identified obliquely, go by several names, and masquerade as each other. Elaborate vocabulary, stylistic experiments, and sheer scale overload the attention, which is further stressed by danger that resolves only to fresh crises and sensitive subjects like interracial relations. Readers who complete *The Last of the Mohicans* will find themselves exhausted, exhilarated, or somewhere in between.

A strategy for managing such an intimidating reading assignment is to classify it. What *kind* of a book is *The Last of the Mohicans?* In literary terms, what is its genre? The short answer, as with most of Cooper's major fiction, is that *Mohicans* is a historical novel. Fictional characters appear in a scenario from the actual past. The novel's subtitle, *A Narrative of 1757,* indicates its setting during the French and Indian War of 1754–63, two generations before Cooper wrote it. The novel's original readers would have had an easier time recognizing the names of actual generals like Webb and Montcalm who appear on these pages. Also, because the French and Indian War was so much nearer—comparable to World Wars I and II for us—they would sense how much it shaped their world. Without that earlier war, the American Revolution might not have occurred a dozen years later.

Other genres inform *Mohicans'* meaning and action. Nations in conflict make the novel analogous to a classical epic (Porte 40). As in an epic, heroic figures represent whole tribes or nations. The title character Uncas of the Delawares and the devious Magua of the Iroquois resemble Achilles and Hector in *The Iliad.* Veterans like Chingachgook and Tamenund share the stature of Agamemnon or Priam, and Leather-stocking makes alliances like a latter-day Odysseus. As in the *Iliad's* war over Helen of

Troy, the heroes and villains of *Mohicans* battle to capture or rescue the Munro sisters, Cora and Alice.

This epic mode elevates *Mohicans* to classic grandeur, but its popularity also resulted from Cooper's experiments with gothic style. Better known now as "horror" but already popular in the 1800s, gothic novels often involved an innocent young woman entering a haunted castle to be threatened by dark forces of the past. Since the American frontier offered few old buildings, *The Last of the Mohicans* relocates the gothic's ominous atmosphere and extreme characters to the forests of North America. These gothic formulas sensationalize the wilderness and develop a color code for imagining interracial relations.

A final piece in the novel's genre-puzzle—romance—accounts for the tug the novel makes at the reader's heart as well as its compelling narrative structure. Romance hints at a forbidden yet noble love glimmering between Cora and Uncas. As a literary term, *romance* describes a quest for an object of desire, like knights in search of the Holy Grail. To read *The Last of the Mohicans* is to journey in search of a beauty that never was, that nonetheless lives in regret and possibility.

POINT OF VIEW: HISTORICAL OMNISCIENCE AND FICTIONAL NAÏVETÉ

Like all the Leather-Stocking Tales, *The Last of the Mohicans* relates events primarily from a third-person omniscient point of view. This expansive storytelling style frames Cooper's trademark landscapes, but it can also shift to spotlight individual characters and actions. This classic technique varies and adapts to meet the special demands of a historical novel that feels intensely personal.

The God's-eye view of world history that opens *The Last of the Mohicans* demonstrates omniscient or all-knowing perspective. The narrator sets the time and place by referring to "the colonial wars of North America" and "the country which lies between . . . the Hudson [River] and [its] adjacent lakes" in present-day upstate New York. As though looking down on a vast map, the narrator previews the route the Munro sisters will take from Fort Edward "along the margin of the Hudson" River to Fort William Henry, about 20 miles north on Lake George. This lofty perspective then descends to the first of these forts to observe the departure of "fifteen hundred men," whom "the forest . . . appeared to swallow up." Narrowing further, the viewpoint then records the actions and speech of another set of characters who are preparing to leave the fort.

Similar panoramas throughout the novel shift focus from settings to individuals. Critics compare Cooper's spacious scans to a wide-screen movie and his spotlighting to a zoom lens. The evacuation of Fort William Henry midway through *Mohicans* follows this pattern. "Living masses of the English . . . near three thousand, were moving slowly across the plain," watched by "the French army" and "a dark cloud of savages" (chap. 18). The viewpoint then zooms to the English "women and children [fleeing] in terror," particularly one wife carrying an infant. The "gaudy colours of [her] shawl" attract the attention of a Huron Indian, whose brutal murder of her and her child triggers a widespread massacre.

The way Cooper coordinates different scopes of perception to create tension and terror anticipates the development of cinematography a century later. Within a year of the novel's publication, Cooper's friend Thomas Cole (1801–48) of the Hudson River School—Romantic artists famous for portraying natural landscapes on large canvases—began a series of paintings based on *The Last of the Mohicans*. Available for viewing on the Internet, Cole's *Landscape with Figures: A Scene from "The Last of the Mohicans"* (1826) and *The Last of the Mohicans: Cora Kneeling at the Feet of Tamenund* (1827) show grandeur and detail faithful to Cooper's word-paintings—even when seen on computer screens.

This pattern of a broad viewpoint tightening to close observation recurs in the knowledge Cooper's narrator brings to *The Last of the Mohicans*. Theologically, *omniscience* refers to infinite awareness and understanding. Cooper's God-like narrator knows not only the past history that leads to the French and Indian War but also the future ahead. During the fort's surrender, the narrator previews that French General Montcalm would, "only two short years afterwards, throw away his life" in the siege of Quebec, and that American military tactics in the French and Indian War continued in "the war of the revolution" two decades later (chap. 15).

But this apparently infinite knowledge has peculiar limits. In the first chapter, the narrator recognizes the historical General Daniel Webb and refers to him by name. But when fictional characters come on the scene, the narrator identifies them with descriptions—Magua is an "Indian runner," Alice is a woman with "golden hair," Cora is "the other." Only after these characters address each other by name does the narrator, as though overhearing them, use their names. A similar pattern occurs in chapter 3. "[Using] an author's privilege [to] shift the scene a few miles to the westward," the narrator relates a conversation between "an Indian" and a "white man." After they call each other by name, the narrator designates the Indian as "Chingachgook," and "the white man . . . we shall call Hawkeye, after the manner of his companions" (chap. 3).

This combination of historical omniscience and fictional naïveté helps manage the storytelling challenges of a historical novel. Narrative tension benefits from some degree of ignorance. An omniscient narrator risks spoiling the story by telling too much too soon. To counter this risk, Cooper tactically delays confirming some knowledge. The narrator, even after learning characters' names, may hesitate to use them. Following the massacre at the fort, "the forms of five men" are "seen issuing from the narrow vista of trees" to search the killing field. The narrator's pause in identifying these characters invests the scene with strangeness, tension, and discomfort. Finally another paragraph adds, "The reader will perceive, at once, in these respective characters, the Mohicans, and their white friend, the scout, together with Munro and Heyward" (chap. 18).

Mohicans achieves similar effects by shifting from omniscient to third-person limited point of view. Limited perspective tells the story through a character's eyes and consciousness. For this purpose Cooper mostly uses Major Duncan Heyward, the Munro sisters' escort. Cooper's original readership would find this white officer and gentleman a comfortable conduit for processing information. Also, Heyward's youth and blandness give him an intelligent naïveté comparable to that of the narrator. Once, Heyward thinks he sees a shockingly primitive Indian camp, only to find he is among a colony of beavers (chaps. 21–22). In the actual Huron village Heyward witnesses a captive warrior's heroic self-preservation—"a light form cleaving the air"—but fails to recognize Uncas in the half-darkness and confusion. Action and point of view climax simultaneously as Uncas reaches safety near a fire whose light reveals him in all his glory (chap. 23). Viewpoint in *Mohicans* again heightens tension by delaying recognition—though such delays may confuse readers used to more direct narration.

A final note regarding point of view is to distinguish Leather-stocking from the narrator. At times it seems like Hawk-eye outtalks the narrator, but overall he functions less as a reporter of events and more like a chorus from classical drama, as his commentary on the speech and action of others reinforces or undercuts themes. In comparison, the historically conscious but fictionally naïve narrator maintains a careful objectivity. Such interplay is further evidence of the range and suppleness of point of view in *The Last of the Mohicans*.

SETTING: AMERICA'S OFFICIAL HISTORY, AND THE GOTHIC WILDERNESS

As a "historical novel," *The Last of the Mohicans* develops settings from two distinct but related categories of literature. The first of these settings derives from history—what *really* happened—which forms a frame for the novel's fictive action. Within that framework, however, the new, unknown fictional story—what *could* have happened—generates another setting of its own. That second setting is less formal and empirical than history, but it feels more immediate and sensational. *Mohicans* repeatedly shifts between these settings' unique symbols and systems of validity to create a hybrid reality on the frontier of fact and fiction.

America's national history contributes to *Mohicans'* status as classic or epic literature. This official backdrop appears at the start of the book or individual chapters. It gains definition from the familiar apparatus of historical knowledge: names like French General Montcalm; surveys of the New York-Canadian border; natural features like the Hudson River or Lake Champlain; structures like Fort Ticonderoga; and recognizable events of war and diplomacy. Along with its subtitle, *A Narrative of 1757*, these materials reveal that *The Last of the Mohicans* takes place during the French and Indian War of 1754 to 1763.

Like all novelists, Cooper takes liberties with history, as when Montcalm leaves his camp in disguise, or when an actual Colonel Monro at Fort William Henry becomes the fictional father of Cora and Alice Munro. Such latitude does not invalidate the picture of history that grows from a novel but reveals the bargains made by a hybrid genre. Historians don't complain as long as fictional events and characters operate within accepted boundaries of fact, changing neither the outcomes of actual events nor the trajectory of actual figures. Historical fiction is less a competitor than a complement to traditional history.

Readers of historical fiction cooperate with this bargain. In *Mohicans'* opening pages, they march through some names and dates. Such strokes set a foundation for a fictional story and invest it with history's grandeur. Soon, though, fictional characters and events appear in more intimate settings—a court, a ship, a town, or a home. In *Last of the Mohicans*, this fictional setting opens when the fictional characters take a separate path through the wilderness. After the English soldiers follow the direct route to Fort William Henry, the crafty Magua guides Major Heyward and the Munro sisters to a shortcut on "a narrow and blind path" that leads through "numberless trunks of trees, that rose in dark lines" (chap. 2).

This "narrow" passage into a "dark" space introduces a popular fictional setting that appears in numberless novels and films. The literary term for such a setting is *gothic*—more casual terms include horror, thrillers, or ghost stories. Gothic style originally refers to the architecture of medieval Europe, which reappears in *Mohicans* as "deep arches of the forest . . . in deceptive shadow" and, at Glenns Falls, "the arches of the cave" (chaps. 8, 10).

In American literature, gothic style is most associated with Edgar Allan Poe, whose poems and tales began to appear the year after *Mohicans*. The gothic literary fashion or genre had begun the previous century, and by Cooper's and Poe's time it followed a set pattern. An innocent young woman enters a large house or castle whose hidden rooms and passageways hold dark and threatening secrets from the past. The gothic's power to thrill audiences by probing repressed fears made it a natural vehicle for Cooper's exploration of America's past in *The Last of the Mohicans*.

Yet Cooper and other writers wishing to set a gothic tale in the New World faced a problem. Few old buildings were to be found on the American frontier. Therefore Cooper relocated the gothic's dark atmosphere and festoons to the "bleak and savage wilderness" (*Mohicans*, chap. 22). At least two other classic texts of American literature had already made similar experiments. *Edgar Huntly* (1799) by Charles Brockden Brown (1771–1810) tracked a "somnambulist" or sleepwalker through an American forest haunted by deranged murderers and marauding Indians. Washington Irving's *Legend of Sleepy Hollow* (1819) took Ichabod Crane through a countryside of spectral legends, hanging trees, and paths menaced by the Headless Horseman. The American forest reappeared as a gothic space as recently as the film *The Blair Witch Project* (1999).

But no work before or since *The Last of the Mohicans* has so ingeniously and extravagantly developed the gothic potential of the American wilderness. Examples of this style in *Mohicans* are too numerous to list, but three scenes demonstrate how Cooper coordinated the gothic with character and theme. The most extensive setting is the hiding place at Glenns Falls. Instead of vaults or tombs as in a gothic building, the characters enter "a narrow, deep, cavern in the rock" (chap. 6). The light-and-shadow dynamic of the gothic appears as "blazing knot[s] of pine" contrast with the "black limestone" of the cave's walls. The "spectral looking figure" of Chingachgook "stalk[s] from out the darkness." This array of gothic conventions climaxes with a favorite gothic sound effect. In horror movies and gothic novels, moments of peace are broken by a scream in the night. In the "dim light" of "the arches of the cave" at Glenns Falls, the fugitives find such a moment shattered by "a cry, that seemed neither human, nor earthly, . . . penetrating not only the recesses of the cavern, but to the inmost heart of all who heard it" (chaps. 10, 6). This cry rises not from some dusty medieval scenario—a victim buried alive or threatened by a malicious dwarf—but from a horse frightened by Indians stalking outside.

Cooper's gothic ingenuity sometimes grows darkly playful, as other settings in *Mohicans* show him stretching this style to comical lengths. In the midst of the forest, an abandoned building looms up to evoke the moldering architecture and bloody history more typical of the European gothic. Hawk-eye leads the party to a "decayed block-house . . . quietly crumbling in the solitude of the forest," a "species of ruins" matching "the gloomy character of the surrounding scenery" (chap. 13). Like a haunted house, the blockhouse is the site of a secret history. Hawk-eye and Chingachgook helped erect this fortification in "the first war in which [Hawk-eye] ever drew blood from man." At the end of Hawk-eye's recollection, the young people find they are sitting on the graves of the dead who were buried there after that fight: "Heyward and the sisters arose on the instant from the grassy sepulchre." The spooked party leaves this "silent grave and crumbling ruin . . . to bury themselves in the gloom of the woods."

The novel's second half includes a final gothic riff when Magua, like Dracula or some other gothic villain in his lair, holds Alice captive in a "cavern in the bosom of the mountain" (chap. 24). As hallways in a gothic castle branch off to innumerable nooks and crannies, Magua's cavern features "natural galleries and subterranean apartments" whose "dark and gloomy passages" are pierced by "shrieks and cries" (chap. 32). Cooper may go a step too far when Hawk-eye, dressed as a bear, discovers that the "apartment" imprisoning Alice has that overworked gimmick of gothic setting and action—a secret passage or "private outlet" through which Magua escapes.

Cooper's extravagance should not distract from the seriousness of the gothic setting to *Mohicans'* characters and themes. This dark alternative to the official chronicle of progress uncovers a nightmare version of history. This alternative American history is generally repressed but always ready to break out. Beneath the standard black-and-white color scheme of the gothic, the lurid red of blood percolates—the spilled blood of violence, the warm blood of life, the shared blood of family or nation. Throughout *Mohicans* the setting turns to blood. Hundreds of Frenchmen find a "sepulchre" in the "silent pool of the 'bloody pond'" (chap. 14). The "soil" at William Henry is "fattened with human blood" (chap. 18). Whites "without a cross" like Hawk-eye, Duncan, and Alice risk their blood on the multicultural frontier. This historical novel makes America feel at once stranger yet more real than the history of the textbooks, as though printer's ink might imbrue our hands with the guilty, angry blood of the past.

PLOT AND STRUCTURE: ROMANCE OF QUEST AND CAPTIVITY

Mohicans' plot, like its setting, shows two faces of the historical novel. Features from earlier narratives lend the story a classical vintage. Yet the story's restless energy shares qualities with popular literature and film. The novel consolidates these various sources and impulses in a perennial model of narrative known as the romance.

In the literary marketplace and everyday speech, a *romance* is a love story for women readers. Adding themes of forbidden love and dark or haunted settings creates a gothic romance like *Jane Eyre* (1847) or *Rebecca* (1938). *Mohicans* makes similar appeals with its story of Cora and Uncas. But for literary criticism, *romance* is not limited to a particular subject like love. Instead it is a pattern of storytelling or narrative. As classified by Northrop Frye in *Anatomy of Criticism* (1957), *romance* is one of four principal narratives in Western literature (the other three being tragedy, comedy, and satire). The romance follows a journey through trials and ordeals in quest of some goal or object of desire. For instance, *Mohicans* opens with Duncan and the Munro sisters traveling through the dangers of the forest to join Cora's and Alice's father at Fort William Henry.

The European Middle Ages provide the original models for the romance narrative—especially tales of chivalry. In *Mohicans* Duncan guards Alice, "dreaming that he was a knight of ancient chivalry, holding his midnight vigils before the tent of a re-captured princess" (chap. 13). Princesses and such paraphernalia shout "romance," but the essential romance *narrative* concerns the recaptured relation. Realizing some dream or object of love, the heroes or heroines of romance overcome a sense of separation or incompleteness. This quest leads them to cross borders, whether the physical or racial boundaries of *Mohicans* or class boundaries in film romances like *Pretty Woman* (1990) or *Working Girl* (1988). Like medieval knights enduring trials, the sisters and their rescuers must overcome Magua's treachery. Cora and Alice reach their father but are recaptured. Their rescuers strive for one "great and engrossing object—the recovery of the sisters" (chap. 22). Uncas races after Cora "as if life to him possessed but a single object" (chap. 32). The romance narrative propels *The Last of the Mohicans* and many other popular stories because its heroes and their goals embody an individual and shared desire for something greater. Whatever it is inevitably slips from the grasp, only to renew the quest or journey.

Whether romance ends comically, as with the marriages in Jane Austen's novels, or tragically, as in Fitzgerald's *The Great Gatsby* (1925) or the film *Titanic* (1997), what marks this narrative's conclusion is a motion or spirit of "transcendence." The medieval knight glimpses the Holy Grail as a sign of a higher realm. In popular romances, characters "live happily ever after" or treasure a special memory of a finer time. At the end of *The Last of the Mohicans*, Alice and Duncan return to "the settlements of the 'pale-faces,'" while Indian maidens sing of Cora and Uncas transcending to an afterlife where the "Heaven of the pale-faces" abuts the Indians' "blessed hunting grounds" (chap. 33).

Part of the historic greatness of *The Last of the Mohicans*, then, is that it relocates the European romance narrative to characters and settings of the New World. But Cooper's romance is not merely a pale imitation of something done earlier and better in Europe. *Mohicans* also incorporates a narrative native to the Americas. Cooper's first readers would have recognized his novel as a captivity narrative. One of America's unique contributions to world literature, a "captivity" typically tells of a white person captured by Indians, followed by ordeals such as assimilation into Indian culture, or goals like escape or revenge. From the colonial era to the early twentieth century, this "vast and enormously popular genre" generated "more than a thousand separate captivity titles" (Haberly 431). *The Narrative of the Captivity and the Restoration of Mrs. Mary Rowlandson*, written by the wife of a Puritan minister in 1682, is the most famous of the historical narratives. The genre's popularity led to its adoption into fiction. Brown's *Edgar Huntly* modeled a captivity episode in the generation before Cooper's. In the twentieth century this tradition continues in classic movies like *The Searchers* (1956), *Little Big Man* (1970), and *Dances with Wolves* (1990).

Mohicans alludes to the captivity tradition and integrates it with other narratives. At Glenns Falls Alice shows herself familiar with the genre's sensational elements by mentioning "those cruel murders, those terrific scenes of torture, of which we read so much" (chap. 6). When the rescuers meet David Gamut near the Huron camp and ask about the sisters' fate, Gamut replies, "They are captives to the heathen" (chap. 22). Chapters set in the Hurons' village resemble actual captivity narratives and refer to Indian practices: "Magua, in obedience to a policy seldom departed from, separated his prisoners" (chap. 22). *The Last of the Mohicans* actually involves two captivity narratives—the first at Glenns Falls, the second following the massacre. As Terence Martin writes, "In the first half of the *Mohicans*, Cora and Alice Munro try to reach their father; in the second half the father (in Cooper's words) is 'in quest of his children'" (1969; 87). Captivity formulas explore the fears and attractions of American Indian life, while its journeys, ordeals, and restorations share obvious parallels with the romance narrative.

Detractors complain that Cooper's stories move slowly, but the opposite impression once prevailed. Though *Mohicans* takes its time "collecting [its] plot" or recovering from major action sequences, perceptions that its plot is slow may result more from Cooper's thick prose (Martin 81). Critical references often characterize *Mohicans*' plot as "captivity, escape, pursuit"—formulas popular in escapist entertainment of our own time. *The Last of the*

Mohicans may be a prototype for modern action novels and movies replete with hostages, rescues, and chases. Such spectacles are rarely remembered for long, but the action in Cooper's novel still matters.

MAJOR CHARACTERS: TITANIC CHALLENGE AND GLORY

Characterization again brings Cooper's reputation into conflict with his achievement. His style of characterization frustrates modern expectations but creates significant figures. Cooper's characters are, in Jane Tompkins's phrase, "storybook savages and cardboard heroes" (95). Yet these characters are also larger-than-life, inspiring fresh analysis in scholarship and classrooms. Comprehending and coping with Cooper's unique style of characterization helps a reader appreciate *Mohicans*' status among his greatest novels.

If characters in *Mohicans* frustrate both critical and popular standards, these eccentricities mark not mere failures in style but the expressions of an alternative system of characterization. Students who enjoy the interior dimensions of modern fictional characters may feel balked by "Cooper's utter lack of curiosity about the inner lives of his characters" (Tompkins 100). On the other hand, readers who enjoy straightforward heroes and villains find that *Mohicans* offers few warm-and-fuzzy protagonists with whom to identify or absolute scoundrels to despise.

As a measure of the differences between popular expectations and what *Mohicans* offers, consider Hawk-eye in the novel in contrast to the character of the same name in the 1992 hit movie *Last of the Mohicans* (directed by Michael Mann). The novel's Hawk-eye is a middle-aged, musty chatterbox. In the movie, Hawk-eye as played by Daniel Day-Lewis is a strapping young aristocrat—Tarzan of North America. Such changes are innocent on their face, and the credits for the movie acknowledge it is based not on Cooper's novel but on a screenplay for an earlier *Mohicans* film from 1936. Hollywood films design characters to reflect the generous self-images that paying customers carry into the theater with their popcorn. Such popularized characters are easily embraced—but just as easily forgotten.

Meanwhile, the novel's characters confront new generations of readers with unexpected meaning. If Cooper's characters are not consumer-friendly and their author "has no interest in the drama of the individual psyche which is the central subject matter of modern fiction," what are the sources of these characters' pleasure and meaning? (Tompkins 100). In her article on "A New Way to Read the Leatherstocking Novels," Tompkins suggests that, rather than "crude caricatures, or defective versions of characters in other novels," Cooper's characters embody "fixed values in a system of value" (106, 113).

Identifying a "system of value" sounds tedious compared to the instant pleasure of identifying with glamorous individuals, but two exercises help the reader appreciate Cooper's unique appeal. One approach is to return to the movie of *Mohicans* to observe the repercussions when seedy old Hawk-eye changes into the Incredible Hunk. Other characters also become simplified and predictable. As the new leading man, Hawk-eye bumps the title character—Uncas—from connecting with Cora. She, in turn, is white-washed to a spunky babe. Uncas is busted to teen sidekick. Chingachgook, formerly Hawk-eye's partner, gets kicked upstairs to the wise-old-man department. And Magua, a voice for the dispossessed, is downgraded to an angry red man. Standing on their own, the characters in the movie confirm what we already think. In the novel, in contrast, each character's complexity grows relative to that of the others. (The film of *Mohicans* that is most faithful to the novel is a silent movie from 1920 directed by C. Brown and M. Tourneur, who retain the original Uncas-Cora pairing and keep Hawk-eye the same age as Chingachgook.)

The characters' numerous disguises and names serve as an index to the novel's interdependent characters and systems. Hawk-eye and David Gamut exchange costumes in the Huron village, where David replaces Uncas as a captive. Hawk-eye and Uncas take turns dressing in a bear-suit while Chingachgook hides out as a beaver. Duncan, made up by Chingachgook, disguises himself as a French faith-healer, then enters a shooting-match to prove he is Hawk-eye. These unstable identities account for the many names by which characters are known. Hawk-eye is Leather-stocking, the scout, "*La Longue Carabine*" or Long Rifle. Uncas is "*Le Cerf Agile*" or Bounding Elk, the "panther of his tribe," the "pride of the Wapanachki," and "the last of the Mohicans." Every name indicates the character's place in another system of signs. At the center of the novel's shifting identities and plots is Magua, also known as Le Renard Subtil or the Sly Fox. In a characterization partly based on "the great Deceiver" (Satan) in Milton's *Paradise Lost*, Magua counterfeits so well that in the Delaware camp his and Uncas's identities as good and bad Indians are briefly reversed.

MAJOR INDIAN CHARACTERS: UNCAS AS NOBLE SAVAGE, MAGUA AS SLY FOX

Another method for identifying systems of value in *Mohicans* is to analyze characters in pairs. As a brief instance, David Gamut and Hawk-eye look alike, but they read the world differently through the book of Scripture or the book of nature. Among other antithetical pairs, Uncas and Magua appear as divergent symbols of Native America, standing on either side of the split in the Western mind when it thinks of Native Americans. As the good Indian or Noble Savage, Uncas lives in nature yet recognizes the better angels of white culture. Magua, in contrast, is the bad Indian thirsty for the white man's whisky and blood in remorse and revenge for the losses inflicted on him and his people.

These opposing figures fulfill the epic and gothic dimensions of the historical novel. As a classical figure, Uncas is a golden youth of "beautiful proportions," like "some finely moulded statue" (chaps. 26, 24). Magua as "the Prince of Darkness . . . plotting evil" invokes the epic stature of the Bible or *Paradise Lost,* but he also functions as a gothic trickster (chap. 27). Like Heathcliff in Emily Brontë's *Wuthering Heights* (1847), he feels dispossessed and determined to regain his birthright, and he and his tribesmen appear as dark images of disorder. The Hurons are "imps," "devils," and "hell-hounds" (chap. 7). Magua, displaying a "dark form and malignant visage," laughs with the "hellish taunt of a demon" (chap. 25). The opposed characters of Uncas and Magua embody competing stories of North America—either a glorious history of one classical civilization built on another, or a rankling nightmare of despoliation and vengeance.

WOMEN CHARACTERS AS FAIR AND DARK LADIES: ALICE AND CORA

Such symbolic oppositions do not say the last word on Uncas's or Magua's development, but they expose a framework that produces these characters' meaning. The Munro sisters similarly pair off as the conventional fair lady and dark lady of literature. Such a division is as deep as legend and as recent as a soap opera. Alice, with "yellow locks and blue eyes," is endearing, but she wilts under pressure (chap. 18). Under the same stresses Cora, with her "dark eye" and "tresses . . . shining and black, like the plumage of the raven," proves reasonable, resourceful, and dangerously attractive (chap. 1).

Cooper elaborates the fair lady–dark lady motif to a daring exploration of a critical American issue. A precedent for this treatment appeared seven years before *Mohicans* in Walter Scott's medieval romance *Ivanhoe* (1819). Its main women characters were the blond Rowena, descended from King Alfred, and Rebecca, daughter of Isaac the Jew. Accounting for Rowena's fairness and Rebecca's darkness, their genealogies also affect their characters and fates. Rowena's social pedigree makes her an attractive partner for any ambitious knight, but her security in the status quo keeps her personality bland and in bounds. Rebecca as a Jewess in medieval England fits in nowhere, which frees her to take chances, to help the rebels—and then to wander off as Ivanhoe marries the safe Rowena.

As with Rowena and Rebecca, distinct bloodlines determine Alice's and Cora's characters and fates. The Munro girls are *half*-sisters, their father reveals (chap. 16). Alice, the younger, was born to Munro's second wife in their native Scotland. That child has a "dazzling complexion" with a "bloom on her cheek," which the gothic color code marks as spiritual purity. Cora says of Alice, "her soul is pure and spotless as her skin!" (chap. 30). Like Uncas, fair Alice contrasts with dark Magua. At Glenns Falls, when danger momentarily appears past, her prayer of thanksgiving renders her angelic: "Her eyes were radiant . . . ; the flush of her beauty was again seated on her cheeks" (chap. 9). But heavenly white is meaningful only in opposition to demonic darkness. Through a crack in the cave wall, Alice sees "the malignant, fierce, and savage features" of the forest demon Magua. Again *Mohicans'* characters create meaning together, not separately.

CORA AS TRAGIC MULATTO

A nearer darkness opposes Alice's fairness. In the first chapter Cooper contrasts the "flush" of Alice's "complexion" with Cora's skin, which is "not brown, but . . . charged with the colour of the rich blood" (chap. 1). After this initial note on skin color, Cora is identified by her "raven . . . tresses," with both Uncas and Magua calling her "the dark-hair." As with Rebecca in *Ivanhoe*, these surface differences index a genealogy that both liberates and condemns Cora.

The story of Cora's conflicted identity is easy for readers to miss because its details are so explosive that Cooper must reveal them indirectly. In hindsight, the story is implicit from the start, but the facts emerge when Heyward asks Colonel Munro for the hand of his daughter in marriage. The scene opens almost comically as the concerned father assumes Heyward is interested in his elder daughter. The mood changes, however, when Heyward indicates he's interested in Alice. The Colonel explains his "offended feeling" by relating the "history" of Cora's birth in the West Indies or Caribbean. Cora's mother was "descended, remotely, from that unfortunate class, who are so basely enslaved" (chap. 16). A few coded details confirm information especially disturbing to Heyward, who is from South Carolina, a center of American slavery. Cora shares the blood of "those unfortunate beings [who] are considered of a race inferior to your own!"

In contrast to Alice's pure whiteness, Cora is colored by African as well as European descent. Identifying this biracial background renders Cora's character more intelligible, along with much else about *The Last of the Mohicans*. Attitudes toward interracial relations continue to evolve, but Americans live in a world shaped by the dynamics that inform Cooper's story. The British and American empires have been multicultural affairs, but their dominant cultures tend to regard races as pure, permanent, and separate from each other. Hawk-eye repeatedly announces, "I am genuine white" with "no cross in his blood"—"a white man without a cross" (chaps. 3, 7). Likewise the Delawares are an "unmixed people," and Chingachgook, averring "I am an unmixed man," calls his son Uncas "the last of the Mohicans" because there are none "of [his] race" with whom to marry and reproduce (Preface, chap. 3). This faith in pure blood is challenged by many mixed-blood offspring in the New World's slave societies and marriages between Indians and whites on the frontier. Yet figures like Cora might find themselves in a limbo between two worlds. For literature, such a character became known as a "tragic mulatto." A light-skinned person of white and black ancestry, the mulatto appears doomed to wander in search of a partner or family who do not officially exist.

Cora's death at the end of *Mohicans* makes her an early example of this tragic type, but the novel glimpses a more redeeming story. The "misfortune of my nature," Cora confesses, leaves her unable to "see the sunny side of the picture of life" (chap. 15). In "the settlements of the 'pale-faces,'" Cora's difference would disqualify her from any successful identity. Ironically, on the American frontier—a world where different races might meet on roughly equal terms—this same difference equips her to survive and find her voice. If the frontier romance involves testing and crossing borders, borders are already crossed in Cora's very being. Absent a place in the existing world order, Cora, like Rebecca in *Ivanhoe*, takes her chances with disorder. When things fall apart, Alice, accustomed to the status quo, faints into "infantile dependency" (chap. 11). Cora observes, inquires, and commands with "the collected and feminine dignity of her presence" (chap. 11). She has no choice but to journey like a knight of medieval romance, testing her spirit and braving the shadow of death. What does she have to lose?

Cora's development on the frontier enlarges to an alternative vision of American society as she challenges moral judgments based on color. In an early chapter, when Alice and Duncan hesitate to follow Magua, Cora asks, "Should we distrust the man because . . . his skin is dark!" Similarly she inquires concerning Uncas, "who, that looks at this creature of nature, remembers the shades of his skin!" (chap. 6). This standard of impartiality extends to whites as well as people of color. When Magua argues to Cora that "the pale-faces, the people of your own colour" gave him "the fire-water" that "made him a villain," Cora ironically replies, "[A]m I answerable that thoughtless and unprincipled men exist, whose shades of countenance may resemble mine?" (chap. 11).

However tragic, Cora's bearing generates a fleeting glimpse of a multicultural America where races meet on intimate terms and elevate each other in common identity. Cooper cautiously develops Cora's relationship with Uncas in glances, brief confidences, and her final, unsuccessful rescue. These evanescent, impassioned contacts create progress in human development. In the cave at Glenns Falls, Uncas, "his dark eye linger[ing] on [Cora's] rich, speaking countenance," serves the ladies in an imitation of European chivalry and "an utter innovation on the Indian customs" (chap. 6).

Outside the cave, when all seems lost and the "men without a cross" prepare to die, Cora comparably "innovates" by speaking out and directing them to escape for aid. As Uncas hesitates, Cora, "perhaps with an intuitive consciousness of her power," instructs him to "go to my father . . . and be the most confidential of my messengers" (chap. 8). Events preclude this special rendezvous between the Scottish-American colonel and the Native American prince, but one fancies Uncas and Munro meeting on terms that might grow to resemble those between Heyward and Munro. Any hypothetical offspring of Cora and Uncas would inherit the three major racial bloodlines of early America: Indian, European, and African— a union that occurs more in real life than in fiction. In popular and classic American literature *The Last of the Mohicans* begins an alternative story of American racial identity.

THEMES AND ALTERNATIVE READING:
MYTH AND HISTORY

Given the oversized characters and issues in *Last of the Mohicans*, classrooms may find more to discuss than time permits. Students preparing essays will find a wilderness of possibilities in which each path may lead to deliverance—or danger. Any bright thread may lead to glorious insight, or become lost or crossed in the novel's thick fabric. Such hit-or-miss qualities discourage formal criticism of *Mohicans*. Instead, the novel's bulk and significance entice cultural and historical analysis. Its heft and clutter give it the scale of myth and the feel of history. Samples from two distinguished Cooper scholars demonstrate how criticism has used these terms to manage the novel's overflow of themes.

Mythic interpretation deepens the cultural importance of a book like *Mohicans* by relating it to influential patterns of Western art or thought.

nvolves a symbolic narrative inher-
B. Lewis, for instance, interpreted
illusory myth of the American as
anches Cooper's complex characters
major appeal of myth criticism.
, *The Last of the Mohicans,* consider
yone can process the phrase "the
never read the book or heard of
n mythic interpretation, the title's
lank]" intones a familiar symbolic
n existence leads every generation
ed and the finer things in life are
Mohicans evokes and echoes that
ild card, people use the phrase to
past greatness, however vaguely

Uncas as Hero: The *Ubi Sunt*
nplifies such criticism. The char-
world" where Uncas becomes a
h fulfills a pattern indicated by
l itself. The Latin phrase "*Ubi*
ise of loss implicit in *The Last*
this formula's classic example
Bygone Times" (1461), which
, ... year?" Cooper relates this motif
.....overs title in an early chapter where Chingachgook, answering a
question from Hawk-eye about surviving members of his family, laments,
""Where are the blossoms of those summers!—fallen, one by one. . . . [M]y
boy [Uncas] is the last of the Mohicans." Such themes of change and loss
gained a special urgency and appeal in the Romantic era—as one grand
example, the final opera of Richard Wagner's *Ring Cycle* is known as the
Götterdämmerung or *Twilight of the Gods* (1876).

By relating *Mohicans* to time-honored themes in world literature, mythic
interpretation lifts the text out of Cooper's unyielding thickets and into the
open skies of memory and imagination. Associations with myth reinforce
the novel's classic significance and touch "something we answer to even
before we have spotted it; some image of experience we know to be fundamentally our own" (Lewis 102). Since the heyday of myth and symbol criticism in the mid-twentieth century, though, another critical movement has
shifted the historical field of comparison for books like *Mohicans*. Instead
of timeless but familiar literary motifs, New Historicism lowers its gaze

to more down-to-earth and controversial historical backgrounds. Relating famous literary works like Cooper's novels to texts and documents that few readers will have previously considered, this method unearths fresh and sometimes disquieting meanings from the contested grounds and events of history.

A chapter entitled "History and Empire" in the 1995 study of *The Last of the Mohicans* by John McWilliams exemplifies New Historicism. McWilliams reviews how *Mohicans* mixes "known facts" with "liberties" in order to reconstruct the French and Indian War from a war between the French and English for control of North America to a "self-destructive civil war between and within the Indian nations" (92, 86). Shifting to the period after the novel's publication in 1826, McWilliams connects Cooper's depictions of Indians to political controversies of the 1820s and 1930s connected to the "Trail of Tears," which relocated Cherokee Indians from the Appalachian Mountains to Oklahoma. Drawing on Cooper's images, "proponents of Indian Removal found it handy to write and speak of Indians as if they were all nomadic hunters, children of the forest." In fact, the Cherokees had "accepted white ways" with a constitution, court system, written laws, English newspapers, and schools. In contrast to the independent and "unmixed" characters of *Mohicans*, the Cherokees had "at least 200 interracial (red and white) married couples" and owned more than a thousand black slaves (104). After the Trail of Tears uprooted and killed a quarter of the Cherokees, former U.S. President Andrew Jackson, the chief proponent of Indian Removal, disdainfully mimicked the language and sentiments made famous by Cooper. "[O]ne by one have many powerful tribes disappeared from the earth," Jackson told Congress, but "true philanthropy" toward the Indian does not lament "the last of his race" (110).

Historically, the impact of Cooper's text is neither as lofty as myth, nor as pure as Alice, but conflicted and fated like Cora. *The Last of the Mohicans* both glorified Indians *and* helped whites accept the Indians' extinction as a natural outcome of American progress. Given such contradictory conclusions, New Historicism duplicates the complexities of Cooper's style and content. Rather than escaping to airy clarity or eternal myth, this method acknowledges the living history and contemporary texts with which classic fiction interacted.

New Historicism also generates new meaning by relating the Indian past imagined by Cooper to Indian life in our own times. A recent historical event refreshes the meaning of the title of *The Last of the Mohicans*. Cooper's Preface notes that the name "'Mohicans'" was "corrupted by the English into 'Mohegan.'" In the 1600s the Mohegans, led by a historic figure named Uncas (who would have been a great-grandfather of the novel's Uncas), were among the first Indian groups in New England to cooperate with Puritan settlers. Later, pressured by white expansion, the Mohegans dispersed, making alliances with tribes like the Delawares and generally disappearing from the records as a distinct group.

Thanks to efforts by tribal elders in Connecticut, however, the United States in March 1994 officially recognized the Mohegan people as a sovereign Indian nation. The indispensable person in this successful campaign was Mohegan Medicine Woman Gladys Tantaquidgeon, who died in 2005 at the age of 106. In recent years the Mohegan Sun casino in Uncasville, Connecticut, has become New England's largest amusement center and home to the Connecticut Sun of the Women's National Basketball Association. What was that about "the last of the Mohicans"? Certainly those Mohegans who are operating the casino are not fleeing white civilization—they're selling tickets! Furthermore, given the mixed-blood status that most American Indians inherit as a fact of their survival, they are probably not "unmixed people" like Chingachgook and Uncas.

Cora and Uncas were the future after all. Yet the pure and noble savages who resisted and died in fiction maintain a stronger place in the literary imagination than the Indians who adapted and survived in fact. *The Last of the Mohicans* raises more questions than it answers and may be wrong as well as right—like all great literature, and like our nation's history, then and now.

HISTORICAL ALLUSIONS AND NAMES IN *THE LAST OF THE MOHICANS*

Packed with detail, *The Last of the Mohicans* refers to many historical places, people, and events. Most readers, especially their first time through the novel, make as much sense as they can from the materials at hand. They work with the context; check footnotes or endnotes; look up a few words; and hope some arcane references aren't essential to understanding. Cooper's 1826 preface acknowledges the need "to explain a few of the obscurities of the historical allusions," mostly relating to names. His 1831 introduction adds, "most of the information necessary to understand [the novel's] allusions [is] rendered sufficiently obvious . . . in the text itself, or in the accompanying notes," which Cooper provided for the first two editions and later editors have augmented. Given the sheer number of references, though, many "obscurities" remain. This section highlights the most crucial allusions and symbols that recur throughout *The Last of the Mohicans*.

Cooper's Preface identifies the novel's "greatest difficulty" as "the utter confusion that pervades the names." The greatest difficulty for a first-time reader is how many ways Cooper can refer to a single character. This affectation rises partly from Cooper's florid romantic style, but various names also identify how each character relates to distinct social groups and their "systems of value."

Here are names and roles associated with characters in *The Last of the Mohicans*, followed by an explanation of major Indian groups in the novel.

MAJOR CHARACTERS AND THEIR ALTERNATIVE NAMES

Hawk-eye, the scout, the Leather-stocking, *La Longue Carabine*, Long Rifle, Nathaniel (Bumppo).

Chingachgook, the Great Snake, *Le Gros Serpent*, the Serpent, Sarpent, the Sagamore.

Uncas, the Bounding Elk, *Le Cerf Agile*, the "panther of his tribe," the "pride of the Wapanachki," "the last of the Mohicans."

Major Duncan Heyward, the "Open Hand"; disguised as a "fool" or "buffoon" who "knows the art of healing," a French-speaking "juggler from Ticonderoga," or a "conjuror" in the Huron camp.

Cora Munro, "the dark-hair," the other, elder, or darker sister.

Alice Munro, the fairer or younger sister.

Magua, the Fox, *Le Renard Subtil* ("the Sly Fox"), *le Subtil*, the Huron (after his tribe of origin).

David Gamut, the psalmist, identified by his pitch-pipe; the use of the word *psalms* associates David with the biblical David, an allusion reinforced when he fights with rocks and a "deer-skin thong" (chap. 32). Compare his appearance and profession to Ichabod Crane in *The Legend of Sleepy Hollow*. ("Gamut," as in the idiom "run the gamut," refers to the accepted range or series of notes in Western music.)

Tamenund, a historical leader of the Delaware Indians, after whom "Tammany Hall" in New York politics was named.

INDIAN TRIBES OR PEOPLES IN *THE LAST OF THE MOHICANS*

With some variations, *Mohicans* follows the Leather-Stocking Tales' division of Algonquian and Iroquois peoples as "good and bad Indians," respectively. The needs of fiction dictate this division far more than any facts of history.

The largest Algonquian tribe in the novel is the Delawares, also known as the Lenni Lenape, originally from the Delaware River area of New Jersey and Pennsylvania. Chingachgook and Uncas are Mohican or Mohegan Indians, originally from New England, who associate with the Delawares. "Wapanachki" inclusively refers to both groups as "eastern peoples."

Iroquois Indians are referred to variously as Mengwe, Mingoes, and Macquas (the name from which "Mohawk" derives). The name of Magua, the Indian villain, may also derive from Macqua, but he is originally a chieftain of the Huron or Wyandotte tribe, who migrated from Lake Huron of the Great Lakes area to merge with the Iroquois in the 1700s.

Traditionally the Delaware-Mohicans were enemies with the Iroquois-Hurons, but much of the novel finds them in a tense alliance. In the final chapters, Uncas leads a Delaware attack on the Huron village holding the Munro sisters.

SYMBOLS: BLOOD AND THE TORTOISE

Symbols in Cooper's novels often appear and as quickly disappear, with little formal development. In *Mohicans*, however, two sets of symbols help unify the novel's sprawling diversity. One of these symbolic systems, mentioned above, is blood, which bubbles up in terms of violence, life, family, or nation. Associated symbols extend from blood's place in the gothic spectrum of color—comparable to the "blood-red moon" shining through the walls of Poe's "House of Usher." The normal gothic color scheme of black, white, and red parallels the novel's interracial relationships: Cora's black and white blood, plus her potential relation with a red man. Duncan reinforces this dual color scheme when he claims "no difference . . . whether the colour of the skin be red, or black, or white" (chap. 23). How consciously Cooper intended such parallels cannot be known. Such ideas, like the Indian maidens singing of Cora and Uncas together, must be "cloth[ed] . . . in the most remote and subtle images" (chap. 33).

Certainly Cooper consciously developed another pervasive symbol in *Mohicans*—that of the tortoise or turtle. This symbol determines the novel's climactic scene, when Uncas as a prisoner in the Delaware camp faces death at the hands of a "fierce and savage" warrior. His executioner suddenly halts and points to "the figure of a small tortoise, beautifully tattooed on the breast of the prisoner, in a bright blue tint." The appearance of this symbol marvelously hushes the throng of Delawares who menaced him. With the tortoise symbol revealed, Uncas "motion[s] the crowd away with a . . . sweep of his arm" and "advance[s] in front of the nation with the air of a king" (chap. 30).

How has the tortoise "on the breast of the prisoner" caused such a magical change? In classical literature, such a moment is labeled a *recognition scene*, as when Odysseus's nurse recognizes the scar on his leg or Oedipus knows that he himself is the murderer he seeks. But what have the Delawares recognized in Uncas's tattoo that makes them accept him as their king? Uncas "point[s] proudly to the simple blazonry on his skin" and speaks figuratively of the tortoise and its mythic role in the Indian world: "my race upholds the earth! Your feeble tribe stands on my shell!" When Tamenund asks, "Who are thou!", Uncas calls himself "a son of the Great Unamis," a word that Cooper footnotes as "Turtle."

The turtle, tortoise, or Unamis is a legendary ancestor or "totem" of the eastern Indians. By showing a tattoo, Uncas claims descent from the most ancient line of Indian rulers and a destiny to lead the Delawares back to glory. Cooper had studied Indian folklore in "diaries, journals, books and correspondence of . . . missionaries who lived among the Delaware, Mohican, and Iroquois" (Alpern, par 6). These sources were not completely reliable, and Cooper adapted these materials to his own needs, but undeniably the turtle carries important weight in American Indian spoken traditions. Of three clans organizing the Delaware, the senior Unami clan claimed descent from "the great Turtle, the primal being, older than the earth . . . who yet bears the world on its back as it stands deep in the primeval ocean" ("The Delaware"). This ancient legend corresponds to a widespread Iroquois creation story in which animals spread mud on the back of "Big Turtle" until the dry land becomes North America: "And the turtle holds the Earth up to this very day" (*Native American Myths*, Pars. 1–10).

Cooper twice foreshadows the climactic appearance of Uncas as the restored leader of "the children of the Turtle" (chap. 30). When the rescuers meet David Gamut near the Huron village, Hawk-eye asks, "Can you say any thing of the totems of their tribe?" Gamut mentions "strange and fantastic images drawn in their paint" representing "the likeness of [a] tortoise!" (chap. 22). Chingachgook exclaims "Hugh!" Heyward, turning to look at the Indian, observes that "the animal just mentioned was beautifully, though faintly, worked in a blue tint, on the swarthy breast of the chief." Hawk-eye adds, "The Sagamore is of the high blood of the Delawares, and is the great chief of their Tortoises!" Later, in escaping the Huron village, Uncas announces he will go to "the Tortoises"—that is, the Delawares— "the children of my grandfathers" (chap. 26).

Like the American flag and other totems, this symbol joins diverse people in a story that extends from a heroic past to a hopeful future. Uncas was "the last of the Mohicans," but his tattoo survived even into the 1992 movie, and today the decor of the Mohegan Sun Casino in Uncasville features symbols of "the sacred turtle." A new story of Native America emerges: the American Indian has not vanished but adapted its culture into the future that has grown on its land. For better or worse, *The Last of the Mohicans* witnesses a union of peoples who give birth to the New World.

8

The Prairie: A Tale (1827)

The Leather-Stocking Tales may be the most famous series of novels in American literature. When well-read people see or hear titles like *The Last of the Mohicans*, *The Pioneers*, *The Pathfinder*, and *The Deerslayer*, they either know or can guess that these books belong to Cooper's saga. But *The Prairie*, published in 1827 as the third of the tales, often elicits a blank stare. This lack of recognition is discouraging, as Cooper was at the height of his powers in the 1820s, and *The Prairie*'s extraordinary features make it one of Cooper's most readable and charming adventures.

However, these same qualities contribute to its status among the last of Cooper's novels to be considered or assigned. Why is *The Prairie* so comparatively obscure? For starters, the title throws readers off. Standard knowledge of the Leather-Stocking Tales starts with their setting in the eastern woodlands—not the Prairie States. But the setting of *The Prairie* in what is now Kansas or Nebraska turns out to be one of the novel's unique attractions and a key to its other rewards.

The Prairie's western setting establishes this novel as the first western— joining Cooper's other firsts like the first modern sea novel (*The Pilot*) and the first spy novel (*The Spy*). John Cawelti classifies all the Leather-Stocking Tales as westerns, given their depictions of a violent symbolic landscape where "civilization and wilderness, East and West, settled society and lawless openness . . . confront each other" (193). In the other Leather-Stocking Tales, though, the frontier is the Old East of wooded mountains and snow-fed lakes. Only *The Prairie* roams to the stark, treeless plains that most Americans associate with the western genre. This change contributes to *The Prairie's* special attractions. The forest settings of the other Leather-Stocking Tales are tense and claustrophobic. The far horizons of *The Prairie* form the wide-open space that Americans imagine when they think of the west. Despite its enormity, that setting is familiar as home for audiences of western movies or novels.

These advantages extend beyond familiarity. *The Prairie's* change of setting counteracts some of Cooper's normal difficulties with plot. The other Tales sometimes unfold so suddenly as to require backtracking and rereading, which detract from the forward motion desirable in an action sequence. The wider scope of *The Prairie* enables characters to see events developing from far away. Where in the other Tales action breaks out violently and mysteriously, here one well-paced scene rolls after another. Prairie fires, bison stampedes, flights for shelter, and defenses of strongholds take place on a scale that is sublime even by Cooper's standards. These features lend the novel a lighter touch than *The Last of the Mohicans*, published only a year before.

The Prairie's back-burner status results also from reasons beyond its unusual setting. Readers with basic knowledge of the Leather-Stocking series may defer this novel because of its unique place in the overall saga. In 1827 Cooper wrote *The Prairie* as a final installment for what was then a *trilogy* of Leather-Stocking Tales. At the novel's end the Leather-stocking character dies of old age. A dozen years later Cooper would add two more tales from earlier stages in Leather-stocking's life, but the author always insisted that "the history of our hero" should determine the order in which the Leather-Stocking Tales are read (1850 Preface). By this ordering, *The Prairie* should be read last. Some well-informed readers may keep this novel on a back shelf, thinking they must read every other tale beforehand.

However a reader approaches it, *The Prairie* offers the usual gifts of a Leather-Stocking Tale and then some. Again it is a historical novel, set during the time of the Lewis and Clark expedition in the western territories acquired by the Louisiana Purchase. The novel has characters of the heroic magnitude one expects from Cooper, but tempered by surprisingly tender complexity. Ellen Wade may be Cooper's most carefully rounded and winning woman character, while the pioneering Bush clan combines brutal lawlessness with the tangled feelings of a big family. The novel surprisingly employs animals as characters, with resulting visual, comical, and sentimental effects. And finally there is the Leather-stocking, here called "the trapper," guiding young lovers to safety and chattering away to the very end. This subtle portrait reveals both the failings of age and its complementary gifts of patience and craft as this ancient American hero manages one last great adventure in *The Prairie*.

POINT OF VIEW: OMNISCIENCE AND ITS LIMITS

The Prairie narrates from Cooper's normal third-person omniscient point of view, with third-person-limited accommodations for special subjects or experiments. The omniscient style appears explicitly at the beginning of the book and some chapters. The novel opens with a God's-eye view of nature and history, scanning "the vast regions" acquired by the Louisiana Purchase a quarter-century earlier and the "emigration" of a "multitude" across its "virgin territory" (chap. 1). Conforming to the framework of a historical novel, the viewpoint drops from this overarching view to ground level to describe a "train of wagons" bearing the fictional Bush family. Chapter 25 similarly begins on a commanding level, raising the "curtain of our drama" on a "landscape" before descending to the fictional "actors." In a climactic battle, Cooper's zoom-lens style shifts from "all the struggles which were made" to "one solitary instance of success" (30).

These shifts of focus help Cooper limit the problems that omniscient perspective may inflict on storytelling. A narrator who sees and knows everything can ruin a good story by revealing answers and outcomes too soon. Another strategy with which Cooper avoids this problem is to shift to third-person limited perspective, which narrates through the eyes or mind of a character. The witnessing of action through a participant who cannot see or know everything creates tension and draws readers to feel more personally involved. Cooper casually adopts and drops limited viewpoints. Different passages in the novel are told from the perspective of the Leatherstocking, the pioneer leader Ishmael Bush, or the Sioux chief Mahtoree. In the final chapter the omniscient narrator reveals that Captain Middleton "is the source from which we have derived most of the intelligence necessary to compose our legend" (chap. 34). A concluding short narrative on Leather-stocking's death and burial is told from Middleton's viewpoint as he visits the Pawnee camp the following autumn (chap. 34).

The Prairie's crime-driven plot and western locale also limit omniscience. The novel tracks two crimes—the kidnapping of Middleton's wife Inez, and the murder of the Bushes' eldest son Asa. In the first of these plots, the Bush family standing at ground level in their stronghold on a rock outcropping see Ellen Wade on "the uppermost crag" observing something they cannot see from their position. Despite their calls to report, she remains "riveted on some remote point of the Prairie" (chap. 8). The suspense of ignorance makes the reader, like the Bushes, wish frantically for Ellen to tell what she sees (her fiancé Paul with Middleton, as is later revealed). Asa's murder is handled with similar skill. The crime occurs outside the narrator's view, but later the Leather-stocking recognizes the spot where Asa was killed, revealing he has seen something the reader has not. When he is accused of the crime, his "short story" confronts the real murderer with the criminal's nightmare: "little did you dream that your motions were watched" (chap. 31). Thus *The Prairie* shifts between omniscient and limited perspective in order to provide or withhold information as the plot requires.

American Indians inspire other artful perspectives. After the bison stampede, the omniscient narrator sees "fifteen or twenty horsemen . . . riding in quick circuits about a noble bull," who is slain by a "thrust from the lance of a powerful Indian" (chap. 19). This plain description creates an impression of the Sioux's stature and rights by transcending a character's prejudices—which appear when the trapper identifies them as "a band of the accursed Siouxes!" Indian characters also speak or reflect from their own viewpoint. Negotiating with the rescuers, the Sioux chief Mahtoree thinks they were neither "hunters [nor] traders, the two characters under which the white men commonly appeared in [Sioux] villages" (chap. 21). Cooper's finest experiment is to report the captivity of Inez and Ellen in Mahtoree's wigwam through his wife, Tachechana, who sees the white women as "beings of an entirely different nature" and a threat to her marriage (chap. 26).

SETTING: FROM PARIS TO THE PRAIRIE, THE FRUITS OF INVENTION

If *The Prairie* is the first western, James Fenimore Cooper was the right author to inaugurate this distinctly American genre. In previous novels Cooper had shown an ability to paint dramatic landscapes with words. The special significance that setting has for the genre of the western is denoted by its very name. The geographical subject of *The Prairie* would lead Cooper to stretch his powers to impressive new dimensions.

The author's first challenge was how different *The Prairie*'s setting would be from that of the other Leather-Stocking Tales, which were set in the author's home territory of northeastern North America. Cooper never visited the western territories of the United States and wrote *The Prairie* while living in Paris. To describe such faraway places, he drew information from published accounts of expeditions, especially those of Lewis and Clark in 1803 through 1806 and Stephen Long in 1819 through 1820. Also, Cooper had met delegations of western Indian chiefs visiting

Washington, D.C., where he heard stories of bison hunts and prairie fires (Muszynska-Wallace 192–95).

These eyewitness accounts gave Cooper a base of hard data. He further compensated for a lack of firsthand experience by imagining the conditions of a strange place in familiar terms and combining them into an overall effect. Cooper had earlier developed such techniques in describing American Indians, whom, as he told a friend, he knew only "from reading, and from hearing my father speak of them." His practice was to outline a few bold and convincing details, then put them into motion in larger scenarios that were similarly sketched. Likewise for *The Prairie* he combined secondhand knowledge into a functioning whole. The result isn't exactly realistic, but, like modern fantasy literature, it keeps enough familiar and exotic forms in play to fabricate an imaginable space.

The setting of *The Prairie* also demonstrates Cooper's inventive powers by appealing to senses in both familiar and surprising ways. Light and darkness heighten tension while concealing the author's ignorance. On one escape the trapper warns, "night must come, and darkness be upon us afore we leave this spot" (chap. 24); in another, sundown "add[s] the mantle of darkness to the other dreary accompaniments of the place" (chap. 11); that darkness is relieved by the familiar "studded vault" of stars (chap. 23). Cooper uses sounds to define the prairie's empty spaces. Dogs howl, donkeys bray, "Indians [raise] a cry," bison "bellow," and the wind carries "strange and unearthly sounds" (chaps. 19, 32). Like a composer, Cooper orchestrates light, sound, and space to produce "spectacle[s] of wild and peculiar grandeur" (chap. 19). When the Bushes approach the thicket hiding Asa's body, diverse effects magnify the terror. "The howls of the dogs became more . . . plaintive, the vultures and buzzards settled so low as to flap the bushes with their heavy wings, and the wind came hoarsely sweeping along the naked Prairie, as if the spirits of the air had also ascended to witness the approaching development" (chap. 12).

Such theatrical apparatus is balanced by the setting's weighty association with American empire. The novel takes place near the Missouri River in the Kansas and Nebraska region, which the Louisiana Purchase added to the territories of the United States in 1803. The following year President Thomas Jefferson commissioned the Corps of Discovery led by Lewis and Clark to survey this land and its inhabitants. The action of *The Prairie* unfolds in the same timeframe as the Lewis and Clark expedition. Dr. Bat dates one of his scientific notes "1805" (chap. 6). Leather-stocking asks Captain Middleton, "Are you of the party which the States have sent into their new purchase to look after the nature of the bargain they have made?"

Middleton replies negatively but acknowledges that "Lewis is working his way up the river, some hundreds of miles from this" (chap. 10).

In hindsight, the setting of *The Prairie* appears as a prophecy of westward expansion or manifest destiny, by which the United States conquered Indian peoples and extended its political and economic system across North America. That movement would climax in later decades with the Oregon Trail, the Mexican War, and the annexation of Texas, California, and other large western states. This expansion led to the United States' Civil War, which was largely incited by questions whether new territories would be slave or free. For instance, the 1820 Missouri Compromise and the Kansas-Nebraska Act of 1854 affected the very area where *The Prairie* takes place. Cooper represents the justice and progress of these historical developments with his usual ambivalence. Western pioneers are primarily represented by the brutish Bush family, who are associated with lawlessness and slavery, while the novel's more civilized characters return to a "government of Laws" in the East (chap. 15).

A final issue associated with the setting is environmental. Readers may be puzzled by references to the prairie as "the American desert, as we . . . call this region" (chap. 10). Today the Midwestern states of Kansas, Nebraska, and Missouri are known as "America's Breadbasket" on account of their agricultural fertility. However, as Henry Nash Smith explains in his classic study *Virgin Land: The American West as Symbol and Myth*, early explorers described the region as "the great American desert." The prairie's absence of trees was regarded as "proof that the area was unsuited to any kind of agriculture and therefore uninhabitable by Anglo-Americans" (203).

The Midwest turned out quite differently, but *The Prairie* remains, like other Leather-Stocking Tales, an important text for ecological criticism. The trapper indicts the "march of civilization" for the "madness of [its] waste" in "scourg[ing] the Earth with axes" and "stripp[ing] . . . the gifts of the Lord without remorse or shame!" (chaps. 6, 8). Several powerful scenes use apocalyptic terms to describe a place that looks like "an ancient country, incomprehensibly stripped of its people and their dwellings" or to prophesy a reversal of that state, when the "wilderness" becomes "a peopled desert" (chaps. 32, 18).

PLOT AND STRUCTURE: FEEBLE MOTIVES AND GRAND ADVENTURES

The plot of *The Prairie* shows Cooper at his bracing best and his brazen worst. Detractors and defenders will find plenty to confirm their outrage or pleasure over this author's plotting. Large-scale military movements and single combat; captivities, escapes, and pursuits; and bravado exercises in unfamiliar genres give evidence of ingenious design and improvisation. Yet Cooper's contrivances for motivation can make one wish to throw his book into a prairie fire.

If you read a Cooper novel with rotten tomatoes in your other hand, *The Prairie* offers fat targets. The motivations behind the novel's main plot are implausible in the extreme. Why do the Bushes carry Inez, Middleton's wife from New Orleans, westward in a special cage? Inez's Catholic priest, Father Ignatius, appears to be at the bottom of this cockeyed scheme. His name echoes that of Saint Ignatius Loyola, implicating an old-fashioned Jesuit conspiracy. Father Ignatius, "frustrated" by Inez's marriage to the Protestant Middleton, hires Abiram White, the Bushes' kinsman and a former slave-dealer, to steal her for an eventual ransom (chap. 15). But at those distances, how did White ever imagine collecting from Inez's wealthy father? Problems with motivation also rise in Inez's captivity by the Sioux chief Mahtoree. Deranged by the "unaccountable loveliness" of this "'flower of the pale faces,'" he dumps his well-connected Indian wife and double-crosses the heavily armed Bush family, whose rifles decimate his warriors (chaps. 23, 26). Similarly, Abiram's murder of his nephew seems an excessive response to Asa's having slapped him and shown "insubordination" regarding his family's involvement in Abiram's kidnapping scheme (chap. 13).

In Cooper's defense, romantic novels often deviate from common sense to set their plots in motion or resolve hopeless predicaments. Like other adventure writers, Cooper speedily disposes of such embarrassments. Overall, *The Prairie* is such a big book that, if a reader suspends disbelief, its flaws fade in comparison to its wonders. Especially if those absurd motivations are forgotten, the action takes on a life of its own.

The Prairie's captivity narrative involving Inez generates Cooper's usual escape-and-pursuit action, as in *The Last of the Mohicans* the year before. But this tale's captivity spins off major plot variations. The Siouxes' abduction of Inez, Ellen, the trapper, Hard-Heart, and others is a familiar Indian captivity scenario. But Inez's initial confinement by the Bushes resembles another distinctly American genre, the Slave Narrative. The ironically named Abiram White was "a dealer in black flesh" (chap. 8). The stresses caused by Inez's captivity lead to the murder of Asa, which in turn spawns a detective story. In two impressive chapters (chaps. 12, 13), the victim's aggrieved parents and brothers ask questions, "look for the signs" of foul play, and examine Asa's corpse for entry and exit wounds. Abiram's misconstructions make the Bushes suspect the trapper, but the Leather-stocking's story of how he trailed Abiram and Asa makes him resemble a classic gumshoe detective who eyewitnesses a crime and exposes the criminal.

A fresh plot development spawned by Asa's murder and its investigation expands the narrative structure of *The Prairie* to an epic scale. While the Bushes search for Asa's body and then for clues, the men Ellen had observed help her and Inez escape from the Bush encampment into the broad plains. As the trapper observes, this group forms—with the Bushes, the Sioux, and the Pawnees—"four parties within sound of a cannon, not one of whom can trust the other" (chap. 19). As the prairie becomes a potential battlefield, Cooper shows his powers of military narrative as these bands capture or form shifting alliances with each other until the climactic battle between the Sioux and Pawnees, who are aided by the Bushes. Yet Cooper again shifts from the grand scale to the individual when the battle begins with single combat between Hard-Heart and Mahtoree as champions of their nations.

A subtle and intriguing aspect of these climactic chapters is how much the trapper appears to design or plan their action. The "artifice of the trapper" leads him to wonder, "If an invention could be framed that could set these Siouxes and the [Bushes] by the ears"; or, "if matters are managed with judgment we may leave these Tetons as the night sets in" (chaps. 19, 20). As in the previous two Leather-Stocking Tales, the title character proves the essential glue for holding together a spacious plot—almost to the extent of writing it himself.

CHARACTERS: OLD AND NEW GENERATIONS

In Cooper's earlier tales, the Leather-stocking was an essential but supporting character. He spoke and acted decisively in the plot, but those plots and their themes centered on other characters. Intending *The Prairie* as a conclusion to the Leather-Stocking saga, Cooper drew the Leather-stocking character into the spotlight, making a final, heroic portrait that started with the novel's opening scene. A "spectacle as sudden as it was unexpected" stops the Bush family as it trudges toward the setting sun. The "human form" of the trapper appears on a wave of the prairie, framed and magnified to "colossal" proportions by the sunset's "flood of fiery light" (chap. 1). Likewise in the final chapter, in the trapper's peaceful death as "last of [his] race," his "body [is] placed so as to let the light of the setting sun fall full upon the solemn features," as the Pawnees and Middleton's military party reverently attend.

In between these epic framing scenes, the Leather-stocking is his usual gabby, crafty self. As in previous tales, he isn't a traditional leading man, but his actions weave together the multiple plots and characters. Beyond "the trapper," *The Prairie* maintains Cooper's signature style of characterization. Yet his peculiarities turn to advantage. Ishmael and Esther Bush, the pioneer patriarch and matriarch, initially appear as stereotypes of a brutish redneck and his shrewish wife. As the novel unfolds, though, both figures gain depth, even poignancy. Their distant kinswoman, Ellen Wade, may be Cooper's most appealing woman character. Other characters more easily take their places in the usual lineup of good and bad Indians, bookish eccentrics, and bold young men and the women who love them. Yet Cooper endows even these stock figures with enough color and expression to contribute to the novel's extravaganza.

THE LEATHER-STOCKING CHARACTER: "THE TRAPPER"

The basic fact regarding the Leather-stocking character in the *Prairie* is that he is a very old man. The novel's action takes place a decade after *The Pioneers*, the first Leather-Stocking Tale, which ended with the Leather-stocking leaving his old haunts in New York State to journey "far towards the setting sun" (*Pioneers* chap. 41). Then, he was already an aged figure. Now, after "ten tiresome years . . . on these open fields," he counts "fourscore and seven winters" or 87 years of age. The costs of living beyond one's time register first in the character's strange lack of a name. Formerly known as Hawk-eye, his failing vision now limits his skill as a hunter. "I am nothing better than a trapper"—a job description that henceforth operates for his name (chap. 1). The physical toll of a long, hard life appears in his "ghastly smile" (chap. 20). Mentally the trapper alternates between forgetting and remembering his past in the forests instead of the plains— "the day has been" (chap. 4). Age only worsens the Leather-stocking's wordiness. As such failings typically provoke aversion or pity, readers may wonder if they can enjoy a book with an eighty-something hero.

But the old man proves so indispensable that the age issue fades. When it surfaces, it sometimes attracts attention to the advantages of age. "Foolish boy, . . . will you never learn to know the wisdom of patience!" the trapper whispers as he cuts the bonds of the captives in the Sioux camp. As soon as they're freed, the young men, "filled with the pride of . . . strength and manhood," wish to fight their way to freedom. But the trapper knows they will be weak from hours of constraint: "he that has seen much, is apt to think much." One of the young men, finding himself "helpless," grudgingly replies, "Truly, old trapper, . . . you have some judgematical notions in these matters" (chap. 29).

THE BUSH FAMILY: PEOPLING THE FRONTIER

The pioneering Bush family initially appears as the worst possible unit to represent the advancing Western civilization. The family's parents—the bullheaded Ishmael Bush and his hellcat wife Esther—bully their children, deprive them of education, and raise them to be as "shiftless and lawless" as themselves (chap. 11). Over the course of the novel, though, members of this family express fundamental decency and depths of feeling that grant them a stature of their own. Most writers of Cooper's status tend to ignore, mock, or scorn such classes of white Americans as the Bushes represent. Cooper's fair play with this family testifies anew to his impulsive but deep generosity.

Preachers and politicians glorify the model of America's western pioneers, but the Bushes force one to rethink. As the first character to appear in *The Prairie*, Ishmael Bush is both heroic and embarrassing. His "vast" physique of "prodigious power" matches the bold outlines of a pioneer as Ishmael advances before his family's wagon train with a rifle in one hand and "a keen and bright wood-axe" in the other. But Ishmael's face is "coarse . . . and vacant," his "intellectual" expression "low, receding, and mean" (chap. 1). This mix of the pioneering and the primitive is reinforced by the name of Ishmael, which the Bible's book of Genesis made a byword for a social outcast. An angel foretells that Ishmael will be "a wild donkey of a man" who will "live in hostility toward all his brothers" yet will also be "fertile" and "the father of . . . a great nation." Ishmael is last seen living in a desert like that the Bush family traverses. (A quarter century after *The Prairie*, Herman Melville would open *Moby-Dick* with the words, "Call me Ishmael.")

Cooper reinforces the biblical allusion by referring to the Bush family as "the tribe of wandering Ishmael" (chap. 4), and he deepens and darkens the portrait of Ishmael Bush as a social outcast by associating him with antigovernment attitudes that accompany America's westward orientation. The Louisiana Purchase's opening of lands to settlement is only one reason that Ishmael emigrates from his native Kentucky. Paul Hover, Ellen's fiancé from Kentucky, associates Ishmael with the murder of "a sheriff's deputy," and Bush admits he "found the law sitting too tight upon me" (chap. 5). For all his resentment of government, however, Ishmael rules his sons with a heavy hand, leading Asa to complain, "You talk of law, as if you knew of none; and yet you keep me down" (chap. 8).

After Asa's murder, though, Cooper redraws Ishmael as an aggrieved father who reveals flashes of decency and grace. After his surviving sons complete Asa's grave, Ishmael "lift[s] his cap . . . to thank them for their services, with a dignity that would have become one much better nurtured" (chap. 13). He wrongly persecutes the trapper for the crime. As soon as he learns the truth, however, he releases the old man and turns his justice on his own kinsman Abiram White. His parting words to his niece are surprisingly self-conscious and gentle: "to you, Ellen, though you may not prize the gift, I say, God bless you" (chap. 31).

Cooper similarly develops Ishmael's wife Esther. First appearing as a "shrill-toned termagant" or nag, her "ingovernable impatience" begins to alternate with better qualities: "working and scolding with equal industry" (chaps. 2, 11). In contrast to the enervated refinements of Inez, she shows the "courage of a frontier-woman" (chap. 12). In a time when women were questioning their legal status in the new nation, such equality of leadership might more likely be found on the primitive frontier than in eastern cities. With a "dress half-masculine, and bearing a weapon," she leads the search party for her eldest son Asa, commanding "Follow *me!*" (chap. 13). Like Ishmael, Esther becomes touchingly vulnerable when her firstborn's body is found. "She threw herself on the earth, and receiv[ed] the cold and ghastly head into her lap. . . . At times, her fingers play'd in the matted hair of the dead, and at others, they lightly attempted to smooth the painfully expressive muscles of its ghastly visage, as the hand of the mother is seen lingering fondly about the features of her sleeping child" (chap. 13).

ELLEN WADE: COOPER'S FINEST WOMAN CHARACTER?

Ellen Wade, a distant relative of the Bushes who travels with their wagon train, disappears for most of the novel's second half, but in the first half she appears as one of Cooper's most appealing heroines. The "outline of her form, her fair hair streaming," her "laughing blue eyes," and "glowing cheeks" give her a bright physical definition that is complemented by an adventurous and conscientious spirit (chap. 8). Nina Baym in an article on Cooper's women characters offers an accurate summary and evaluation of this character. Ellen "bound[s] about the prairie like a young antelope," Baym writes, "strong, healthy, busy, noisy, sneaking away from the encampment at night to meet her lover, minding the battalion of little Bush children, talking back to men. . . . the 'new woman,' woman in a democracy, woman as free spirit" (708).

AMERICAN INDIAN CHARACTERS AND PEOPLES

The Prairie is the only tale not to feature Chingachgook, who perished in *The Pioneers*. The Leather-stocking's other Indian companion, Uncas, died in *Mohicans*. Instead of being part of an interracial buddy team, the trapper in *The Prairie* works alone. But his fluency in the Pawnee and Sioux languages suggests that the trapper regularly interacts with Indians in the new territories. These tribes' representatives divide to Cooper's familiar good and bad Indians. The Pawnees take over the Delawares' and Mohicans' previous roles as noble savages, while the Sioux assume the Iroquois' status as lustful cheats. This fundamental division characterizes all of Cooper's descriptions as he zigzags from humane sympathy and informed anthropology to sensational stereotypes.

Cooper's descriptions of American Indian characters and peoples in *The Prairie* conform to his practice in other Leather-Stocking Tales and to the requirements of the historical novel. Anthropological details pulled from accounts of western expeditions embellish his descriptions of Plains Indians. But the needs of romantic characterization and plot lead him to simplify Indian peoples and their representatives into heroes and villains. For instance, his overall descriptions of the Tetons or Sioux respect this great nation's power and resources. As a brief background, the Sioux are a widespread and powerful people made up of many local groupings (Teton, Oglala, Brule, Yankton). But the Sioux live not only in their own culture but also in white stereotypes. Featured in films like *Dances with Wolves,* the Sioux are the people most white Americans imagine when they think of Indians. Their men were horseback warriors who sometimes wore feathered headgear, and their people lived in mobile lodges popularly known as tepees. Famous as the principal tribe in the Indian victory at Custer's last stand, the Sioux's great leaders included Sitting Bull, Red Cloud, and Crazy Horse. Their outstanding literary figures include Black Elk, Zitkala-Sa, Dr. Charles Eastman, Vine Deloria, Jr., and Paula Gunn Allen.

Cooper's composition of *The Prairie* preceded these developments in the Sioux's history. His primary source for depicting the Sioux as a formidable and dangerous people was the tense 1804 encounter near the Missouri River between the Lewis and Clark expedition and the Teton Sioux, who controlled trade in that area. In its broadest descriptions *The Prairie* depicts features of Sioux life in such a way as to give the impression of an established and sophisticated culture that, despite its appearance of "chaos" to white eyes, acts with "alacrity and intelligence" (chap. 29). The novel mentions their "war songs and sacred rites," the "lodge of Mahtoree" with its "sacred medicine bag," and the "great pipe of his people" as they meet in council (chaps. 29, 26, 27).

When Cooper focuses on individual Indians or engages the familiar mechanisms of the captivity narrative, however, he resorts to fictional formulas. Rhetorical descriptions he formerly applied to the Iroquois or Hurons now brand the Sioux as gothic fiends or "demon-like looking figures" (chap. 5). Suspenseful scenes early in the novel find Mahtoree repeatedly described as a "wily snake" or "reptile" who "worm[s]" his way among the sleeping Bush family: "he stalked through the encampment, like the master of evil" (chaps. 3, 4). His "fierce, dark, visage," like that of the Huron Magua in *Mohicans*, is disfigured by a "bayonet scar" (chap. 20). Again like Magua, Mahtoree is a skillful politician and orator whose lust for a mysterious pale-face woman makes him an especially dangerous sort in Cooper's book.

Sioux women embody another division between good and bad Indians. Tachechana or "the Skipping Fawn," Mahtoree's "most favored" wife, is a young Indian woman with an eye of "sweetness and playfulness" and a voice like the "melody of the forest" (chap. 25). The attractive and adaptable figure of a young Indian woman also appears in *Pathfinder* as Dew-of-June and in *Deerslayer* as Chingachgook's fiancée Hist. But older Indian women are another matter. The "wrinkled and cruel minded squaws" of the Sioux have an "insatiable desire for cruelty." These "raging she-bears" stimulate the Sioux warriors' "deeply seated love of vengeance" (chaps. 27, 29). Yet even these hackneyed characterizations find Cooper rendering a note of objective fairness when "the ferocious hags" sing "a low, monotonous song" that "recall[s] the losses of their people, in various conflicts with the whites" (chap. 29).

The Pawnees are less complicated because Cooper focuses on a single representative of the tribe as his novel's requisite noble savage. Living in areas now marked by the states of Nebraska and South Dakota, the Pawnees—also referred to as "Loups"—were traditional enemies of the Sioux. "The Pawnees are a wise and a great people," the trapper says. Hearing tales of "a great warrior of [their] race," the rescuers repeatedly encounter a single Pawnee with "a striking air of dignity and fearlessness" (chap. 18). This warrior is "Hard-Heart," whose name derives from his "fortitude" (chap. 28). Like Chingachgook and Uncas as "the last of the Mohicans," the isolation of Hard-Heart from any larger tribal life endows him with purity and loftiness. Also like Uncas and Chingachgook in various Tales, "the light and Apollo-like person of Hard-Heart" can only be compared to the "models of antiquity": "The outlines of his [face] were strikingly noble, and nearly approaching to Roman" (chaps. 25, 18). The trapper inquires whether he and the Pawnees may be related by blood to the Delawares or Mohicans. In contrast to Mahtoree's "selfish" and carnal motives, Hard-Heart shows the "romantic honor" and "courtesy blended with reserve" that distinguished Uncas (chaps. 26, 30, 34). His chivalrous "deference to age" leads Hard-Heart to serve the trapper as a son, restoring Leather-stocking's earlier union of white and Indian cultures (chap. 18).

MINOR CHARACTERS: THE ANIMALS OF *THE PRAIRIE*

Aside from *The Prairie*'s inventive uses of sound, its most agreeable surprise is its use of animals as characters and plot devices. Serious literature
normally defers animals to the realms of comic relief or sentimentality.
The Prairie is not above such usage, especially with Dr. Bat and his donkey Asinus. Dr. Bat is another of Cooper's regrettable efforts at a comic
eccentric. As with Captain Cap in *The Pathfinder*, no amount of critical
interpretation can redeem this character's tiresome wordiness.

But his appearance astride Asinus aligns him with a tradition of literary
lunatics and their moth-eaten mounts, from Don Quixote on Rocinante, to
Ichabod Crane on Gunpowder and, in *Last of the Mohicans*, David Gamut
on Miriam. Dr. Bat sitting on his ass—a term for donkey derived from the
beast's Latin name of asinus—provides Cooper with numerous opportunities for sophomoric puns and allusions. Dr. Bat's ass earns its prominence
throughout *The Prairie* by resolving the great scene of the bison stampede.
The trapper, Paul, Middleton, and Dr. Bat strive to ward off the "dark mass
of bodies" from Ellen and Inez, who stand with Asinus. All seems lost
when "a furious bull dart[s] . . . through . . . with the velocity of the wind,"
but at that moment "Asinus . . . lift[s] his voice in the midst of the uproar."
His "alarming and unknown cry" causes the "most sturdy and furious of
the bulls [to] tremble" and the "stream" of the massive herd to divide into
"two dark columns" that sweep around the human party (chap. 19).

That plot gimmick works just well enough to conclude a spectacular
crisis in a semi-comical way. Elsewhere in *The Prairie* Cooper's animals
play in more serious turns of the plot. The Leather-stocking's dog Hector,
who previously appeared in *The Pioneers*, is joined by one of his offspring,
a "pup" accompanying Middleton. These dogs often fill conventional animal roles, whose sentimentality or comedy links human characters to animal or physical nature. Such human-animal dynamics converge twice in
plot developments, once when Hector in the Sioux camp whines as an
echo to Hard-Heart's otherwise inexplicable hearkening as the Pawnee
forces prepare a surprise attack (chap. 28).

The other such moment occurs during the initial tension over Asa's dis-
appearance, as the Bushes search the prairie. Just when the investigation
stalls, Hector and the pup emerge from the background, chasing a deer
over a near hill. The "younger dog suddenly bounded from the course, and
uttered a cry of surprise. His aged companion stopped also, and returned
panting and exhausted to the place where the other was whirling around . . .
apparently in mad evolutions" (chap. 12). Both dogs howl, and as the wind
sweeps "dusky and ragged" clouds overhead, the Bushes force the pup to

enter a nearby thicket flocked by "a thousand carrion birds." Hidden in the darkened foliage, the pup gives another "alarmed and startling howl," followed by the cries of the Bush boys as they discover and drag out their brother's body. "The whole truth is out," Ellen later says (chap. 14). None of the characters or their relations can be the same. "The dogs uttered a long and closing howl and then breaking off, together, they disappeared on the forsaken trail of the deer" (chap. 12).

Cooper's invention imitates the surprising complexity of life. Humans join other animals in the texture of nature, even its shadow of death. Throughout the novel characters discuss the mercy of killing the feeble Hector or the rascally Asinus—as though nonhuman animals live always on that threshold. At the end, the trapper sits dying in the Pawnee camp with "the figure of a hound" that turns out to be "only the skin of Hector stuffed by Indian tenderness and ingenuity" (chap. 34). Is this strange element a sick joke, a "pious fraud," or only another incomprehensible layer of the great world through which dogs, deer, and people pass?

THEMES: CALL THE LAW!

Like the other Leather-Stocking Tales, *The Prairie* boldly confronts what it means to define our people and land as "American." The novel fulfills the artistic commandment to present life as it is. Conflicting rights and desires breed and shape its themes. Every self-evident truth depends on or contends with other truths. The one inescapable fact of the novel is the expansion of the United States across the natural landscape of North America and into the cultural landscape of Native America. This fact drives nearly every question. Given the new culture's inability to imagine staying where it is, what laws or restraints can it observe?

"America has grown . . . to be a country larger than I once had thought the world itself to be," observes the Leather-stocking (chap. 7). The "garden of the Lord was the forest," but now the woodlands ring to "the sounds of axes, and the crash of falling trees" (chaps. 19, 2). The irony is that, as a "pathfinder," the Leather-stocking himself opened the way for the forest's devastation—a pattern that resumes on the prairie. When the trapper guides the Bushes to a camping site, they cut down its trees, leaving the place "as if a whirlwind had passed" (chap. 2). Eyeing the "worthless and deserted logs," the trapper mutters, "Often have I seen the same before, and yet I brought them to the spot myself" (chap. 7).

The Leather-stocking's experience recounts the social transformation—from forest to farm, town, city, suburbs, and sprawl—that inevitably follows the frontier. Continual westward development was driven especially by "the increasing and unparalleled advance of population" (Cooper, Preface to *The Prairie*). The Bushes count "eighteen open mouths to feed"—numbers that would support the trapper's threat to the Sioux, "if one white skin dies, a hundred spring up" (chap. 8, 29). *The Prairie's* expression of progress as a dilemma makes the novel a pioneering text of ecological consciousness. "The wisdom of the Lord hath set bounds to [man's] evil workings," the trapper observes (chap. 22). Condemning the sight of "the wilderness deformed," he prophesies an apocalyptic judgment: "What this world of America is coming to . . . the Lord, he only knows" (chap. 23).

Law might control reckless desire and prevent such dire outcomes. But on the multicultural frontier of *The Prairie*, law takes so many forms that only individual power and inclination determine limits. An "American borderer" like Ishmael Bush lives "without restraint" and "beyond the reach of law" (chap. 6). The trapper has also fled a bad experience with Eastern laws (as seen in *The Pioneers*). These very different men meet in agreement that "in this land of America, . . . man is left greatly to the following of his own wishes, compared to other countries, and happier, . . . and more manly, and more honest too, is he for the privilege" (chap. 31). Yet limited government creates a vacuum in which primitive or regressive forms of law prevail. In the ungoverned American west, "what might be called the Prairie law" is that "might is right . . . , and what the strong choose to do, the weak must call justice" (chaps. 7, 18).

Another, equally primitive code is that of family blood and honor. When Ellen informs the trapper that the loss of her immediate family made her join the Bushes, he replies, "you left a friend behind you that is always bound to look to the young and feeble, like yourself." When she asks of whom he speaks, he continues: "The law—'Tis bad to have it, but, I sometimes think, it is worse to be entirely without it" (chap. 2). The desperate needs that drive westward expansion break even the law of blood kinship. Ishmael "cast off his own aged and failing parents, to enter the world unshackled and free" (chap. 13). When Abiram is convicted of killing his nephew Asa, his sister Esther frets, "My blood, and the blood of my children is in [Abiram's] veins." Abiram claims, "A man is surely safe among his kinsmen!" Ishmael can only respond, "So thought my boy!" (chap. 23).

Law unifies the white men only when they use it against the Indians, who fight among themselves instead of unifying to fight the white intruders. The Sioux Chief Mahtoree "had heard of a Great Council . . . when the [Spaniards] had sold to the [Americans] their incomprehensible rights over those vast regions, through which his nation had roam'd, in freedom, for so many ages" (chap. 21). Hard-Heart inquires, "And where were the chiefs of the Pawnee Loups, when this bargain was made! . . . Is a nation to be sold like the skin of a beaver!" (chap. 18). The trapper ponders the alternative: "Could the red nations work their will, trees would shortly be growing again . . . and woods would be whitened with Christian bones" (chap. 25). As things stand, the "Great Prairies appear to be the final gathering place of the red men" (Introduction). But "that engrossing people [i.e., white pioneers and settlers] were daily encroaching on their rights, and reducing the red-men of the West, from their state of proud independence to the condition of fugitives and wanderers" (chap. 33). The greatness of a book like *The Prairie* is not that it exposes the New World's sins but that it unblinkingly acknowledges that such sins are inseparable from the greatness claimed.

ALTERNATIVE READING: IS *THE PRAIRIE* SCIENCE FICTION?

James Fenimore Cooper is well known as the father of several fictional genres: the spy novel, the sea novel, the American historical novel, and, with *The Prairie*, the western. Is it possible also to claim that the first great American novelist helped found science fiction or fantasy? Cooper won't displace Jules Verne or H. G. Wells among the fathers of science fiction, but the question raises a platform for examining a popular genre and how it may meet a classic text like *The Prairie*.

Genre, defined as a type or class of literature, is an indispensable building block in literary criticism. When you ask a friend, "What kind of book is that?" you're discussing genre. A book review immediately notes the genre of the text under consideration: biography, history, memoir, poetry, or fiction—or what kind of fiction? Serious, formula, thriller, romance, detective, science fiction? Genre is basic, and students of literature constantly develop their ability to identify its various forms and their conventions.

Yet genre studies are not a focus of systematic teaching and scholarship. Formal study of genre sometimes annoys students for appearing to put a vital text in a confining box. Genre's negative cachet among scholars derives partly from its elementary quality but also from its instability. If "the novel" is a genre, are the detective novel and the gothic novel subgenres, or genres of their own? Is *The Prairie* a historical novel, a western, a fantasy, or all three? A single text usually involves multiple genres, whose definition may depend on more variables than can be separated or accounted for—subject, audience, history, packaging, internal form. In brief, genre studies spawn too many possibilities for systematic and conclusive analysis.

Consequently, the subject usually serves not as a landing point but as a launching point for other questions and issues.

With such an attitude, genre's simplicity and fertility may turn to strengths. Most readers have basic knowledge of genre boundaries. Bookstore clerks easily direct one: "Those first shelves are Literature, but if you keep walking you'll see the Science Fiction." Such shared knowledge allows genre studies to reach across areas that usually have little to do with each other and invite them to share each other's light.

In the present case, a dialogue might capitalize on *The Prairie*'s status as the first western and remark the resemblance between westerns and science fiction. This analogy gained wide currency in the 1970s with the appearance of George Lucas's original film of *Star Wars*. Numerous reviewers categorized it as "a western set in space," citing the resemblance of the alien bar scene to a wild-west saloon; Han Solo's boots, holster gun, and cowboy code of honor; and Luke Skywalker's vow of revenge when his stepparents' frontier home is burned. The television show *Star Trek* had already been described by its creator Gene Roddenberry as "Wagon Train to the stars"—*Wagon Train* being a 1950s TV western (Gibbeman par. 7). Later, postapocalyptic films like *Mad Max* would, like *The Prairie*, feature stark settings, chases, gunplay, and "Indians" in biker leather. Anime shows like *Cowboy Bebop* (1998) and cyberpunk novels like William Gibson's *Neuromancer* (1984) with its "console cowboys" relocate the western to outer space, cyberspace, or both.

The field of comparison may also be reversed by relating the features of science fiction back to *The Prairie*. The standard science fiction hero is "the Competent Man"—handy with ray guns, bare fists, rewiring, or computer codes. This model retrofits easily to the Leather-stocking as an all-purpose frontiersman. Patrician or predatory aliens find ideological equivalents in Cooper's good-or-bad Indians. Like many science fiction novels, *The Prairie* is one in a series.

The reward of such comparisons is immediate—and a little obvious. Genre is indeed a fecund subject, but as examples multiply, attention dwindles. Rather than persisting past a point of diminishing returns, criticism can take advantage of the common ground the exercise has established by refocusing on a formal element. One such element—metaphor or analogy—is common to all literature, including westerns, but it is particularly essential to science fiction.

Metaphor and analogy are related figures of speech by which an unknown entity is explained or described in terms of something known. When in *The Prairie* the Sioux hold the Bushes at bay with a confusing series of feints, the action concludes in just such a clarifying figure: "the

Tetons … darted across the Prairie … as directly and nearly with the velocity of the arrow, that has just been shot from its bow" (chap. 20). The mysterious behavior of the Tetons gains definition from the familiar model of "bow," "arrow," and "darted." Because such metaphorical patterns help process new data, they often serve as explanatory devices for science and, by extension, science fiction. "The sky above the port was the color of television, tuned to a dead channel": the famous opening sentence from Gibson's *Neuromancer* uses an everyday electronic descriptor—"dead channel"—to picture a near-future gone haywire.

Like a science fiction author, Cooper in *The Prairie* imagined a setting that was then being explored, but which he and his audience might never experience directly. Like Gibson, Cooper used a metaphor familiar to his time by styling the prairie as an ocean or sea. "The earth was not unlike the ocean," the narrator says of the land crossed by the Bushes. "There was the same waving and regular surface, the same absence of foreign objects, and the same boundless extent to the view" (chap. 1). The prairie doesn't become the sea, but the reader apprehends the landscape in customary terms. Later the family's "stout and armed men" move toward the Sioux "as a squadron of cruisers … steer[s] across the waste of waters towards [a] convoy." The "three groups now resembled so many fleets at sea" (chap. 20). As a navy veteran and inventor of the sea novel, Cooper easily developed such a metaphor, and his trans-Atlantic readers, accustomed to travel by water and to news of decisive military conflicts at sea, were comfortable processing it.

The Prairie's metaphorical extension of sea fiction to the western joins a larger evolutionary process when later writers translate the western to science fiction. In the late nineteenth and early twentieth centuries the western reached its popular zenith in dime novels and early cinema. During this span, Verne and Wells founded science fiction. In 1912, another American author took the western to another planet. Edgar Rice Burroughs (1875–1950) is today remembered almost exclusively as the creator of Tarzan. In his lifetime, though, he was well known for his many science fiction or fantasy novels, especially the eleven-volume series concerning the adventures of an Earth man on the planet Mars or "Barsoom."

Burroughs's "space operas" share many elements and formulas with the western: desert landscapes, captive women, a final showdown. The first of his Barsoom series, *A Princess of Mars*, made such parallels explicit. Published early in the same year that Burroughs would publish *Tarzan of the Apes*, *Princess* begins with John Carter, a former soldier in the Civil War, prospecting for gold with a friend in Arizona, where Burroughs had served in the U.S. Cavalry. This land is "haunt[ed]" by "hostile Indian[s]" much like

Cooper's Sioux or Iroquois: "vicious marauders" who "torture . . . every white party" (2). After the Apaches capture, torture, and kill his friend, "half a thousand red warriors" chase Carter to the mouth of a mountain cave (4). From that cave the "Arizona moonlit landscape" resembles "some dead and forgotten world, so different" from "any other spot upon our earth." Suddenly Carter is mysteriously transported, a process he describes with the classic occult analogy of magnetism: the "large red star" of Mars "seemed to call across the unthinkable void" and "to draw me as the lodestone attracts a particle of iron." Carter awakens on another "strange and weird landscape" that does not appear very different from the one he has left. "I knew I was on Mars" (9–11).

Even if you buy the magnet business, metaphorical analysis reveals that Carter has not landed on another planet. Instead, writes critic Fred G. See, Carter's adventures take place in "another West, . . . a West which he calls 'Mars'" (64). Three generations earlier the Leather-stocking had gone west from his original frontier to give the wild life a final chance. In the intervening century the American frontier closed. Burroughs's disillusioned veteran first follows Leather-stocking into a western desert, but soon he finds himself on another unknown frontier.

Like Cooper, Burroughs verified the reality of this new territory with information from explorers. In the decade before *A Princess of Mars*, the eminent American astronomer Percival Lowell (1855–1916) published *Mars and Its Canals* (1906) and *Mars as the Abode of Life* (1908), which popularized a theory that dying Martian civilizations had built vast irrigation projects in the form of "canals." Much as Cooper based *The Prairie*'s "waving plains, tall grass," and "mirages" on explorers' accounts, Burroughs has Carter report, "Twice we crossed the famous Martian waterways, or canals, so-called by our earthly astronomers" (Muszynska-Wallace 194, 197; Burroughs, *Princess* 76).

However validating, such details are only seasoning for dishes demanded by human appetite and crafted in the kitchens of metaphor. The heart's desire to live forever and overcome the terrors of death opens a space that *The Prairie* and *A Princess of Mars* take their turns filling. Where Cooper deployed seafaring metaphors from his youth in the U.S. Navy, Burroughs creates Mars in the image of Arizona. Except for a "veneer of exotic detail, nothing is changed," See writes in "Edgar Rice Burroughs and the West Beyond the West." The Martians met by Carter "roam an enormous tract of arid and semi-arid land" (31), much as the Sioux and Pawnee traversed the "endless wastes" and "immense regions of Louisiana" (*The Prairie*, chap. 10).

Metaphor extends the known to the unknown, introducing our normal habits of thought to fresh experience—yet also threatening to reduce all New Worlds to the same old story. Cooper's and Burroughs's heroes cross the "gloomy wastes" like knights crossing the wasteland in search of the Holy Grail, facing death that their souls may be reborn (chap. 11). Both novels follow Cooper's standard plot of captivity, escape, and pursuit. Chapters 16 and 17 of *A Princess of Mars* are titled "We Plan Escape" and "A Costly Recapture." As See concludes, "What happens on Mars is not after all much different from any number of American captivity narratives" (66). When Carter and his princess are under attack by unfriendly Martians, he recommends saving some bullets for an honorable suicide, "as did those brave frontier women of my lost land, who took their own lives rather than fall into the hands of the Indian braves" (54). In Burroughs's story of "loss, suffering, threat and trial, which the Western scene reveals and the Martian romances ceaselessly repeat," green Martians are only Indians of a different color (See 63). Like the Apaches Carter fled, they "inflict death on their prisoners of war in various ingenious and horrible ways" (19). Observing the grand entrance of a Martian army, "I could not but be struck with the startling resemblance the concourse bore to a band of the red Indians on my own Earth" (111).

May we then claim Cooper as a founder of science fiction or fantasy? Or do we reclassify John Carter's adventure on Mars as just another western? This exercise won't add another "first" to Cooper's list. Denying that accolade may measure a difference between classic and pulp fiction. At the end of *The Prairie*, the trapper dies. "In high-brow literature, the idea of death . . . return[s] . . . once and for all to its limitations, from which the popular text serially releases it" (See 69–70). In *Princess*, John Carter is revealed to be immortal. He rescues his princess but loses her again when he returns to Earth as mysteriously as he left—until the next Barsoom adventure turns him around to be reborn all over again. The trapper, stopped from talking at last, clears a path for something new—which, a dozen years later, turns out to be two more Leather-Stocking Tales from the hero's youth: *Pathfinder* and *Deerslayer*. Metaphor has cast a bridge between *The Prairie* and *A Princess from Mars*, between westerns and science fiction, between past and future, between death and denial—as long as we never stop reading and writing.

9

The Pathfinder: or, The Inland Sea (1840)

In 1827 Cooper apparently concluded the Leather-Stocking Tales with *The Prairie*, his third installment in the series. That epic novel traced the Leather-stocking's last days on the western plains in the early 1800s. "The trapper," as he was called, died at *The Prairie*'s end as a new generation of settlers stood by to inherit the American land from the old pioneer and his Indian comrades.

Thirteen years later, however, Cooper surprised the literary world by resurrecting a younger Leather-stocking. The appearance in 1840 of *The Pathfinder; or, The Inland Sea* was one of many turns Cooper's career took after *The Prairie*. Living in Europe from 1826 to 1833, Cooper published more popular sea tales along with political commentary and novels on European history. Audiences reacted to these latter developments with hostility or indifference. Announcing in 1834 that he would abandon the writing of fiction, Cooper devoted himself to social criticism, travel writing, and a *History of the Navy of the United States of America* (1839).

After returning to America, however, Cooper resumed fiction-writing. If *Pathfinder* aimed to reclaim his earlier audience, such expectations were not entirely disappointed. The French novelist Balzac exulted, "Cooper becomes once more the great Cooper. The descriptions of the forest, the waters of the river, and the falls, the wily schemes of the savages" (197). Yet the overall reception for *Pathfinder* and the next Leather-Stocking Tale, *The Deerslayer* (1841), disappointed Cooper. Among "all those . . . who have read the three first books of the series," he complained in his 1850 preface to the collected tales, "not one in ten has a knowledge of the existence even of the two last" (vi).

Cooper's perception of neglect for *The Deerslayer* is surprising, as many later readers rate that last tale among the author's exemplary productions. If Cooper's contemporaries overlooked *The Pathfinder,* however, readers today evidently follow their precedent. By all appearances, teachers assign and scholars discuss *Pathfinder* less frequently than any other Leather-Stocking Tale.

Why? Reading this novel helps fans understand why some critics disparage Cooper's works. *Pathfinder* stretches the author's bothersome traits to excruciating lengths while withholding his usual rewards. Leather-stocking himself—here called "Pathfinder"—disappears for chapters at a time, and Chingachgook shows up only briefly. Meanwhile, the characters who fill their places lack comparable stature. A baffling hash of a book, *The Pathfinder* mixes genres, belabors its worst materials, and interrupts its best plot lines.

Yet these very qualities make reading *The Pathfinder* a remarkable journey for those willing to slog through. The book's diverse materials affirm Cooper's astonishing range and facility. As for rewards, the opening and ending thirds of the novel feature scenes of striking imaginative power. As Balzac suggested, Cooper's word-paintings remain richly affecting, and the storms and ships he depicts on Lake Ontario resemble the maritime mysteries of Edgar Allan Poe (e.g., "Ms. Found in a Bottle" [1833] and "Descent into the Maelstrom" [1841]).

How may one account for such variety in a single text? Evidently Cooper intended to mix genres. His early audience was built on "romances of the forest" and "romances of the sea." In an 1839 letter to his publisher, Cooper ventured, "I think the Pathfinder will be a selling work" not only for reintroducing "[our] old acquaintance the Leatherstocking in the person of the Pathfinder" but also for its "union of Indians and sailors" (443). The story opens in the familiar forest pathways that characterize other Leather-Stocking Tales. But its subtitle—*The Inland Sea*—confirms its nautical spin by referring to Lake Ontario, the easternmost Great Lake. *The Pathfinder's* central third follows a ship transporting British forces who battle storms and treason in the French and Indian War.

This diversion dislocates Leather-stocking from his familiar environs and pursuits. The combination of romances of forest and sea leads to "romance" in another sense. Pathfinder, instead of serving as an avuncular guide to young heroes and heroines, himself falls in love. The object of his affection is a spirited and attractive woman, Mabel Dunham. Her character rarely transcends sentimental formulas, but her prominence leads Cooper to develop, as in no other tale, extensive scenes of a woman thinking and acting on her own. Such unusual features make *The Pathfinder* a fascinating miscellany of genres and styles.

POINT OF VIEW: FROM SOCIAL OMNISCIENCE TO A LIMITED PRIVACY

Most of *The Pathfinder* is narrated from a third-person omniscient point of view, in which a disembodied narrator describes characters primarily from external appearances rather than interior psychology. This perspective, along with first-person viewpoint, was standard practice in many popular novels of the early 1800s. With variations, Cooper uses it in nearly all of his fiction.

Two effects make the third-person omniscient a useful vehicle for Cooper's tales. Omniscient or all-seeing perspective observes action like a wide-screen movie camera tracking people on the move through vast landscapes, as in films like *Dances with Wolves* or *Braveheart*. In the historical novel *Waverly* (1814), the British novelist Walter Scott used such a technique to describe battles between English and rebel forces in Scotland. Cooper skillfully adapted this point of view for the military maneuvers, perilous journeys, and spacious landscapes of his frontier and sea romances. *Pathfinder* employs this technique strikingly in the opening chapters, where Leather-stocking and others help Mabel escape a river ambush to join her father at Fort Oswego.

Third-person omniscient also excels at depicting populous social scenes in which characters' speech and gestures declare their identities and, to an extent, their inner states of mind. Cooper found this style comfortable for novels of manners like *Precaution* and *The Spy*. In *Pathfinder* he relocates it to the frontier of North America. The novel's richest social scene is a "shooting match" at Fort Oswego. Like medieval ladies attending jousting tournaments in Scott's *Ivanhoe*, the spectators—officers' wives, Mabel, and the common soldiers' wives—seat themselves on planks according to "the etiquette of rank" (chap. 11). Everything glitters, but all is witnessed from outside.

By 1840, however, fashions in literature were changing. As fiction matured, perspective became more personal. Third-person limited point of view focuses selectively on the internal consciousness of individuals. Fiction by Nathaniel Hawthorne such as *The Scarlet Letter* would influence this style's development. Abandoning the omniscient's wide scope, limited viewpoint deepens psychological intensity. The resulting ambiguities appeal to modern tastes for irony and self-deception.

In several chapters near the end of *Pathfinder*, Cooper experiments with third-person limited perspective. After the main characters journey to a small English-held island in Lake Ontario and are besieged by Iroquois and French forces, Mabel Dunham, the youthful object of Leather-stocking's affections, becomes separated from her protectors and shuts herself in a fortified blockhouse. The scenes that follow are among the novel's most compelling. As Mabel watches through the blockhouse's peepholes, her painfully limited perspective becomes identical with her struggle to survive. Mabel never achieves the depth of a Hester Prynne, but such experiments help *Pathfinder* become the most psychological of the Leather-Stocking novels.

SETTING: ESCAPING HISTORY FOR THE SUBLIME

The action of *The Pathfinder* is easy to locate on a map, in history, or relative to other Leather-Stocking Tales. These backgrounds qualify *Pathfinder*, like most of Cooper's fiction, as a historical novel. Ultimately, though, this tale's settings have less to do with history and more to do with psychology.

Geographically, *The Pathfinder* takes place around or on Lake Ontario, easternmost of the Great Lakes of North America. In the opening scenes Pathfinder and his friends canoe down the Oswego River, which empties into southeastern Lake Ontario. Their goal is Fort Oswego, located on the Ontario shoreline in upstate New York. Middle chapters find Leather-stocking and party crossing Lake Ontario in a sailing ship named the *Scud*, which wanders near Niagara Falls and French-controlled Fort Frontenac at modern Kingston in Ontario, Canada. Eventually the party lands at a ficti-tious "Station Island" in the historic area known as the Thousand Islands. (This region became a resort for Gilded Age tycoons, one of whose chefs concocted Thousand Island salad dressing.)

The Pathfinder's setting brings Leather-stocking and Chingachgook in contact with their perennial enemies, the French and Iroquois. The Great Lakes now form a natural boundary between the United States and Canada. During *Pathfinder*'s action in the late 1750s, the area was a battle-ground in the French and Indian War (1754–63). As recent for Cooper and his readers as World War 1 (1914–18) is for people today, this conflict between the British and French empires led to the American Revolution a dozen years later.

Pathfinder's action around Forts Oswego and Frontenac broadly conforms to the dynamics of the French and Indian War, but Cooper takes liberties with chronology and characterization. The Indian aspect of the war refers to alliances by Native Americans with colonial forces. Historically, different Iroquois groups shifted back and forth between the English and the French. But *Pathfinder* identifies all Iroquois—a.k.a. "Mingos"—as minions of the French, making them easy-to-identify enemies for English-speaking characters as well as for Chingachgook of the Delawares, their traditional foes.

Cooper also heightens *Pathfinder's* impact by placing its events soon after those of *The Last of the Mohicans*, his 1826 bestseller. That novel takes place earlier in the French and Indian War, and *Pathfinder* refers directly to *Mohicans'* tragic couple, Cora and Uncas (chaps. 4, 27). Overall, though, the novel's action seems less consequential than in *Mohicans*, where Uncas's death ends hope for a unified Indian nation.

The most persistent theme in *Pathfinder's* setting is Mabel's reaction to the wild beauty of the Great Lakes region. The key word in her reaction is "sublime" or "sublimity," a Romantic idea of an awesome beauty that inspires a mix of fear and exaltation. Thus Mabel, observing the lake and forests from Fort Oswego, feels her "blood thrill" at "the real sublimity that belonged to the scene" (chap. 8). This "feeling for the poetry of this beautiful earth of ours" recurs several times, and the apparent ghost ship that passes on Lake Ontario stimulates similar "wild and appalling" feelings (chaps. 8, 17, 25).

PLOT AND STRUCTURE: NAVIGATING AN INLAND SEA OF LOVE

The Pathfinder's plot divides to three major movements. The first third describes Mabel's escort through a river ambush to Fort Oswego, where her father urges his old friend the Leather-stocking to propose marriage. In the middle third, the river party undertakes a sailing expedition across Lake Ontario on a ship called the *Scud*. The final third lands the party on Station Island, where they are besieged by the French and Iroquois.

For modern readers, the first and final thirds of *Pathfinder* will likely prove more interesting than the maritime journey midway through. The escape-and-pursuit action that characterizes other Leather-Stocking novels energizes the river ambush, while Mabel's captivity in the final third deepens the psychological focus.

The middle third concerning the journey of the *Scud* will strain the patience of readers who are unfamiliar with seafaring terminology and indifferent to seafaring. Such materials must have been less tedious for readers of Cooper's time, who would find reading about boats and navigation comparable to our pleasure today in "techno-thrillers" by authors like Tom Clancy.

Even with a dictionary to help with nautical terms, the sailing scenes of *The Pathfinder* suffer from heavy-handed plotting. Jasper Western, skipper of the *Scud*, is falsely suspected of treason with the French. Cooper depicts Jasper as so transparently honest and the reasons for suspecting him so flimsy, that his wrongful arrest, the incompetent takeover of his ship, and the expedition's subsequent dangers are more irritating than suspenseful. Some powerful scenes remind us that Cooper invented the modern sea novel, but *The Pathfinder*'s long passages on the lake may make you feel like jumping overboard.

Uniting the novel's diverse movements is Leather-stocking's growing love for Mabel, their contrived engagement, and her subsequent release. Given that the man is twice Mabel's age, this plot's interest is strained to begin with. Any chance for it to develop as compelling fiction is lost with the wanderings of the *Scud*, when both characters disappear below decks. When Cooper revives the love story, it is too late to regain lost momentum. Yet in this crisis the Leather-stocking exposes aspects of heart and mind unseen in any previous tale.

CHARACTERS: ALL FOR LOVE ON THE FRONTIER

The Leather-stocking is the most original, compelling, and developed character in *The Pathfinder*. Cooper's methods for creating his depth and vitality illuminate why the novel's other characters fail to gain comparable stature. Most of those characters function as *types* who appear on the scene preformed and preprogrammed—little they do or say will stray far from an audience's expectations. Predictability makes types popular in their own time. In today's action films, wisecracking musclemen and protective moms provide assurances that movies will follow a familiar path to a routine outcome. But later generations tend to dismiss such figures as stale formulas.

One such character is Mabel Dunham, the novel's female lead and the object of Pathfinder's affections. Mabel is bright, appealing, and inoffensive, but few readers will remember her for long after closing the book. Her wary reactions to the older Leather-stocking's love are understandable, honorable, and unsurprising in everything but their detail. For a minor character, such predictability conveniently moves the plot forward. For a major character like Mabel, the cost of such simple virtue is that she develops little complexity or resonance. Though one may admire her perfection, it functions as a shield against empathy and shared identity.

This surface style works best in animated social scenes like the shooting match, where Mabel finds herself in an ambiguous position, fitting in with neither the soldiers' drab wives nor the snobbish wives of the officers. As the child of an enlisted man she is not a lady, but her good education and manners make her a special case. Jasper wins the match and gives her the scarf or "calash" he wins as a prize. When an officer's wife offers to buy it and Mabel demurs, the lady claims the offer is null and void if the calash touches Mabel's head—a needless insult that Mabel meekly acknowledges. But a hint of rebellion and vanity marks her final gesture: in front of the wives, "she placed the forbidden garment over her well turned shoulders, where she kept it a minute, as if to try its fitness, and then quietly removed it, again" (chap. 11).

This gesture's deftness displays Cooper's fine social observation and brings Mabel to dear life. In less animated scenes, overworked formulas limit her development. After her father is mortally wounded, Mabel comforts and prays for him at length. The moment is serious, but its privacy is never penetrated. As a result, a psychological and spiritual event of potential intensity is witnessed from outside, like a scene from the sentimental fiction or theater of the time. The reality of the faithful daughter remains confined within its type.

Pathfinder has none of Mabel's attractiveness, but his awkwardness makes him more vulnerable. An older man pursuing a younger woman involves a "wince factor," but complexity requires error. In changing from a confident outdoorsman to a victim of love, Pathfinder veers from self-control to delusion and finally back to discipline. Despite his loss of dignity, Pathfinder makes the novel's outcomes less predictable and more significant.

Such development elevates an otherwise lumbering novel. Pathfinder's ability to love Mabel enhances her stature as well as his own. In contrast, her eventual marriage to Jasper is honorable but unaffecting. Pathfinder returns to his old, heroic, all-male world, but even that gains depth from his struggle. Trying to comprehend the nature of love, he can only compare it to how he lived before with Chingachgook and his son Uncas, who died in *The Last of the Mohicans*.

In the entire book, the emotion of no scene surpasses that during the river ambush when Leather-stocking, thinking Chingachgook was captured or killed by the Iroquois, sees him returning safely. "Chingachgook—my brother!" the Pathfinder says in a trembling voice, "Chief of the Mohicans! my heart is very glad. Often have we passed through blood and strife together, but I was afraid it was never to be so again."

Like an old hunting buddy, Chingachgook accepts his friend's concern with a grunt and shifts the attention to his trophies. "Mingos—Squaws! Three of their scalps hang at my girdle." Such bonding and bloodshed won't suit everyone's taste, but it can't be read with indifference. At length, though, Cooper's economy in representing Chingachgook becomes too much of a good thing. Reported to be scouting, tracking, or "on the lookout" (chap. 19), the Great Serpent vacates so that Pathfinder can consider a new partner. The novel suffers for his absence, supporting D. H. Lawrence's assertion that in the Leather-Stocking Tales "the figures of Natty and Chingachgook[,] two childless, womanless men, of opposite races" are "the abiding thing": "All the other loves seem frivolous."

ROLE OF MINOR CHARACTERS: LESS CAP, MORE TUSCARORA

The mixed-up plots and genres of *Pathfinder* weaken the novel's minor characters. Some with real potential disappear, only to reappear after the reader forgets about them. This mismanagement is especially regrettable in Cooper's Indian characters.

Among the minor characters of European descent, Lieutenant Muir and the cold-blooded Captain Sanglier declare their villainy by aligning with the French and Iroquois. English-speaking minor characters like Mabel's father Sergeant Dunham or his commanding officer Major Lundie are sturdy and conscientious. Lundie's entanglements with Muir through their Scottish background, along with his bookish reflections in his "movable hut" of a headquarters, lend depth and humor to his brief appearance.

Two other male characters play central roles in the middle chapters involving the *Scud*. Jasper Western, known as Eau Douce or Sweet Water for his navigation of the fresh-water Great Lakes, fits Cooper's norms for romantic leading men: occasionally moody or rash, but honorable and eligible to marry.

Charles Cap, also known as Salt Water because he captained ships on the ocean, is one of Cooper's regrettable efforts at developing a character for comic relief. Like Dr. Bat in *The Prairie*, "Cap" is a pompous, clueless know-it-all who interrupts the plot's promising dialogues and plots. An article by Sargent Bush, Jr. redeems this character's presence as a preview of Cooper's "increasingly critical" attitudes toward America's "provincial small-mindedness" and "tendency to base rash action on unfounded suspicions" (267, 269, 271). As a factor in *The Pathfinder* itself, however, Cap is past redemption. A reader quickly learns to dread his "long and desultory conversation" (chap. 14). Yet Cooper undercuts any pleasure in regarding him as a villain by making him Mabel's uncle and repeatedly assuring the audience that the old windbag means well. Worst of all, Cap's inane suspicions of Jasper justify the novel's wrongheaded chapters on the *Scud*. If there is a single figure whose absence would make *Pathfinder* a better book, that character must be "Captain Rude" (chap. 28).

Conversely, if *Pathfinder* has characters whose systematic development might redeem the novel, those characters are the remarkable husband-wife team of Arrowhead and Dew-of-June. They are Tuscarora Indians, who fled to the Great Lakes region from North Carolina in the early 1700s to escape colonial warfare, slave-dealing, and land encroachment. As speakers of an Iroquoian language, the Tuscarora joined the Iroquois Confederacy, expanding its Five Nations to Six Nations. Readers of Cooper's time might have known that the Tuscarora fought on the colonists' side in the American Revolution.

Such backgrounds give Arrowhead and Dew-of-June the potential to transcend Cooper's standard division between good and bad Indians. As the novel opens, Arrowhead guides Mabel and Cap to Fort Oswego, but when he and Dew-of-June vanish, Arrowhead is suspected of steering the party into the Iroquois ambush. Later, on the Scud, Arrowhead plays both sides and manipulates the love-struck Pathfinder in one of the novel's most intriguing psychological scenes (chap. 15). Later, the plot retrofits a regrettable plot device when Dew-of-June tells Mabel, "Arrowhead love pale face girls," raising Cooper's old specter of interracial marriage (chap. 20). By the novel's end, Arrowhead is a shadowy bogeyman bolting into the woods in a vain attempt to save his scalp from the Great Serpent.

The same specter proves the undoing of June. Her ingenious arrivals and departures and her improvisations of signals and language brighten the novel's later chapters. Further, June's alliance with Mabel begins an interracial friendship between women to match that of Leather-stocking and Chingachgook. After her extended mourning of Arrowhead, though, the book doesn't know what to do with her. Interracial marriage was a fact on the real American frontier, where June might have made a good wife for a white pioneer. But her status as an Indian woman only seals Cooper's standard doom for Native Americans: "the double loss of husband and tribe produced the effect that Pathfinder had foreseen. She died" (chap. 30).

THEMES: THE GIFTS OF LOVE AND NATURE

The Pathfinder's most ambitious theme is significant but elusive: how do different people love, or even get along? The novel explores the "nature" of various sorts—Indians and whites, outdoorsmen and townspeople, even freshwater and saltwater sailors—as well as their possible relations. Such issues may seem timeless, but America's ever-changing frontier and its people's struggles for independence and self-government constantly change the terms of discussion. How may conflicts be decided on merits rather than on simple tradition or convenience? How do we honor the rights of others to be equal yet different? Cooper rarely offers solutions, but *The Pathfinder* shows again how well he registers the creative tensions of American life.

Leather-stocking discusses such subjects in terms of different people's nature or "natur'." (The apostrophe may indicate a dialect pronunciation, like "critter" for "creature.") His belief that human nature is plural complicates the American ideal that all human beings, "created equal," share similar values. Such topics arise when Chingachgook returns from battle bearing one or more "reeking scalps." City slickers gasp in horror, but Leather-stocking rationalizes his friend's actions by reference to "Indian natur'." If whites want Chingachgook to protect them, part of the bargain is that he scalps his enemies.

Such compromises complicate universal law. "In truth, while all men act under one common law that is termed human nature," Cooper writes, "the varieties in their dispositions, modes of judging, feelings and selfishness are infinite" (chap. 10). In addition to "Indian natur'," the novel considers "christian natur'," "Scotch human nature," and "a Pale face's natur'," as well as various "gifts" (chap. 9, 10, 18).

Such a pluralist standard creates a wide range of social adaptations, among them a tendency toward equality and meritocracy. Frontier folk, thrown together in rough conditions, make their mark not by inherited rank or property but by merit or skills: "the woods bring men to a level" (chap. 9). Cooper notes the "indifference with which [Pathfinder] regarded all distinctions that did not depend on personal merit" (chap. 9); "in his eyes, rank had little or no value" (chap. 11). Thus the "impartiality" of the shooting match attracts "men, whose . . . subsistence equally depended on skill in the use of their weapons" (chap. 11).

If Cooper celebrates the equalizing tendencies of American life, he also represents conservative reactions. Human nature in "varieties [that] are infinite" may sound like multicultural tolerance. When, however, Mabel speculates that "a hunter" like Leather-stocking "may find a mate" among "Indian girls," Leather-stocking replies, "Kind must cling to kind, and country to country"; "Like loves like" (chaps. 15, 18). The Leather-stocking, as in other tales, wishes to preserve the social order with which he is familiar.

But Mabel tests the limits of such traditional wisdom. Hearing English plans to disrupt French aid to the Iroquois, she questions "the difference . . . between an Englishman's and a Frenchman's employing savages in war." Her father replies, "[A]n Englishman is naturally humane and considerate, while a Frenchman is naturally ferocious and timid." Mabel finds this "all unintelligible" (chap. 19).

Similarly in the blockhouse when Mabel asks Dew-of-June to help her save English or "Yengeese" soldiers, June answers, "June no Yengeese; June, Tuscarora—got Tuscarora husband—Tuscarora heart—Tuscarora feelings—all over Tuscarora" (chap. 23). Again Mabel can only act "bewildered," but to her credit she has struggled to imagine a universal sense of law that might extend justice and prevent bloodshed. This attempt to think more maturely and inclusively contrasts with limits in Leather-stocking's thought.

SYMBOLS AND ALLUSIONS: AN "OCEAN OF LEAVES"

Cooper rarely crafts symbols whose development corresponds carefully with a character or plot across the length of a book, as Hawthorne would do in *The Scarlet Letter* ten years later. If Cooper is conscious of symbols, he develops them opportunistically, not systematically. The blockhouse that shelters Mabel in later chapters of *The Pathfinder* may symbolize her perspective as a woman in frontier warfare, and her father's death in the well of that blockhouse may be additionally expressive, as it frees her from obligation to marry the Leather-stocking. But such symbols are the reader's responsibility, not Cooper's, as he neither elevates nor belabors them.

The Pathfinder's subtitle, *The Inland Sea*, highlights a complex symbol in the novel's plan for a "union of Indians and sailors." Twice Cooper juxtaposes the frontiers of forest and water. In the first chapter Mabel's "eye range[s] over an ocean of leaves," and in another sublime moment from the ramparts of Fort Oswego she finds herself looking from the "dense, interminable forest" to "a field of rolling waters." Nature, Cooper writes, "[set] two of her principal agents in bold relief to each other . . . ; the eye turning from the broad carpet of leaves, to the still broader field of fluid" (chap. 8). The concept of forest as sea, and Lake Ontario as another frontier, is promising as a device for imposing formal unity on Cooper's ambitious novel. In his third Leather-Stocking Tale in 1827, *The Prairie*, Cooper similarly juxtaposed the Midwest's rolling fields and wagons with the ocean's waves and ships. In *Pathfinder*, however, internal affairs at the fort soon distract the narrator's attention. When the narrative returns outdoors, it fails to redevelop this symbol.

Cooper treats systematically what Sergeant Dunham calls "the signs and symbols of [a soldier's] honorable trade" (chap. 9). Cooper often introduces military characters by observing marks of rank or the threat-level of Indians' war paint. The only puzzling allusion to such a symbol is the "halbert" or "halberd," a staff-like weapon that in earlier centuries became the emblem of a sergeant. This symbol appears repeatedly in *Pathfinder* to recall that Mabel is the daughter of an enlisted man—not of an officer and gentleman. "I am in an awkward position, for while I am not good enough to be the wife of one of the gentlemen of the garrison," Mabel notes, "I am too good to be the wife of one of the common soldiers" (chap. 14). In the novel's denouement, however, such symbols vanish-like those of the Middle Ages in *Ivanhoe*. Mabel and Jasper leave the frontier to become a merchant family in New York City, where new symbols of rank would be studied by later novelists like Edith Wharton and Henry James.

ALTERNATIVE READING: ADAM WITHOUT EVE

The Pathfinder's outsider status as the least popular Leather-Stocking Tale puts it into a position to differ with a critical consensus on Cooper's series. The most prevalent notion of Leather-stocking's significance is that associated with the title of R. W. B. Lewis's *The American Adam* (1955), which saw Cooper's hero as "an Adamic person, . . . at home only in the presence of nature and God" (89). Though Lewis qualified this idea as a "noble but illusory myth," many have uncritically celebrated this theme. But a counter-tradition of criticism perceives the social costs of a hero who is "at home only in the presence of nature and God." Leather-stocking's courtship tests his ability to live with others, making this Tale a central document for a case that Cooper criticizes rather than celebrates the American Adam.

The narrator in *Pathfinder* describes the Leather-stocking as "a sort of type of what Adam might have been supposed to be before the fall," carefully adding, "though certainly not without sin" (chap. 9). Such a characterization leads one representative critic to write that *Pathfinder* and *Deerslayer* exalt "an idealized hero, who, separated from both traditional and white societies, embodied only the best qualities of both cultures" (Cawelti 202).

As with Professor Bush's reading of Charles Cap as a critique of American "small-mindedness,", Cooper uses Leather-stocking's "best qualities" to cast the American character into critical relief. This critique partly derives from Cooper's long stay overseas, his longer feud with his American critics, and his increasing dismay over "the American people['s] anti-intellectuality, their disregard for law, and most serious, their utter indifference to highly articulated and generally recognized social formulations," writes Robert

Zoellner. These same negative qualities were "given vivid personification in Leatherstocking" (412). In *Pathfinder*, Cooper discredited these anti-social values by highlighting his central character's inability to manage complexities of class, race, and family life as the frontier is settled. Cooper presents the Leather-stocking as "an incomplete being," David W. Noble wrote of *The Pathfinder*, continuing: "nature is no substitute for what God has given man: the possibility of love and families and civilization" (in Axelrad, 197).

The Leather-stocking's inadequacy as a model also appears psychologically. Zoellner restyles the ideal of the American Adam alone with God and nature as a case of arrested development. A "system of moral imperatives essentially infantile" cause "the crises which both characterize and determine Natty's moral nature" in the tales (401). Supporting this conclusion, Cooper notes that Pathfinder's "mind [is] almost infantine in its simplicity and nature." Cooper tempers this characterization by noting "emotions so painful and so deep, that they seemed to harrow the very soul," but concludes, "in this respect the Pathfinder was a mere child" (chap. 18).

Concluding passages of *Pathfinder* reinforce the American Adam's essential childishness. Not only Leather-stocking but Huck and Tom in *Huckleberry Finn* (1884), Rabbit in John Updike's *Rabbit, Run* (1960), and Yossarian in Joseph Heller's *Catch-22* (1961)—all prefer to flee modern society rather than engage it to a larger benefit. That may be American, but an American Adam tells only half the story of Adam and Eve. *Pathfinder's* last glimpse of Leather-stocking comes when Mabel returns to the frontier and sees him staring at her from afar, unwilling to speak—like a child angry at his mother (chap. 30). Mabel and Jasper, on the other hand, "resembl[e] Milton's picture of our first parents, when the consciousness of sin first laid its leaden weight on their souls" (chap. 29). Adam and Eve leave the American garden to enter the new frontier of international commerce. Leather-stocking rejoins Chingachgook in their shrinking wilderness, an innocent boys' world that, without women, could not survive for long.

10

The Deerslayer: or The First War-Path (1841)

The Deerslayer was the last of the Leather-Stocking Tales to be written—but should it be read first?

Is *The Deerslayer* "a crime against the language," as Mark Twain wrote, or, in D. H. Lawrence's phrase, "a gem of a book"?

These are only the first pieces of the puzzle presented by Cooper's final performance in the Leather-Stocking Tales. Reception of *The Deerslayer* has always been of two or more minds. The novel seems built of a million parts, most of them brilliant, yet some so unrewarding as to imperil the whole. As ever with Cooper, the critical mind finds innumerable tantalizing threads and bold experiments—yet frustration to any final theme, shape, or design. Ultimately the novel's sprawl and improvisation seem, like all of Cooper's texts, to imitate the American experience, particularly our conflicting and extreme impulses toward diversity, nature, God, and honor on our constantly changing frontier.

But *The Deerslayer* is not just a mind game. More than any other Leather-Stocking Tale, it makes a feast for the senses and a petition to the soul. Gorgeous scenery shimmers or flashing action leaps from nearly every page. Boldly drawn characters desire all things beautiful and just—or, in some cases, anything immediately gratifying. The novel magnifies their yearnings with one exquisite image after another, building a mystic sense of humanity's place in the world. Characters speculate on an afterlife that could satisfy their aspirations for rightful justice and inclusive mercy.

Anyone who enjoys escaping into splendid language, sublime nature, daredevil storytelling, and higher visions may find *The Deerslayer* the most consistently readable and rewarding of the Leather-Stocking Tales.

Like all of Cooper's works, *The Deerslayer* may also test one's endurance. Lengthy dialogues and time-killing distractions distend the novel's concluding chapters. The climactic suspense over whether or how the Hurons will kill "Deerslayer"—this novel's name for the Leather-stocking—is frustrated by most readers' knowledge that this character appears as an older man in the other Leather-Stocking Tales.

But also as usual, Cooper's exasperating tendencies reward patience in surprising ways. This author's idiosyncrasies and excesses testify to a strangeness that must have been essential to his successes—and the late filibustering may only reinforce the seriousness of what is at stake. A coda to *The Deerslayer*'s last chapter exemplifies creative brilliance with the most astonishing vision possible: a glimpse of the Leather-Stocking Tales' heroic dead, momentarily resurrected.

The novel frames these ups and downs in a larger puzzle box of questions about literary quality, which inevitably dog Cooper. After *The Last of the Mohicans*, *The Deerslayer* may be Cooper's second most famous title—but for bad reasons as well as good. One positive reason is the title: *The Deerslayer*, like *The Pathfinder*, simply *sounds* like a Leather-Stocking Tale.

But *The Deerslayer*'s fame is widespread for an embarrassing reason as well. Many educated people who will never read a book by Cooper are familiar with *The Deerslayer* because of Mark Twain's notorious satire of the novel, "Fenimore Cooper's Literary Offenses" (1895). As reviewed earlier, Twain's satire is funny but fundamentally unfair. Published four decades after Cooper's death, the essay amounts to propaganda for the Realistic style with which Twain and others supplanted Cooper's Romanticism. Fair or not, the effect of Twain's attack is that many students of literature recognize *The Deerslayer*—but only as a book to be mocked.

With the passing of Realism, though, *The Deerslayer* gained fresh respect. This resurgence began with *Studies in Classic American Literature* (1923) by D. H. Lawrence, a major British author of the early twentieth century. Admiring *Deerslayer* as the "most fascinating Leatherstocking book," Lawrence urged that it be read as "a myth, not a realistic tale." In the mid-twentieth century Lawrence's appreciation contributed to analysis of myths and symbols in the new academic field of American Studies.

Lawrence's essay posed yet another puzzle concerning this novel's place in the Leather-Stocking saga. Cooper's preface designates that "*The Deerslayer* is properly the first in the order of reading, though the last in that of publication." Lawrence, though, reviewed the tales in order of publication, starting with Leather-stocking's appearance as an old man in *The Pioneers* and ending with the "fresh youth" of *The Deerslayer*. That order aligned the tales' progress with "the true myth of America": "they go backwards, from old age to golden youth." This chapter's Alternative Reading explores this reversal of Cooper's intentions.

In order to complete the puzzle of *The Deerslayer*, it is necessary to recognize how much Cooper continued to experiment. Cooper in his fifties already stood as America's foremost author in the Romantic tradition, which began in Europe late in the previous century. Yet the trans-Atlantic book trade that sold Cooper's American version of Romantic literature to Europe continued to bring European Romanticism to America. *The Deerslayer* explicitly indicates this influence in the epigraphs or quotations that head each chapter. Shakespeare and Milton dominate the procession as in all his novels, but Cooper now cites a pantheon of Romanticism: Wordsworth, Chatterton, Coleridge, Scott, Shelley, and Byron.

Acknowledging this tradition adds a final clue. *The Deerslayer*, praised by Allan Nevins as "the most romantic of Cooper's narratives of the American frontier," seems sometimes to have steeped too long in a formulaic Romanticism (Afterword 535). The first three Leather-Stocking Tales in the 1820s were boldly romantic in scale and characterization, but their action had centered on historical events. In the 1840s Cooper reset *The Deerslayer* and *The Pathfinder* outside time or history. These tales escape into an Edenic American world separate from our own. With this change, their manner becomes increasingly "stylized"—they increasingly conform, that is, to styles or patterns rather than to nature or reality.

The resulting set pieces make one blink with wonder—or they make one wonder if *The Deerslayer* is so much fluff. The courtly, even biblical language of the characters is the most persistent unreality, as when Judith says to Deerslayer, "you see I have lighted the lamp and put it in the cabin of the ark" (chap. 24). Twain jeered, "To believe that such talk really ever came out of people's mouths" Yet such talk is perfectly consistent and honest on its own terms in the text. Lawrence compared the novel's overall attainment to "paste," or artificial jewelry: "It is a gem of a book. Or a bit of perfect paste. And myself, I like a bit of perfect paste in a perfect setting, so long as I am not fooled by the presence of reality."

This confection never entirely dissolves into mush, as Cooper parlays well-practiced techniques into unexpected areas. When *The Deerslayer* appeared in 1841, American literature and culture were on the threshold of extraordinary changes. Among these changes was the Transcendentalist movement of New England, which turned Romantic themes to higher purposes. The same decade saw a widespread "Spiritualist" movement, in which mediums and trance-speakers communicated with the dead. (Cooper himself later participated in séances.) Such profound, eccentric exploration of another world animates *The Deerslayer*. The novel's imagery hovers on the border of nature and spirit. Characters ponder the fate of the dead, who live again in the never-land of this wilderness or the next. Completing the Leather-Stocking Tales, *The Deerslayer* makes a final move to new imaginative frontiers.

POINT OF VIEW: FURTHER EXPERIMENTS IN OMNISCIENCE AND ITS LIMITS

As with all the Leather-Stocking Tales, Cooper frames *Deerslayer* in a third-person omniscient or "all-knowing" perspective. From this point of view, a novel's narrator can behold any scene without being exclusively attached to a single character, as in the first-person or the third-person limited perspectives. Also as usual, Cooper adapts this viewpoint to his novel's special conditions.

Third-person omniscient viewpoint implicitly violates two standard rules of modern literary fiction, but a wider view excuses both flaws. First, omniscient style is old-fashioned, but Cooper's career started when such a style was normal. Even today this narrative technique remains standard in popular fiction like Tom Clancy's *Hunt for Red October* or Dan Brown's *Da Vinci Code*. *The Deerslayer* now survives as serious or academic fiction, but Cooper was a popular novelist in his day. Cooper's third-person omniscient also fails a modern test of narrative integrity on account of its inconsistency. This restless and innovative author always experimented with the materials at hand. Finally, the skills that Cooper had developed by the time he wrote *The Deerslayer* delightfully demonstrate that one pleasure of third-person omniscient perspective is that it may contain all the others.

As his first variation on the third-person omniscient style, Cooper begins *Deerslayer* with a bird's-eye view of its time and place: "between the years 1740 and 1745" in one of the "broad belts of the virgin wilderness" in today's New York State. Since *Deerslayer* takes place before the largest events of American history and in an unsettled and uncontested region, this overview is briefer than in other tales. In a couple of pages the narrator descends to Cooper's mid-level perspective, which has been compared by many observers to a movie camera. "Voices [are] heard calling to each other"—two foresters emerge from the thick woods to a clearing that serves as a stage. Such settings and perspectives shift quickly, as in chapter 10 where the viewpoint moves back and forth between Hetty Hutter finding her way through the shoreline forest and her sister Judith on the lake in her family's "ark" or houseboat. This mobile omniscient narrator may also break free from the characters' time-frames. Once, when discussing the strangeness to the Indians of a chess-piece carved as an elephant, the narrator fast-forwards to a day when "the progress of civilization" would bring circus elephants to bathe in the lake.

For purposes of suspense or taste, *Deerslayer*'s narrator sometimes limits omniscience. When characters from the ark investigate the "castle" to see if Indians are hiding inside, the characters waiting outside hear "a heavy thud" and other noises that make "the whole interior [of the other building] seem alive" (chap. 19). To increase suspense, the narrator does not immediately witness what makes these noises. Twice in that sequence the narrator backtracks to reconstruct how sudden or inexplicable acts became possible. The narrator also withholds—for the sake of "the more tender-minded and more timid"—a visual description of the concluding bayonet massacre of the Huron Indians, which "the trunks of the trees, the leaves, and the smoke . . . concealed" (chap. 31).

Like *Pathfinder* the previous year, *Deerslayer* in 1841 experiments with third-person limited perspective. Third-person limited point of view is not identical with first-person. Without using the first-person pronoun "I" or speaking directly in a character's voice, it remains limited to a single character. Authors like Nathaniel Hawthorne began developing this more modern style in the 1830s and 1840s. In *Deerslayer*, Cooper inhabits the consciousness of individual characters for extended periods. These experiments appear particularly when Deerslayer—as the Leather-stocking character is called—is alone in his canoe on the lake. When his low-life companions go on a nighttime scalping expedition to the Huron camp, the narrator reviews Deerslayer's reflections on "the prejudices of the frontiersmen" and the "shadowy and fantastic forms around the lake." The narrator verges on an internal viewpoint: "once he thought he heard the cracking of a dried twig, but expectation was so intense it might mislead him" (chap. 6).

Perhaps the most interesting of Cooper's variations in perspective occurs when he experiments with a limited point of view, only to revert to omniscience. After the Hurons capture the men on the scalping expedition, Deerslayer reports the fact to one of the men's daughters. From his limited perspective, Deerslayer anticipates a lack of "feminine apprehension and concern" since the women are "accustomed to the hazards . . . of a frontier life." But the elder daughter Judith acts "distressed." Deerslayer attributes her "agitation" to her "filial love" for her father, but the omniscient narrator knows what Deerslayer fails to comprehend. Judith is "influenced by feelings that were novel to her"—her love for Deerslayer, which his limited viewpoint cannot perceive.

SETTING: HISTORICAL FACTS AND
TRANSCENDENTAL NATURE

Cooper's scenery, always his greatest attraction, glows with fresh intensity in *The Deerslayer*. The special effects of the novel's setting suggest influences ranging from the author's biography to his continued cultivation of the Romantic style.

Biography never completely explains literature, but Cooper's special relation to the scenes of *The Deerslayer* helps account for the skill and feeling that animate the novel's setting. The deftness with which Cooper draws nature to elicit visual and emotional responses owes much to skills mastered over two decades of professional authorship. But Cooper's personal investment in this setting guaranteed he wasn't going through the motions. *The Deerslayer* takes place at Lake Otsego, where Cooper's father built Cooperstown, where Cooper grew up, and where Cooper returned a few years before starting this novel. The "scene of the tale," Cooper acknowledges in the novel's preface, "is intended . . . to be a close description of the Otsego prior to the year 1760, when the first rude settlement was commenced on its banks." A familiar landmark, Otsego Rock, becomes "the rendezvous rock" at which Deerslayer meets Chingachgook (Preface chap. 8). "It stood, and still stands, for we are writing of real scenes" (chap. 9). Familiarity must have aided his descriptive abilities. Having just turned fifty, though, Cooper may tapped deep recollections of the place to which he was brought as an infant—"a time when nine-tenths of the shores of this lake were in the virgin form" (Preface). Using the Algonquian word for God, Chingachgook looks at this "panorama" of "lake, hill, and heavens" and exclaims, "This is the country of the Manitou!"—the Great Spirit (chap. 25). "Among ourselves," Hurry Harry says of himself and the other white pioneers, "we've got to calling the place the 'Glimmerglass'" (chap. 2).

Such images of primordial nature form powerful symbols for Romantic literature. The American wilderness was a significant backdrop in all the Leather-Stocking Tales, but their action also took place within recognizable historical events, such as the French and Indian War for *Mohicans* and *Pathfinder*. In contrast, *Deerslayer* is set *before* the conquest and development of North America. "The hand of man had never yet defaced or deformed any part of this native scene," which had not been beheld by "the eyes of twenty white men" (chaps. 2, 1). According to Romanticism, such a scene gains value by remaining separate from the corrupting influences of economic exploitation and urban civilization.

But this "reign of nature" also presents problems for a descriptive writer (chap. 2). Beyond its instinctive appeal, how does one make an unknown, unpopulated world interesting to a reader? Cooper frames his portraits of nature in concepts familiar to his readers. Most obviously, he associates nature directly with standard artistic styles, patterns, or scenes. He depicts trees around the lake as "Rembrandt-looking" or as a "drapery of pines," while a glorious dusk resembles "an Italian or Grecian sunset" (chaps. 2, 15, 22). Cooper also suggests a "scene . . . such as a poet or an artist would have delighted in" by intoning aesthetic terms such as the "quaint, picturesque, and ornamental" (chaps. 3, 19).

Another technique Cooper uses to invest nature with feeling is to describe it in terms of the gothic—that dark and thrilling style in which haunted spaces objectify our repressed fears and desires. Washington Irving pioneered this technique in *The Legend of Sleepy Hollow* when Ichabod Crane rode by night on a forest trail haunted by the headless horseman. Cooper himself took the gothic forest to daring extremes in *The Last of the Mohicans*. In *Deerslayer* Cooper acknowledges this style and its derivation from Gothic architecture as "the arches of the woods . . . cast their somber shadows": "It was probably from a similar scene that the mind of man first got its idea of the effects of Gothic tracery and churchly hues; this temple of nature producing some such effect, so far as light and shadows were concerned" (chap. 27).

Gothic motifs in *Deerslayer* dramatize natural scenery, a family mystery, and interests in the afterlife. Gothic twists and turns appear as "mazes of the forest" or the "tangled labyrinth of a small swamp" (chaps. 10, 1). Deerslayer's search for the Hutters' ark at "Rat's Cove" finds a latent threat in nature (chap. 3). The "place . . . truly seem[ed] to be a stream lying in ambush"; the "gloomy character of the shaded river added to the uneasiness" as "the shadows of the woods [grew] still more somber and gloomy" (chaps. 3, 4). "Muskrat Castle," the Hutter family's home at the center of the lake, has conventional gothic features including "a dark, massive chest" holding clues to the family's legacy (chap. 2). At the novel's end the Hutters' "castle" fulfills its gothic profile as "a picturesque ruin" (chap. 32). *Deerslayer's* most intriguing gothic feature may be the Hutters' "family burying ground" in the waters of the lake—"graves [that] could not be found" when Leatherstocking returns years later (chaps. 21, 32).

Deerslayer's natural setting also extends into sunnier, less gothic realms of the spirit—a development that reflects or anticipates Transcendentalism. Five years before *Deerslayer*, Ralph Waldo Emerson published his Transcendentalist manifesto *Nature*, which claimed, "Nature always wears the colors of the spirit." Scenes in *The Deerslayer* find the world "pervaded by the holy calm of nature" (chap. 2). When Hetty sings, "the holy strain [arises] singly on the breathing silence of the wilderness" (chap. 5). Like the

Transcendentalists, Cooper's novel and title character describe nature in religious terms. Deerslayer says of the lake, "this very spot would be all creation to me" (chap. 32). The sense of "a world by itself" and Glimmerglass's "mirrorlike" reflection of the spirit anticipates the "perfect forest mirror" of another lake described the next decade by Henry David Thoreau in *Walden* (chaps. 4, 2).

As at Walden Lake, where "a field of water betrays the spirit that is in the air," *Deerslayer*'s poetry forms on the frontier between lake and sky. Cooper's prose enters a spiritualized realm as its imagery crosses one material element with another. At dawn "even the atmosphere seem[s] to possess a liquid lucidity" (chap. 19). When the Hutter sisters row their canoe over their mother's grave in the lake, the physical image imprints as in a vision: "the girls float[ed] seemingly in air, above the place of the dead, so buoyant was the light vessel that held them, and so limpid the element by which it was sustained" (chap. 22).

By crossing two elements, the setting creates an *objective correlative* for the spiritual challenge and opportunity of a frontier. In 1919 T. S. Eliot defined an objective correlative as a "set of objects" or "situation" that constitutes "the formula of [a] particular emotion." In *The Deerslayer*, the frontier becomes an objective correlative for the meeting of spiritual and physical nature. Deerslayer crosses that frontier when he claims the Bible "can't be truer than that which God has printed with His own hand"— that is, the world itself (chap. 24). The novel's characters frequently discuss the farther frontier of an afterlife where white and Indian souls can meet—"our heaven is [the Indians'] land of spirits," a "path . . . traveled by all colors alike" (chap. 25). There Chingachgook "shall chase a sort of spirit deer" and God will reign as the "Chief of all who live, red or white, or what color they may [be]" (chaps. 25, 11).

Such speculations echo and fade compared to the image of Hetty rowing out over her mother's grave "after nightfall, and carefully anchoring her canoe so as not to disturb the body." Holding "fancied conversations with the deceased [and] sing[ing] sweet hymns to the evening air," she "mingl[es]" the "Christian lore received in childhood" with the "Indian traditions" she has learned at the lake, whose "clear water . . . was almost as pure as air" (chap. 21).

PLOT AND STRUCTURE: A GAME OF CHESS?

Twain in "Fenimore Cooper's Literary Offenses" treats *Deerslayer*'s plot as farce, with Cooper's Indians playing Keystone Kops. Admittedly the novel tests the limits of probability—like all Romantic literature. But with

Deerslayer, Twain chose the wrong target. Of all the Leather-Stocking Tales, this novel's plot appears to be the tightest, or at least the most conscientiously planned. At times, the narrative structure of *Deerslayer* draws so much attention to its devices that it resembles a "meta-fictional" exercise of contemporary or postmodern literature.

The meta-fictional symbol for *Deerslayer*'s plot is the game of chess. Cooper himself was a lifelong chess player—to the extent that, immediately after exchanging their marriage vows, he and Mrs. Cooper played a match with each other. In *Deerslayer*, the Hutters' "dark, massive chest" opens to reveal "a set of chessmen" made of "ivory, much larger than common" (chap. 13). The characters don't know what they've found. Chingachgook shows special "admiration and delight" over the "pawns, which were armed as archers," but Deerslayer condemns the chessmen as "idols." Ultimately the group concludes that the pieces make "some unknown game."

These "toys of civilized life" immediately serve as items of trade in a diplomatic exchange (chap. 13). Deerslayer uses the set's end-pieces (the rooks or castles, carved in the form of elephants) to ransom Thomas Hutter and Hurry Harry from the Hurons. These and other pieces of the chess set resurface in various scenes of the novel.

Since chess is a war game, comparisons with larger conflicts in *The Deerslayer* may be coincidental. But the symmetries of the novel's plot offer the satisfactions of a well-played game. The white men treat canoes like chess pieces by scheming to move or protect them from capture. Hutter accounts, "There's not a canoe on the lake that I don't know where it's hid" (chap. 5). Deerslayer constantly plans strategy, as when he considers "it more than possible that the succeeding night would bring matters to a crisis" (chap. 8). The chapters describing that night and the following day demonstrate rare excellence in plotting.

Chapter 9, for instance, resolves one crisis and reports an earlier one, only to conclude with yet another. Evoking the deception and precision of chess, Deerslayer pilots the ark in a "crablike movement" to pick up Chingachgook at "the rendezvous rock" at sundown, just as the latter escapes from the forest and pursuing Hurons (chap. 8). With "a slight scream, and then a joyous laugh," Judith calls, "You have got your friend, and we are all safe!"

Deerslayer and Chingachgook, after polite introductions to the Hutter sisters, share recent developments. For fear of boasting, the white man resists sharing the news that earlier in the day for the first time he had killed a man—a Huron warrior—in battle. But Chingachgook's "two black eyes [glisten] on him, like the [eye]balls of the panther," and Deerslayer confesses the truth. Meanwhile, through the thickening darkness the ark follows "a narrow stripe of water . . . where the dim light that was still shed from the heavens fell upon its surface in . . . a sort of inverted Milky Way." Suddenly the men and Judith become aware of "a spectral outline of a human form, standing on the water." Judith's mentally challenged younger sister has launched a canoe toward the Huron camp in order to visit her captive father. "Hetty . . . stood erect, a finger pressed on her lips," and the Deerslayer feels "apprehension that all his foresight in securing the canoes would be defeated" (chap. 9).

Deerslayer's meticulous planning, seasoned with impulsive surprises, refresh a plot that might otherwise merely rehearse Cooper's routine action of captivity, escape, and pursuit. As in the rendezvous with Chingachgook at sundown, many of the story's events are coordinated with astronomical phenomena. In subsequent chapters, two captivity narratives converge, as Hetty brings news that the Hurons are also holding Chingachgook's fiancée, who will meet her man on shore at the rising of "a large, bright star." The exact movements of chess and the heavens translate to fictional action as Deerslayer transports his friend to this rendezvous with "utmost skill and precision," so that the "canoe seemed to move by instinct" (chap. 16). Yet when they arrive at the shore, they discover that the Hurons have moved camp, disconcerting their strategy.

Like *The Pathfinder* the year before, *Deerslayer* thus opens with panache. The earlier tales built their action with sometimes excruciating slowness but climaxed in grandly significant actions. These later tales open with headlong action and tight turns—but then both lose steam for long and crucial stretches. The Hurons capture Deerslayer during his rescue of Chingachgook's fiancée Hist, upon which the novel enters a painfully distended sequence of concluding maneuvers. First Deerslayer, on "furlough" from the Hurons, engages nearly every other character in an all-nighter of earnest dialogues. The subjects of these talk-a-thons are worthy, but no one would wish them longer. And if they're not torture enough, when Deerslayer is bound by the Hurons for actual torture, the novel resorts to a tiresome procession of time-killing devices in order to make his rescue plausible. Even then, when soldiers arrive to bayonet the hapless Hurons, the rescue has the appearance of a deus ex machina —a contrived solution to an apparently insoluble difficulty.

For all the brilliance of its opening half, *The Deerslayer* becomes a difficult novel to finish. Cooper's ingenious chess game of maneuvers and checks dwindles to what Twain called "his little box of stage-properties" or "cunning devices, tricks, artifices for his savages and woodsmen to deceive and circumvent each other with." The outrageous highlight of such stage-craft occurs when an enraged Huron hurls his tomahawk at Deerslayer, who catches it by the handle and "[throws] back the weapon at his assailant. . . . The keen little ax struck the victim in a perpendicular line with the nose, directly between the eyes, literally braining him on the spot" (chap. 27). Except for the faux exactitude of "perpendicular," the scene is only a variation of Hard-Heart's "braining" of Weucha in *The Prairie*. Three chapters later, a treasonous Delaware "cast[s] his knife at the naked breast" of Chingachgook; it misses, of course, but immediately "a similar weapon glanced from the hand of the Serpent, and quivered in the recreant's heart" (chap. 30). *The Deerslayer*'s game of chess degenerates to *Mortal Kombat* with retro technology.

But if all praise for Cooper must be qualified, no condemnation can be absolute. For all the delay and overindulgence of its final chapters, *The Deerslayer* finally makes an extraordinarily graceful exit for American literature's greatest epic.

CHARACTERS IN *THE DEERSLAYER*

With a few exceptions, the characters or types of characters in *Deerslayer* are familiar from other Leather-Stocking Tales. Cooper varies and refreshes their familiar roles, however, by making them serve as interlocking pieces in the novel's elaborate puzzle or by intensely examining the psychological and spiritual makeup of each. Some characters are discussed elsewhere in this chapter. Following are descriptions and analyses of *Deerslayer*'s most extraordinary individuals.

DEERSLAYER: YOUNG MAN WITH A GUN

Even though *The Deerslayer* is the last of the Leather-Stocking Tales to be written, its title character is much younger than in any other novel in the series. As in those other Tales, the young Leather-stocking remains Cooper's most interesting character—interesting above all because, as in the other novels, Cooper makes him right more often than wrong yet rarely makes him entirely likeable. In his early twenties, he appears fresh in both senses of the term. On one hand, he is "a young man of truth" whose life in the forest has protected him from "temptation to go wrong" (chaps. 4, 3). On the other hand, he is fresh like a young man whose insistence on being right verges on self-righteousness.

Deerslayer's innocent effrontery wins the reckless adoration of Judith, herself a fallen woman who wants to start over as Eve to his Adam. But two elder or father figures in the story perceive Deerslayer as an impertinent punk. Judith's stepfather Thomas Hutter reflects that "the difference in their views on the morality of the woods had not left much sympathy between them"—even after Deerslayer has helped free him from the Hurons (chap. 19). Similarly the Huron chief Rivenoak finds something to resent in the young man's superiority. When Deerslayer denies Rivenoak's accusation of boasting on account of his white "gifts," the chief replies, "My young paleface *boasts* he is *no* boaster" (chap. 30).

These differing reactions to Deerslayer pose the central question of his character: Will he be a lover or a warrior? The answer plays out in two parallel initiation stories. All cultures have initiation rituals to mark young people's maturation as representatives of adult society. Stories abound in which experience forces youths to abandon innocence or ignorance and to grow into an adult version of themselves. In *The Deerslayer*, the young Leather-stocking undergoes twin initiations. One he accepts as his personal destiny—the other he rejects. His choice models a special masculine fantasy that prevails in American literature and popular culture.

Like a medieval knight on a quest, Deerslayer seeks initiation into manhood as a warrior. *The Deerslayer*'s subtitle, *The First War-Path*, identifies this mission on the part of Deerslayer and his partner Chingachgook. In the opening scene the rugged outdoorsman Hurry Harry asks Deerslayer why he has never "hit anything human" with his rifle and urges him to "wipe that disgrace off your character." Before another day passes, Deerslayer in self-defense kills a Huron warrior, who uses his last words to complete the young man's initiation ritual by giving him a new name. Calling "Deerslayer" a "good name for [a] boy" but a "poor name for [a] warrior," the dying man dubs his young gunman "Hawkeye, as the youth was then first named, for in afteryears he bore the appellation throughout all that region" (chap. 8). ("Hawk-eye" is Leather-stocking's name in *The Last of the Mohicans*, written 15 years earlier in Cooper's time but happening about 15 years later in fictional time. *Mohicans* spells Hawk-eye with a hyphen, which *Deerslayer* elides)

The initiation Deerslayer refuses is marriage with a woman. When Judith Hutter considers abandoning the lake after the death of her stepfather, she asks her sister, "Where is the man to turn this beautiful place into . . . a Garden of Eden for us?" (chap. 22). Deerslayer gives every appearance of being "the man," especially because his innocence represents a redeeming change from Judith's tainted past. The youth speaks with "untaught natural courtesy" and has "a window in his breast, through which the light of his honesty was ever shining" (chap. 9). But when Judith expresses to him "how completely I desire to be nothing but your wife," he cannot recognize her desire, much less act on it (chap. 31). At Harry's first mention of Judith, Deerslayer says, "I would think no more of such a woman but turn my mind altogether to the forest" (chap. 1). Comparably, when the Hurons offer to spare Deerslayer if he will marry an Indian woman whose husband he killed, he "prefer[s] death to her embraces": "I may never marry; most likely Providence, in putting me up here in the woods, has intended I should live single" (chaps. 28, 27).

Leather-stocking's choice to be initiated into adulthood as a warrior but not as a lover models an important form of masculine behavior for American literature and popular culture. As described by Leslie Fiedler in *Love and Death in the American Novel* and Richard Slotkin in *Regeneration through Violence: The Mythology of the American Frontier*, this model of American manhood rejects the settled life of civilization, symbolized by the domestic life of women. Instead, this masculine self seeks always to escape to a frontier where men prove their mettle through redemptive violence and survival.

The resulting ideal of manhood finds itself on a frontier between natural grace and social imbecility. When he discusses heterosexual relations, Deerslayer appears "obtuse on a point on which men are usually quick enough to make discoveries" and displays a "childish simplicity of character . . . so striking that it frequently appeared to place him nearly on a level with the fatuity of poor Hetty" (chaps. 17, 22). This inability to imagine complex human relations turns him to the wilderness. "All is contradiction in the settlements, while all is concord in the woods," Deerslayer rhapsodizes; "the whole Earth is a temple of the Lord to such as have the right mind" (chap. 15).

Deerslayer models American manhood most provocatively by loving neither woman nor nature as much as his gun. In the novel's opening dialogue he swears, "I live by the rifle," and his elegance with this instrument defines the American hero. "To cock and poise his rifle were the acts of a single moment and a single motion," Cooper writes of the shot by which Deerslayer earns his new name (chap. 7). Such deadly grace led Lawrence to style the Leather-stocking as "a saint with a gun." Since Cooper's time, America has worshipped a procession of sharp-shooting demigods: Dead-Eye Dick, Shane, Gary Cooper in *High Noon*, John Wayne in *The Man Who Shot Liberty Valance*, Clint Eastwood's Man with No Name or Dirty Harry, and Mel Gibson in *Lethal Weapon*.

This identification of heroism with gunplay extends to considerations of race and gender. "A redskin is by no means as certain with powder and ball as a white man," Deerslayer consoles the dying Huron. As Indian torture provokes "his peculiar notions of the duty of a white man," he "experience[s] a sort of melancholy pleasure in the idea that he was to fall by a weapon as much beloved as the rifle" (chap. 29). As a sexual symbol the gun seems undeniably masculine, yet it may substitute for women. Deerslayer rejects Judith but accepts her gift of her stepfather's legendary rifle "Killdeer," making him "the King of the Woods" (chap. 23). When Deerslayer, under the Huron sentence of death, wills Killdeer to Chingachgook, he implies that the gun should be more valuable to his friend than his fiancée. Chingachgook, feeling "a little hurt at his friend's lowering his betrothed to the level of a gun," replies, "Wife dear to heart; rifle good to shoot." In the novel's coda, when Leather-stocking as "the Hawkeye" returns to the ruined ark by the lake, his "heart . . . beat quick as he found a ribbon of Judith's fluttering from a log" and "knotted it to the stock of Killdeer" (chap. 32). It will require a future historian to explain the consuming love of American men for their guns. That historian might begin his research by reading *The Deerslayer*.

JUDITH HUTTER: "THE WILD ROSE"

Most readers will like Judith Hutter more than Deerslayer does—and probably more than they like the Deerslayer himself. Deerslayer is prejudiced by Hurry Harry's gossip that "Judith has had *men*," and her own memory is shamed by images of visiting "officers" and "gallants" from "forts on the Mohawk [River]" (chap. 1). Yet Judith, from the first appearance of her "singularly handsome and youthful female face" framed by leaves and a window of the ark, seems vivacious and appealing—as even the blasé Deerslayer remarks at several points. Besides, Judith seems equal to anything the frontier throws at her. She has been "known to kill a deer" with a rifle and to win canoe races across the lake (chaps. 13, 20). When the ark is attacked and a Huron falls from the trees to the deck, Judith "rushe[s] from the cabin" and, "throwing all her strength into the effort, she pushed the intruder over the edge of the scow, headlong into the water" (chap. 4).

Judith's desire always to have something better than her frontier life has created an indefinite shadow of dishonor that damages her prospects. She asks Deerslayer, "Do you believe all you hear about a poor motherless girl?" (chap. 16). The "severe lessons of female morality and propriety" prevent Deerslayer from accepting her as a wife; neither can she "rescue herself from a future she dreaded" (chaps. 21, 32). Cooper's language and Judith's fate seem so final as to create resentment, but the assumptions behind these judgments differ little from the moral framework of any modern soap opera or telenovela. Overall Judith's persona is not rendered with enough depth to reverse Cooper's own reputation for drawing flat women characters. But the novel invests her with irrepressible energy and need. These drive her so repeatedly to rise against her social limits that a reader must extend sympathy to her as a character one will never entirely understand or forget.

HETTY HUTTER: THE GIFT OF UNREASONING

The extraordinary character of Hetty Hutter shows Cooper's daring invention at work again in *The Deerslayer*. "An idiot she could not properly be termed," Cooper writes. Today Hetty might be designated as "mentally disabled," but "differently abled" describes her better. She demonstrates remarkable resilience and a range of gifts, from cooking to keeping secrets, singing, or preaching as the situation requires.

Hetty also represents an early example of a sentimental character type that would become prominent in nineteenth-century fiction: a disabled or dying child with special spiritual powers or insights. Tiny Tim of Charles Dickens's *A Christmas Carol*, which appeared two years after *The Deerslayer*, is this type's most famous specimen. *Uncle Tom's Cabin* (1852) by Harriet Beecher Stowe also featured an inspired but sickly child who preaches to slaves from her deathbed. Later variations on this type may include idiot savants in films like *Forrest Gump* (1994) and *Rain Man* (1988).

Hetty's special condition earns her the liberty of the Huron camp. As Deerslayer explains, "a redskin looks upon a being thus struck by God's power as especially under his care" (chap. 1). Her condition is comparable to earlier Leather-Stocking Tales when other Indians treated David Gamut (*Last of the Mohicans*) and Dr. Bat (*The Prairie*) with a "species of religious reverence" (chap. 10). The morning after she escapes the ark on a canoe, she even keeps company with a family of bears.

This gentle and whimsical stereotyping of Hetty seems consistent with the times in which Cooper wrote. But Hetty's love for Hurry Harry tests the limits implicit in her "atmosphere of pure morality" (chap. 4). Anticipating the discomfort normal people still feel in thinking of disabled people as sexual creatures, Judith "dislike[s] to hear [Hetty] talking" of Harry, which is "not suitable to [her] innocence" (chap. 22). With no obvious resolution forthcoming, Hetty, like similar characters, dies at the novel's end—evidently by a shot from Harry's rifle. Her deathbed scene mixes uncommon elements with end-of-life formulas. The "pure, excellent, sinless creature" confesses to earlier thoughts of suicide: "Once I thought of burying myself" (chap. 31). As in the Hollywood film *Ghost* (1990), she concludes with a spiritualistic entrance to the afterlife: "I see Mother, now, bright beings around her in the lake" (chap. 32).

As in many of his experiments with issues ahead of his time, Cooper's characterization of Hetty, like that of Judith, finally observes contemporary limits. Nonetheless he engages subjects and their contexts with courage, energy, and invention. Hetty enters and exits a surprising number of scenes, often serving ingenious roles for the plot. Her speeches contribute to the tedium of the concluding chapters, but overall her character shows Cooper ahead of his time, taking risks in another unknown area that later writers would develop.

AMERICAN INDIAN CHARACTERS: CHINGACHGOOK, HAPLESS HURONS, AND HIST

As the last and most romantic Leather-Stocking Tale, *The Deerslayer* features Indian portraits that tell more about fiction than about actual Native Americans. Cooper's well-practiced mastery of this imaginary subject appears especially in his treatment of Chingachgook. By this point in his career, however, Cooper has cooked up so many noble and ignoble savages that he sometimes serves stale leftovers. The villainous Hurons zigzag from bloodthirsty craftiness to slapstick fiasco. Such stereotypes test a modern reader's patience but also reward it, as the novel contains one great surprise in Chingachgook's fiancée Hist, a fictional portrait of an American Indian woman with a mind and voice of her own.

Cooper's writing is rarely more efficient and confident than when he describes Chingachgook, but at this stage the Great Serpent's tragedy has been told. He appears more prominently in *Deerslayer* than he did in *The Pathfinder* a year earlier. In both novels he adds beauty and gravity to any scene. In these later tales, the Delaware functions as a superbly realized stock figure who can support the plot and its characters without demanding too much attention for himself. This demotion is understandable, for Chingachgook threatens to steal any scene in which he appears. Leaping from "the rendezvous rock" to the Hutters' ark, he immediately appears as "a noble, tall, handsome, and athletic young Indian warrior" or later, "in his scanty native attire, an Apollo of the wilderness" (chaps. 9, 14). As in the other tales, he expresses "Indian gravity and finesse" through gesture, and when he speaks, "Chingachgook, as usual, speared his words" (chaps. 9, 25). Given free reign, Chingachgook would take over any novel. Therefore Cooper either reserves him, or reduces him to comedy (twice dressing the chief in European clothing) or romance (chap. 12).

The "bad Indians" of *The Deerslayer* are similarly half-hearted. Using the good-and-bad divisions established in previous Leather-Stocking Tales, the Indians who control the shore are tentatively identified as "Iroquois, or Hurons" (chap. 10). Historically, the Canadian Hurons consolidated with the Iroquois Confederation in the mid-1700s. In *The Last of the Mohicans*, the Hurons were the original tribe of Magua, who represented the effects of dislocation and political upheaval during the French and Indian War. In *Deerslayer*, though, the Huron identification serves only as a recruitment device for some dependable villains. With no disrespect to any historical Indians, *Deerslayer*'s fictional Hurons appear potentially more comic than diabolic. This "small fragment of a tribe" was "hunting more comic than diabolic and fishing" when "the breaking out of hostilities between the English and French" found them on the wrong side of the border. Instead of crossing back to Canada, the band confuses pursuers by turning south "to strike a hostile blow before it finally retired" (chap. 11). The band bivouacs in "fifteen or twenty low huts—perhaps kennels would be a better word," where "all [is] dark, covert, and cunning, like its owners" (chap. 11). This forlorn band is led by Rivenoak, who like Magua is a resilient politician.

Aside from their potential to capture, torture, or otherwise threaten Deerslayer and his friends, the prime rationale for the Hurons' presence is the Mohican maiden they hold captive—Chingachgook's fiancée Hist. One of Cooper's best women characters, Hist is humorous, eloquent, and resourceful, as lovable and spirited in her context as Ellen Wade in the first half of *The Prairie*. When the gigantic Hurry Harry rashly shoots a Huron woman, Hist, "with a fearlessness that did credit to her heart," challenges him, "Why you so wicked, great paleface?" (chap. 19). That fearlessness turns to the great paleface's advantage in a subsequent Huron ambush that incapacitates Harry and knocks him helpless into the water. Hist "watche[s] Hurry as the cat watches the mouse," and with "instinctive readiness" throws a rope where he can catch it with his teeth and be dragged to safety (chap. 20).

Hist's stature and vitality climax a surprising trend in the Leather-Stocking saga. The first two tales—*Pioneers* and *Mohicans*—depict Indian women only incidentally. In *The Prairie*, though, Cooper briefly but affectingly engages the viewpoint of Tachechana, young wife of a Sioux chieftain, who suddenly finds two white women captive in her wigwam. Their lack of a common language precludes opportunity for cooperation, but thirteen years later in *Pathfinder*, Cooper advances this identity to its next stage, as the Tuscarora Dew-of-June speaks enough English to warn the novel's white heroine, Mabel Dunham, that June's husband "Arrowhead love pale face girls." With her ingenious signals, candid advice, and sisterly care, June begins an interracial alliance with Mabel like that between Leather-stocking and Chingachgook. *The Deerslayer* takes the final step in this progression when Hist, befriending Hetty at the Huron camp, says, "You paleface, I redskin; we bring up different fashion. Deerslayer and Chingachgook great friend, and no the same color" (chap. 10).

THEMES: FRONTIER LAW

All the Leather-Stocking Tales launch so many ideas and story-lines that a single controlling theme seems contrary to their spirit and practice. *The Deerslayer* provides an additional frustration to such analysis: the first half's pure style anticipates what T. S. Eliot later observed of the novels of Henry James—that they reveal "a mind so fine that no idea could violate it." Innumerable threads in *The Deerslayer's* early chapters shine and stand out briefly, only to be reabsorbed immediately in the writing's tight weave.

The Deerslayer's second half, however, becomes increasingly didactic. Magisterial epigrams question the "right to judge of those who are believed to be standing at the judgment seat of God" (chap. 21). The narrator observes in Judith "the goading of the worm [i.e., conscience] that never dies" (chap. 21). The overwhelmingly verbose dialogues the night before Deerslayer returns to face his sentence of torture may lead some readers to wish the Hurons would call him in early. Characters bare their souls or advise one another on honor, ethics, and the afterlife. "Above all, never do anything in bitterness," Deerslayer winds up one dialogue with Judith (chap. 24); in another, when she "burst[s] into tears," he confesses, "I have overdone the advice" (chap. 26). Admittedly the young man is facing the executioner, when last words enjoy a special value, but it's almost as though he doesn't want his friends to miss him. As soon as he catches his breath, he lays into Chingachgook concerning "the manner in which you red men treat your wives"—a subject on which Hetty also admonishes the poor chief (chap. 31).

Controlling this thematic gusher requires a conceptual model or governing metaphor. For *The Deerslayer*, like all the Leather-Stocking Tales, such a metaphor is provided by its setting: the frontier. In a cross-cultural zone, diverse forces must meet as in a Darwinian landscape of survival and potential evolution. In such a place, no one can see everything or be entirely right, but the violence latent in every situation forces everyone to seek certainty, safety, power, or flight. What law can fairly govern those who cross the frontier's lines? What law is there at all?

Part of *Deerslayer's* seductive enchantment is its comparative escape from the decisive collisions of history that, in *The Last of the Mohicans*, briefly resurrect the Delaware nation or, in *The Prairie*, shake the western tribes' fragile insularity. Yet even *The Deerslayer's* pure land is invaded by the historical issues that occupy all the tales. *Deerslayer* dawns in a phase of the frontier so early as to entertain a dream of innocent contact like that figured in the first Thanksgiving for the Pilgrims and Indians at

Plymouth. A factor in this impression is the negligible number of people inhabiting the continent. The "eyes of twenty white men" have not set eyes on the lake called Glimmerglass (chap. 1). The Hurons' inane intrusion at the lake becomes acceptable if "the reader remembers the vast extent of the American wilderness at that early day, . . . [when] it was possible for even a tribe to remain months undiscovered" (chap. 11). In this momentary balance of power, Indians outnumber whites and coequal partnerships like that between Hist and Hetty or Deerslayer and Chingachgook are conceivable. At the novel's end all the parties evacuate the lake; even after "fifteen years had passed away," at the return of Hawkeye and Chingachgook, "All here was unchanged" (chap. 32).

As in *The Prairie*, however, change is in the air. "When we gaze at the east we feel afraid," says the Huron chief; "canoe after canoe bringing more and more people . . . , as if their land was so full as to run over. The red men are few already" (chap. 27). If the Indians are to be "run over" by "more people" like Deerslayer and his friends, what kind of justice will prevail?

The vacuum prospers frontier justice, the struggle for survival of the fittest in which might becomes right. Hurry Harry warns Deerslayer early in the novel, "when we live beyond law, we must be our own judges and executioners" (chap. 1). Given the foregone expansion of white population, Deerslayer's warning to Judith prophesies the impact on the Indians: "unequal matches, like unequal friendships, don't often terminate kindly" (chap. 24).

Cooper sets the tone for such an outcome as Indians and whites represent different threat-levels of lawlessness. Indians in *Deerslayer* concern themselves with opportunities for matchmaking and collecting scalps from traditional enemies (chaps. 28, 30). The Hurons' determination to torture Deerslayer before "go[ing] back and see[ing] to their own business" in Canada hits the captivity narrative's formulaic fright-buttons. Yet they seem to torture less out of bloodthirstiness than as a political ritual. Torture sounds lawless, but *Deerslayer* repeatedly observes the "grave usages of the American aborigines" and their "rigid regard to honor" as they prepare for the ceremony (chap. 27). Furthermore, Huron justice is surprisingly flexible. Rivenoak offers to overlook Deerslayer's killing of their warrior if he marries the warrior's widow and helps support the couple's surviving children: "blood for blood is one law; to feed her children another" (chap. 27).

In contrast to the Indians' courteous savagery, most of the white men shown in the novel appear dangerously wild and lawless. Deerslayer is the partial exception, of course, but his ideal behavior derives from romantic traditions of knightly honor. Like white-hatted cowboys in westerns or film noir detectives, he operates according to a personal code of chivalry based on romantic doctrines of innate individual goodness. The minimal society of the frontier allows his honor to shine more purely and brightly. Yet his refusal to marry the Indian widow shows him to be far more "rigid" in his ethics than the Hurons, and extravagant plot mechanisms are required to rescue him from his chosen doom.

Deerslayer attributes his morality to "a law, and a lawmaker, that rule across the whole continent" (chap. 1), but other white men in the novel easily ignore this transcendent regime. The ungoverned nature of the frontier seems to attract adventurers whose honor is already compromised and susceptible to further corruption. Hurry Harry March, like Billy Kirby in *The Pioneers*, is a "handsome barbarian" who reigns in the "rude sports of wrestling and jumping then so common in America, more especially on the frontiers" (chaps. 19, 20). His "wrestling" escalates to "assaults and batteries," requiring him to break out of "two or three" colonial jails (chap. 11). The narrator identifies Hurry with "men who dreaded the approaches of civilization as a curtailment of their own lawless empire" (chap. 2). Bringing "all the prejudices and antipathies of a white hunter," Hurry "put[s] the whole family of red men . . . [outside] the category of human rights" (chap. 3).

Despite his racism, Hurry Harry at first seems only innocently reckless, like an oversized boy. When he meets another "fearful mixture of good and evil" in Thomas Hutter, however, the two men's criminal tendencies gain critical mass (chap. 5). Hutter's "good" side is his care for Judith and Hetty. Later in the novel, when the Hurons threaten the Hutter sisters, Hurry similarly incites himself: "white nature . . . won't let him desert females of his own race" (chap. 23). Hutter's past as a pirate or "freebooter" suggest his "bad" side (chaps. 1, 24). Their checkered pasts, their reflexive solidarity with family and race, and their corresponding mistrust of any governing authority make pioneers like Harry and Hutter resemble the Bush family in Cooper's *The Prairie*, who escaped the law of the settlements for a west governed only by personal, family, and tribal law.

Such men must be respected for their physical strength and courage, but to see them as representatives of a law superior to that of the Hurons is unimaginable. Their disdain for others and vulnerability to temptation makes the frontier less a place of advancing civilization than a high-crime district governed by "the principle of retaliation." These frontiersmen destabilize their social environment even more in times of war, which is "regarded as the means of lawfully revenging a thousand wrongs, real and imaginary" (chap. 5). On a midnight mission with Deerslayer to retrieve a canoe, Hutter and Harry deviate from the settled plan. Motivated by no "other desire than a heartless longing for profit," they go on a scalping raid to collect bounties from the colonial government. The Huron women and children are their targets—"them that have neither souls nor names," as Hurry says (chap. 23). For all Deerslayer's virtue, his only possible means for dissuasion would be to overpower them, and he doesn't yet have Killdeer. The first woman Hutter tries to scalp turns out to be Hist. The Leather-stocking may be the ideal man for the frontier, but most of the men who lead this transformation are driven by greed into a zone where lawlessness is rewarded. An experience imagined as chess deteriorates to a game without rules.

SYMBOLS: MODERN AND FOLK ASTRONOMY IN *THE DEERSLAYER*

As action in *The Deerslayer* shifts from canoes on the lake to captivities in the Huron camp, the game of chess and the oversized ivory pieces from Hutter's chest recede from attention. But another surprising mathematical device organizes the action: *astronomy*—a subject that would soon gain increasing prominence in American literature and culture. This unpredictable motif actually emerges early in the novel—in one instance just before the chess set is revealed. Judith draws from Thomas Hutter's chest "one of the mathematical instruments that were then in use among seamen" (chap. 13). Evidently an astrolabe for navigating by the stars, this mechanism is recognized by Deerslayer as resembling the instruments used by "surveyors."

This instrument of celestial navigation provides an early clue to astronomy as a plot device for establishing time and place in *The Deerslayer*. Human cultures have historically used the heavens to direct their seasonal migrations, planting schedules, or religious observances. Compared to earthly nature like land, water, air, plants, and animals, however, the sky's beauty and value cannot be bought, sold, or redeveloped. As a result, the heavens retain a uniquely poetic or spiritual nature. Cooper as a Romantic novelist indulges this special quality, but he does so with an impressive knowledge of astronomy, a subject whose popularity was then increasing in European and American culture.

When, for instance, Hist as a captive of the Hurons relays Chingachgook a message to meet her at a particular time and place, this romantic rendezvous seems lighted and uplifted by its connection to the heavens. Hetty confides to the Delaware, "there is a large bright star that comes over the hill about an hour after dark . . . and just as that star comes in sight, she will be on the point where I landed last night" (chap. 13). Cooper shows off his evident study of astronomy by interjecting, "Hist had pointed out the planet Jupiter, without knowing it."

As the novel's tactics shift from protecting canoes to negotiating with the Hurons, astronomical timekeeping becomes a natural clock for working out exchanges between peoples of different cultures who share the same sky. Only a day before Hist sent her message to Chingachgook, he had intersected with Deerslayer at the rendezvous rock "at sundown," as planned. In the subsequent darkness, as related above, the ark navigated by following "a narrow stripe of water . . . where the dim light that was still shed from the heavens fell upon its surface in . . . a sort of inverted Milky Way" (chap. 9).

Like chess, astronomy provides a structure for guiding human actions, but such mathematical templates can be upended by circumstance. Clouds make the "whole vault of heaven seem a mass of gloomy wall" as Deerslayer and Chingachgook set out to retrieve Hist (chap. 15). "In vain did the Delaware turn his head eastward to catch a glimpse of the promised star" (chap. 16). At last "the selected star was glittering among the branches of a pine. This was every way a flattering omen" (chap. 16). But Hist doesn't show: "the Indians had suddenly removed their camp to the . . . very projection of land, where Hist had given them the rendezvous." Hist "look[s] up through the branches of the trees, as if endeavoring to get glimpses of the star she had herself named as the sign for meeting," but she finds herself watched by an "old hag" identified as "Shebear" (chaps. 15–17).

Deerslayer continues to position and pace its action by celestial phenomena, and once the Leather-stocking offers Chingachgook and Hist a brief lecture on basic astronomy (chap. 25). Despite appearances, Deerslayer explains, the earth turns around the sun rather than the sun moving around the earth. This lecture partly amounts to more of Cooper's didacticism, but his use of astronomy in his narrative also shows his innovation. Cooper's lifetime coincided with a heroic age in European astronomy, marked by the development of advanced telescopes and discovery of new planets. Lacking a single astronomical observatory, the United States lagged embarrassingly in such endeavors, but the 1840s—the decade of *The Deerslayer*—saw the American Observatory Movement, which instituted the nation's later leadership in astronomical research and space exploration.

More impressive than Cooper's learning in modern astronomy is his sensitivity to American Indian knowledge and use of the heavens. In recent decades such traditions in non-Western or prehistoric cultures have entered anthropology and the history of science as "ethnoastronomy" and "archaeoastronomy." Cooper appears proud of modern astronomy, but his representation of American Indians referring to the sky for their own purposes gives fresh testimony of this author's generous nature. Hist didn't know she made a date by a planet rather than a star, but it served her purposes nonetheless. Earlier in the chapter with Deerslayer's astronomy lecture, Chingachgook appears "studying the shores of the lake, the mountains and the heavens." He explains to Hist the time settled for Deerslayer's return to the Huron village: "'When the sun is thus,' continued the Delaware, pointing to the zenith by simply casting upward a hand and finger by a play of the wrist" (chap. 25). When Deerslayer enters the Huron camp, "the oldest of their number cast his eye upward at an opening in the trees and pointed out to his companions the startling fact that the sun was just entering a space that was known to mark the zenith" (chap. 27).

Chess admirably refocuses humanity's warlike ingenuity to a nonviolent game, but its success as a model of the frontier is limited by the fact that some cultures know the game and some don't. But the sun rises (or the earth turns) regardless of our cultural and intellectual framework. *Deerslayer* imagines another symbolic system for transcending violence and disorder. The morning after the battle between the English and the Hurons, "that star which had been the guide of Hist rose on a scene as silent as if the quiet of nature had never yet been disturbed by the labors or passions of man" (chap. 32).

ALTERNATIVE READING: DEATH OF THE AUTHOR AS LIFE FOR THE READER

This final chapter opened with a paradox: "*The Deerslayer* was the last Leather-Stocking Tale to be written—but should it be read first?" Admittedly the question affects only those headstrong bibliophiles who plan to march through all five tales. Yet its answer elevates *The Deerslayer's* mysterious conclusion and exposes a postmodern literary heresy. That conclusion is the novel's epilogue, inexplicable without reference to the other tales. That "heresy" is an invitation to party in the mausoleum of classic literature for the sake of lighting one's own sacred fire. "The death of the author" enables the "birth of the reader."

This *Companion* supports literature's classic regime in its premises and structure. "The author still reigns in histories of literature," wrote Roland Barthes in his eponymous 1968 essay, "The Death of the Author" (143). Each volume of the *Student Companions to Classic Writers* introduces the life and career of the author as a foundation for evaluating literary productions. As Michel Foucault wrote in another founding text for this theory, "the name of the author remains at the contours of texts—separating one from the other, defining their form, and characterizing their mode of existence" (123). Most curricula and anthologies of historical literature organize themselves by authors, whose creative authority becomes mythic if not God-like.

"Stories of heroes gave way to an author's biography," Foucault adds (115). For Barthes, "the author, when believed in," holds "the same relation of antecedence to his work as a father to his child" (144).

If "the author" stands secure on a platform of institutional practices, individual heroism, and family dynamics, "The Death of the Author" sounds like an assassination conspiracy. Yet this theory's premises and conclusions are surprisingly matter-of-fact, democratic, and empowering. No one would argue that the Leather-Stocking Tales might exist without Cooper or that he might have written *Huckleberry Finn*. Instead the theory protests any attempt to reduce interpretation of Cooper's texts to the conscious or unconscious intentions of someone who did, in fact, die more than a century and a half ago. "To give a text an Author is to impose a limit on that text," writes Barthes (147).

As soon as the freeing of literature from an author's intentions is entertained in theory, one sees it everywhere in practice. For instance, this *Companion* respects Cooper for composing the Leather-Stocking Tales but defies his instructions for the order in which to read them. As reviewed in chapter 5, Cooper wanted readers to encounter the tales not in the "desultory and inartificial manner" in which they were written, published, and read, but according to "the career of their principal character." Following this injunction, "*The Deerslayer* is properly the first in the order of reading, though the last in that of publication" (Preface to *The Deerslayer*).

Long ago such questions fell from Cooper's hands into those of his Tales' devoted readers. "A text's unity," according to Barthes, "lies not in its origin but in its destination" (148). In *Studies in Classic American Literature* (1923), D. H. Lawrence ignored Cooper's directives and celebrated the tales' "desultory" or random order as "a decrescendo of reality, and a crescendo of beauty." Lawrence does not track the Leather-stocking from youth in *Deerslayer* to old age and death in *The Pioneers* and *Prairie*. Rather, *The Pioneers* "start[s] with actuality" as the rowdy frontier is settled, while *Deerslayer* ends the series as "a lovely myth" rather than "a realistic tale." Overall the Leather-Stocking Tales "go backwards, from old age to golden youth. That is the true myth of America." This "lovely myth" gained such supremacy in twentieth-century studies of Cooper that the author's contrary instructions became something of a dead letter. A recent study by Geoffrey Rans likewise ignores the author's designs and renews the historical order on behalf not of myth but of readers, then and now. "Few readers of *The Deerslayer* could be unaware in 1842 of Natty's fate in *The Pioneers* of 1822," he writes. "For Cooper's readers today . . . the order of publication [is] the best one," because "the order of composition enforces the reader's making of the text" (19, xvii).

Thus "the death of the author" does not deny the creative force behind the text but opens forward to the creativity imparted by its reader. This theory does not depose one ruler only to impose another. As Foucault warns, "Writing unfolds like a game that inevitably moves beyond its own rules and finally leaves [any limits or orders] behind" (116). In this spirit of gamesmanship, the *Student Companion to James Fenimore Cooper* offers a concluding exercise to honor the author's intentions before witnessing how his text inevitably exceeds them. For purposes of space, this exercise concentrates on *The Deerslayer*'s extraordinary epilogue, which returns to the scene of the novel's action while previewing glories yet to come—in tales a reader may already know.

Composing *Deerslayer* as the first Leather-Stocking Tale, Cooper writes a creation story for a past he has already authored, which is also a future that his fictional characters have yet to live. The novel gives Leather-stocking a new name and arms him with Killdeer, which defines his profile in every adventure. *Deerslayer* as the new first Leather-Stocking Tale seems most engaged, however, with preparing for the tale that is second in either reading order but arguably the greatest of all: *The Last of the Mohicans*. Any anticipation of that sequel must prepare for the advent of its title character. *Deerslayer* succeeds spectacularly at making Hist a wife worthy of Chingachgook and a mother dear and brave enough to bear and rear that novel's title character, Uncas.

Cooper intended that such prefiguring would benefit readers other than those described by Rans, who remembered the previous tales. Cooper's Preface to The Leather Stocking Tales, besides previewing these tales as the "works" that would "outlive himself," envisioned "a generation . . . now coming on the stage" who would read "the several tales . . . arranged solely in reference to their connection with each other." However, the fresh "generation" who would follow this order may not have been the readers Cooper imagined. Such family collections as the one he prefaced prepared for his demotion to the status of children's author. Only generations later would the developing academic fields of American Literature and American Studies revive interest in Cooper as a serious writer for grownups.

The bright pieces of *The Deerslayer* spin together long enough to enchant a child at the dawn of life and literature, or a veteran who reads to remember that "golden youth." The novel ends so miraculously that one cannot entirely deny Cooper's intentions even as it enables readers to fabricate their own. After Leather-stocking spurns Judith a final time and the last visitors exit the novel's scene and action, *The Deerslayer* adds nine paragraphs that form either a prologue to the novels yet to be read or an epilogue to that passage now completed.

Fifteen years later, "on the eve of another, and still more important war," Hawkeye and Chingachgook revisit the lake (chap. 23). Cooper projects them "to rush into new adventures" in the French and Indian War and the next Leather-Stocking Tale. But if, as Barthes wrote, "the true place of the writing . . . is reading," many will already have witnessed that war by reading *The Last of the Mohicans* to its tragic end.

The Deerslayer and all the Leather-Stocking Tales end with a vision as sudden, sublime, and fleeting as Hamlet encountering the ghost of his father, or Magdalene meeting the risen Christ outside his empty tomb. A "stripling" accompanies "the Hawkeye" and "his constant friend Chingachgook." He is "Uncas, the last of his race . . . for Hist already slumbered." Neither slain by Magua nor enamored of Cora, "the youth" repairs one of the old canoes, from which his father and godfather indicate the point on the lake where they sought his mother at the rising of a star. The story is retold. The dead live again.

Bibliography

PRIMARY BIBLIOGRAPHY

In chronological order of publication under the following headings, this bibliography lists James Fenimore Cooper's major published works. Following MLA style, publishing information is not provided for texts over a century old.

The Leather-Stocking Tales

The Pioneers: or The Sources of the Susquehanna: A Descriptive Tale (1823).
The Last of the Mohicans: A Narrative of 1757 (1826).
The Prairie: A Tale (1827).
The Pathfinder: or, The Inland Sea (1840).
The Deerslayer: or The First War-Path (1841).

Current Collections of the Leather-Stocking Tales

The Leatherstocking Tales I: The Pioneers, The Last of the Mohicans, The Prairie. Ed. Blake Nevius. New York: Library of America, 1985.
The Leatherstocking Tales II: The Pathfinder, The Deerslayer. Ed. Blake Nevius. New York: Library of America, 1985.

Other Forest Romances

The Wept of Wish-ton-Wish, 1829.
Wyandotté; or, The Hutted Knoll, 1843.
The Oak Openings; or, The Bee-Hunter, 1848.

Sea Novels

The Pilot: A Tale of the Sea, 1823.
The Red Rover, 1828.
The Water-Witch; or, The Skimmer of the Seas, 1830.
Homeward Bound; or, The Chase: A Tale of the Sea, 1838.
The Two Admirals, 1842.
The Wing-and-Wing; or, Le Feu-Follet, 1842.
Afloat and Ashore; or, The Adventures of Miles Wallingford, 1844.
Miles Wallingford, 1844. [sequel to *Afloat and Ashore*]
Jack Tier; or, The Florida Reef, 1848.
The Sea Lions; or, The Lost Sealers, 1849.

Current Collection of Cooper's Sea Novels

Sea Tales: The Pilot, The Red Rover. Eds. Kay Seymour House and Thomas
    Philbrick. New York: Library of America, 1991.

The Littlepage Manuscripts

Satanstoe; or, The Littlepage Manuscripts: A Tale of the Colony, 1845.
The Chainbearer; or, The Littlepage Manuscripts, 1845.
*The Redskins; or, Indian and Injin: Being the Conclusion of the Littlepage Manu-
    scripts*, 1846.

Other Fiction by Cooper

Precaution: A Novel, 1820.
The Spy: A Tale of the Neutral Ground, 1821.
Tales for Fifteen, 1823 (published under pseudonym of "Jane Morgan").
Lionel Lincoln; or, The Leaguer of Boston, 1825.
The Bravo, 1831.
The Heidenmauer; or, The Benedictines, A Legend of the Rhine, 1832.
The Headsman; or, The Abbaye des Vignerons, 1833.
The Monikins, 1835.
Home as Found, 1838.
Mercedes of Castile; or, The Voyage to Cathay, 1840.

Autobiography of a Pocket-Handkerchief, 1843.
The Crater; or, Vulcan's Peak: A Tale of the Pacific, 1847.
The Ways of the Hour, 1850.

Nonfiction by Cooper

Notions of the Americans: Picked Up by a Travelling Bachelor, 1828.
Letter to General Lafayette, 1830.
A Letter to His Countrymen, 1834.
Sketches of Switzerland, Parts One and Two, 1836.
Gleanings in Europe, 1837.
Gleanings in Europe: England, 1837.
Gleanings in Europe: Italy, 1838.
The American Democrat: or, Hints on the Social and Civic Relations of the United States of America, 1838.
The Chronicles of Cooperstown, 1838.
The History of the Navy of the United States of America, 2 vols., 1839. 2nd ed., 1840. Abridged ed., 1841. 3rd ed., 1847. Posthumous ed., 1853.
Ned Myers; or, A Life Before the Mast, 1843.
Lives of Distinguished American Naval Officers, 1846.

Posthumous Nonfiction Publications

The Eclipse, 1869. (Account of the 1806 solar eclipse seen from Cooperstown, written c. 1834, published posthumously).
Old Ironsides, 1853.
New York; or, The Towns of Manhattan, 1864.

"The Writings of James Fenimore Cooper": Critical Editions of Cooper's Works by SUNY and AMS presses

James Franklin Beard (1919–1989), editor of the *Letters and Journals of James Fenimore Cooper*, founded the project "The Writings of James Fenimore Cooper" in the 1960s to establish critical editions of Cooper's major works. This project has continued under Editors-in-Chief Kay Seymour House and Lance Schachterle. Following is a list of the project's volumes in print, in chronological order of publication. For more details, visit the organization's website at <http://www.wjfc.org>.

Gleanings in Europe: Switzerland. Eds. Robert E. Spiller, James F. Beard, Kenneth W. Staggs, and James P. Elliott. Albany: State U of New York P, 1980.
The Pioneers, or the Sources of the Susquehanna. A Descriptive Tale. Eds. James Franklin Beard, Lance Schachterle, and Kenneth M. Andersen, Jr. Albany: State U of New York P, 1980.

Gleanings in Europe: England. Eds. Donald A. Ringe, Kenneth W. Staggs, James P. Elliott, and Robert D. Madison. Albany: State U of New York P, 1981.

Gleanings in Europe: Italy. Eds. John Conron and Constance Ayers Denne. Albany: State U of New York P, 1981.

The Pathfinder, or the Inland Sea. Ed. Richard Dilworth Rust. Albany: State U of New York P, 1981.

Wyandotté, or The Hutted Knoll. A Tale. Eds. Thomas and Marianne Philbrick. Albany: State U of New York P, 1982.

Gleanings in Europe: France. Eds. Thomas Philbrick and Constance Ayers Denne. Albany: State U of New York P, 1983.

The Last of the Mohicans: A Narrative of 1757. Eds. James A. Sappenfield and E. N. Feltskog. Albany: State U of New York P, 1983.

The Prairie, A Tale. Ed. James P. Elliott. Albany: State U of New York P, 1983.

Lionel Lincoln; or, The Leaguer of Boston. Eds. Donald A. and Lucy B. Ringe. Albany: State U of New York P, 1985.

Gleanings in Europe: The Rhine. Eds. Thomas Philbrick and Maurice Geracht. Albany: State U of New York P, 1986.

The Pilot; A Tale of the Sea. Ed. Kay Seymour House. State U of New York P, 1986.

The Deerslayer or, the First Warpath. Eds. James Franklin Beard, Lance Schachterle, Kent Ljungquist, and James Kilby. Albany: State U of New York P, 1987.

Satanstoe; or The Littlepage Manuscripts: A Tale of the Colony. Eds. Kay Seymour House and Constance Ayers Denne. Albany: State U of New York P, 1990.

The Two Admirals, A Tale. Eds. James A. Sappenfield and E. N. Feltskog. State U of New York P, 1990.

Notions of the Americans: Picked up by a Travelling Bachelor. Ed. Gary Williams. Albany: State U of New York P, 1991.

The Red Rover, A Tale. Ed. Thomas and Marianne Philbrick. State U of New York P, 1991.

The Spy: A Tale of the Neutral Ground. Ed. James P. Elliott, Lance Schachterle, and Jeffrey Walker. New York: AMS, 2000.

Afloat and Ashore, or The Adventures of Miles Wallingford. 2 vols. Eds. Thomas Philbrick and Marianne Philbrick. NY: AMS, 2004.

SELECTED HISTORICAL, BIOGRAPHICAL, AND SECONDARY BIBLIOGRAPHY

In chronological order of publication under the following headings, this bibliography lists major books and articles that aid in the study of Cooper's life and writings. Though not comprehensive, these listings refer to authoritative collections and studies that have been either reviewed by this author or cited frequently by dependable sources.

Biographies, Letters, and Journals

Beard, James Franklin, ed. *The Letters and Journals of James Fenimore Cooper.* 6 vols. Cambridge, MA: Harvard UP, 1960–68.

Cooper, James Fenimore [grandson], ed. *Correspondence of James Fenimore-Cooper.* 2 vols. New Haven: Yale UP, 1922.

Cooper, Susan Fenimore. *Small Family Memories.* 1883. in *Correspondence of James Fenimore-Cooper.* Ed. James Fenimore Cooper [grandson]. New Haven: Yale UP, 1922. 7–72.

Grossman, James. *James Fenimore Cooper.* New York: William Sloane Associates, 1949.

Long, Robert Emmet. *James Fenimore Cooper.* New York: Continuum, 1990.

Memorial of James Fenimore Cooper. New York: G.P. Putnam, 1852. James Fenimore Cooper Society Webpage. Annotated by Hugh P. MacDougall, 2001. 15 Feb. 2005. <http://external.oneonta.edu/cooper/biographic/memorial.html>.

Railton, Stephen. *Fenimore Cooper: A Study of his Life and Imagination.* Princeton: Princeton UP, 1978.

———. "James Fenimore Cooper." *Antebellum Writers in New York and the South.* Ed. Joel Myerson. Dictionary of Literary Biography 3. Detroit: Bruccoli Clark/Gale, 1979. 74–93.

Spiller, Robert E. *Fenimore Cooper: Critic of His Times.* New York: Minton, Balch, 1931.

———. "James Fenimore Cooper, 1789–1851." *American Writers: A Collection of Literary Biographies.* Vol. 1. Ed. Leonard Unger, New York: Scribner's, 1974. 335–57.

Taylor, Alan. *William Cooper's Town: Power and Persuasion on the Frontier of the Early American Republic.* New York: Knopf, 1995.

Wallace, James. "Biographical Information." Web site: *James Fenimore Cooper: Home as Found.* 8 Jan. 2005. <http://www2.bc.edu/~wallacej/jfc/ jfcbio.html>.

Web Sites Devoted to Cooper and His Works

The James Fenimore Cooper Society Webpage. <http://external.oneonta.edu/cooper/>.

"The Writings of James Fenimore Cooper." <http://www.wjfc.org/>. (Homepage for ongoing project to establish scholarly editions for Cooper's works through SUNY and AMS presses. Includes information on special library collections of Cooper's papers.)

Reuben, Paul P. "Chapter 3: Early Nineteenth Century—James Fenimore Cooper." *PAL: Perspectives in American Literature—A Research and Reference Guide*. By Reuben. 1 Aug. 2005. <http://www.csustan.edu/english/reuben/pal/chap3/cooper.html>.

General Studies of Cooper's Writings

(Some of the texts listed here cover other authors or works in addition to Cooper.)

Adams, Charles Hansford. *"The Guardian of the Law": Authority and Identity in James Fenimore Cooper*. University Park: Pennsylvania State UP, 1990.

Axelrad, Allan M. *History and Utopia: A Study of the World View of James Fenimore Cooper*. Norwood, PA: Norwood Editions, 1978. 20 Feb. 2005. <http://www.oneonta.edu/external/cooper/writings/utopia.html>

Bewley, Marius. *The Eccentric Design: Form in the Classic American Novel*. New York: Columbia UP, 1959.

Chase, Richard. *The American Novel and Its Tradition*. Garden City, NY: Doubleday, 1957.

Collins, Frank M. "Cooper and the American Dream." *PMLA* 81 (1966): 79–94.

Cooper, James Fenimore. "Preface to the Leather Stocking Tales." 1850. *The Deerslayer*. New York: Scribner's, 1927. v–viii.

Daly, Robert. "From Paradox and Aporia to Cultural Hybridization and Complex Adaptive Systems: New Theories and the Uses of Cooper at the Present Time." *James Fenimore Cooper: His Country and His Art* 10. Papers from the 1995 Cooper Seminar. Ed. Hugh C. MacDougall. The State University of New York College at Oneonta. Oneonta, New York. 23–31. 7 May 2005. <http://www.oneonta.edu/~cooper/articles/suny/1995suny-daly.html>.

Darnell, Donald. *James Fenimore Cooper: Novelist of Manners*. Newark: U of Delaware P, 1993.

Dekker, George. *James Fenimore Cooper: The American Scott*. New York: Barnes and Noble, 1967.

Dekker, George, and John P. McWilliams. Introduction. *Fenimore Cooper: The Critical Heritage*. London: Routledge and Kegan Paul, 1973. 1–53.

Fields, Wayne. Introduction. *James Fenimore Cooper: A Collection of Critical Essays*. Ed. Wayne Fields. Englewood Cliffs, NJ: Prentice-Hall, 1979.

Fiedler, Leslie A. "James Fenimore Cooper: The Problem of the Good Bad Writer." *James Fenimore Cooper: His Country and His Art*. Papers from the 1979 Conference at State University College of New York, Oneonta and Cooperstown. Ed. George A. Test. 1–10. 7 May 2005. <http://www.oneonta.edu/~cooper/articles/suny/1979suny-fiedler.html>.

Franklin, Wayne. *The New World of James Fenimore Cooper*. Chicago: U of Chicago P, 1982.

House, Kay Seymour. *Cooper's Americans*. Columbus: Ohio State UP, 1963.

———. "Cooper's Females." *James Fenimore Cooper: His Country and His Art, or Getting Under Way*. Papers from the 1978 Conference at State University of New York College at Oneonta and Cooperstown, New York. Ed. George A. Test. 35–44. 12 Sept. 2005. <http://www.oneonta.edu/~cooper/articles/suny/1978suny-house.html>.

———. "Cooper's Status and Stature Now." *James Fenimore Cooper: His Country and His Art*. Papers from the Bicentennial Conference, July 1989, State University College of New York, Oneonta and Cooperstown. Ed. George A. Test. 1–11. 12 Sept. 2005. <http://www.oneonta.edu/~cooper/articles/suny/1989suny-house.html>.

Lewis, R. W. B. *The American Adam: Innocence, Tragedy, and Tradition in the Nineteenth Century*. Chicago: U of Chicago P, 1955.

Lowell, James Russell. *A Fable for Critics*. 1848.

MacDougall, Hugh P. "Reading Cooper For Enjoyment." Cooper Society Webpage. 1999, revised November 2002. 15 Dec. 2004. <http://external.oneonta.edu/cooper/introduction/reading.html>.

McAleer, John J. "Biblical Analogy in the Leatherstocking Tales." *Nineteenth-Century Fiction* 17 (1962): 217–35.

McWilliams, John P., Jr. *Political Justice in a Republic: James Fenimore Cooper's America*. Berkeley: U of California P, 1972.

Nevius, Blake. *Cooper's Landscapes: An Essay on the Picturesque Vision*. Berkeley: U of California P, 1976.

Noble, David W. "Cooper, Leatherstocking and the Death of the American Adam." *American Quarterly* 16 (1964): 419–31.

Peck, H. Daniel. *A World by Itself: The Pastoral Moment in Cooper's Fiction*. New Haven: Yale UP, 1977.

Person, Leland S., Jr. "*Home as Found* and the Leatherstocking Series." *ESQ: A Journal of the American Renaissance* 27.3 (1981): 170–80.

Philbrick, Thomas. *James Fenimore Cooper and the Development of American Sea Fiction*. Cambridge: Harvard UP, 1961.

Porte, Joel. *The Romance in America: Studies in Cooper, Poe, Hawthorne, Melville, and James*. Middletown, CT: Wesleyan UP, 1969.

Ringe, Donald A. "Cooper Today: A Partisan View." *James Fenimore Cooper: His Country and His Art*. Papers from the Bicentennial Conference, July 1989, State University College of New York, Oneonta and Cooperstown. Ed. George A. Test. 162–171. 15 Dec. 2004. <http://www.oneonta.edu/external/cooper/articles/suny/1989suny-ringe.html>.

———. *James Fenimore Cooper*. Boston: Twayne, 1988.

———. *The Pictorial Mode: Space and Time in the Art of Bryant, Irving, and Cooper*. Lexington: UP of Kentucky, 1971.

Thorp, Willard. "Cooper Beyond America." *James Fenimore Cooper: A Re-Appraisal*. Ed. Mary E. Cunningham. 154–171.

Walker, Warren S. *James Fenimore Cooper: An Introduction and Interpretation.* New York: Barnes and Noble, 1962.

Wallace, James D. *Early Cooper and His Audience.* New York: Columbia UP, 1986.

Winters, Yvor. "Fenimore Cooper or The Ruins of Time." *In Defense of Reason.* Denver: U of Denver P, 1947. 176–99.

Zhang, Aiping. "James Fenimore Cooper: A Rediscovered American Writer in China." *James Fenimore Cooper Society Miscellaneous Papers* 14 (August 2001): 10–16. 30 Jan. 2005 <http://www.oneonta.edu/external/cooper/articles/ala/2001ala-zhang.html>.

Collections of Essays on Cooper and His Works

Clark, Robert, ed. *James Fenimore Cooper: New Critical Essays.* London: Vision, 1985.

Cunningham, Mary E., ed. *James Fenimore Cooper: A Re-Appraisal.* Cooperstown, NY: New York State Historical Association, 1954.

Dekker, George, and John P. McWilliams. *Fenimore Cooper: The Critical Heritage.* London: Routledge and Kegan Paul, 1973.

Fields, Wayne, ed. *James Fenimore Cooper: A Collection of Critical Essays.* Englewood Cliffs, NJ: Prentice-Hall, 1979.

Verhoeven, W. M., ed. *James Fenimore Cooper: New Historical and Literary Contexts.* Amsterdam: Rodopi, 1993.

The Spy: A Tale of the Neutral Ground (1821)

Contemporary Reviews

Edgeworth, "Letter to 'an American Lady.'" *Port Folio* 16 (1823): 86. Excerpted in Dekker and McWilliams, *Fenimore Cooper: The Critical Heritage,* 67–68.

Gardiner, W. H. Rev. of *The Spy. North American Review* 15.26 (July 1822): 250–82. Excerpted in Dekker and McWilliams, *Fenimore Cooper: The Critical Heritage,* 55–66.

Criticism

Beard, James Franklin. "Cooper and the Revolutionary Mythos." *Early American Literature* 16 (1976): 84–104.

Cawelti, John G., and Bruce A. Rosenberg. *The Spy Story.* Chicago: U of Chicago P, 1987.

Cooper, James Fenimore. Introduction [1831]. *The Spy: A Tale of the Neutral Ground.* Ed. James P. Elliott, Lance Schachterle, and Jeffrey Walker. New York: AMS, 2000. 12–16.

———. Introduction [1849]. *The Spy.* Ed. Elliott, Schachterle, and Walker. 17–21.

———. Preface to the Second Edition [1822]. *The Spy.* Ed. Elliott, Schachterle, and Walker. 6–7.

———. Preface to the Third Edition [1822]. *The Spy.* Ed. Elliott, Schachterle, and Walker. 9–11.

———. "To James Aitchison" [1821]. *The Spy.* Ed. Elliott, Schachterle, and Walker. 1.

Crawford, T. Hugh. "Cooper's *Spy* and the Theater of Honor." *American Literature* 63.3 (1991): 405–19.

Dekker, George. "James Fenimore Cooper and the American Romance Tradition." *James Fenimore Cooper: New Historical and Literary Contexts.* Ed. W. M. Verhoeven. Amsterdam: Rodopi, 1993. 19–29.

Elliott, James P. Historical Introduction. *The Spy: A Tale of The Neutral Ground.* Ed. James P. Elliott, Lance Schachterle, and Jeffrey Walker. New York: AMS, 2002. xiii-xxxv.

Fink, Robert A. "Harvey Birch: The Yankee Peddler as an American Hero." *New York Folklore Quarterly* 30 (1947): 149.

Harris, Edward. "Cooper on Stage." James Fenimore Cooper Society Web page. 1 Feb. 2005. <http://www.oneonta.edu/~cooper/drama/stage.html>.

Lee, A. Robert. "Making History, Making Fiction: Cooper's *The Spy.*" Verhoeven, 31–45.

McTiernan, Dave. "The Novel as 'Neutral Ground': Genre and Ideology in Cooper's The Spy." *Studies in American Fiction* 25.1 (1997): 3–21.

Ringe, Donald. "The American Revolution in American Romance." *American Literature* 49 (1977): 352–65.

Rosenberg, Bruce A. *The Neutral Ground: The Andre Affair and the Background of Cooper's The Spy.* Westport, CT: Greenwood, 1994.

Schachterle, Lance. "Cooper's *Spy* and the Possibility of American Fiction." *Studies in the Humanities* 18.2 (1991): 180–99.

St. Armand, Barton Levi. "Harvey Birch as the Wandering Jew: Literary Calvinism in James Fenimore Cooper's *The Spy.*" *American Literature* 50 (1978): 348–68.

Stafford, David. *The Silent Game: The Real World of Imaginary Spies.* Athens, GA: U of Georgia P, 1992.

Verhoeven, W. M. "Neutralizing the Land: The Myth of Authority and the Authority of Myth in Fenimore Cooper's *The Spy.*" *James Fenimore Cooper: New Historical and Literary Contexts.* Ed. W. M. Verhoeven. Amsterdam: Rodopi, 1993. 71–87.

Wallace, James D. "Cultivating an Audience: From *Precaution* to *The Spy*." Clark, 38–54.

The Leather-Stocking Tales

Axelrad, Allan M. "Wish Fulfillment in the Wilderness: D. H. Lawrence and the Leatherstocking Tales." *American Quarterly* 39 (1987): 563–85.

Baym, Nina. "The Women of Cooper's Leatherstocking Tales." *American Quarterly* 23 (1971): 696–709.

Cawelti, John G. *Adventure, Mystery, and Romance: Formula Stories as Art and Popular Culture*. Chicago: U of Chicago P, 1976.

Fiedler, Leslie. *Love and Death in the American Novel*. New York: Criterion, 1960.

Frederick, John T. "Cooper's Eloquent Indians." *PMLA* 71 (1956): 1004–1017.

Kelly, William P. *Plotting America's Past: Fenimore Cooper and the Leatherstocking Tales*. Carbondale: Southern Illinois UP, 1983.

Kolodny, Annette. *The Lay of the Land: Metaphor as Experience and History in American Life and Letters*. Chapel Hill: U of North Carolina P, 1976.

Lawrence, D. H. "Fenimore Cooper's Leatherstocking Novels." *Studies in Classic American Literature*. 1923.

Martin, Terence. "Beginnings and Endings in the Leatherstocking Tales." *Nineteenth-Century Fiction* 33 (June 1978): 69–87.

Nevins, Allan. Preface and Introduction. *The Leatherstocking Saga*. Ed. Nevins. New York: Pantheon, 1954.

Pearce, Roy Harvey. "Civilization and Savagism: the World of the Leatherstocking Tales." *English Institute Essays 1949*. Ed. Alan S. Downer. 1950. New York: AMS, 1965. 92–116.

———. "The Leatherstocking Tales Reexamined." *South Atlantic Quarterly* 46 (1947): 524–36.

———. "The Metaphysics of Indian-Hating: Leatherstocking Unmasked." *Historicism Once More: Problems and Occasions for the American Scholar*. Princeton, NJ: Princeton UP, 1969. 109–136.

Rans, Geoffrey. *Cooper's Leather-Stocking Novels: A Secular Reading*. Chapel Hill: U of North Carolina P, 1991.

Slotkin, Richard. *Regeneration through Violence: The Mythology of the American Frontier, 1600–1860*. 1973. New York: HarperPerennial, 1996.

Smith, Henry Nash. *Virgin Land: The American West as Symbol and Myth*. New York: Vintage, 1950.

Starna, William J. "Cooper's Indians: A Critique." In *James Fenimore Cooper: His Country and His Art*. Papers from the 1979 Conference at State University College of New York, Oneonta and Cooperstown. Ed. George A. Test. 63–76. Available on James Fenimore Cooper Society Webpage at <http://www.oneonta.edu/~cooper/articles/suny/1979 suny-starna.html>.

Smith, Henry Nash. "Consciousness and Social Order: The Theme of Transcendence in the Leatherstocking Tales." *Western American Literature* 5 (1970): 177–94.

Twain, Mark. "Fenimore Cooper's Literary Offenses." *North American Literary Review* 156 (July 1895): 1–12.

Zoellner, Robert. "Conceptual Ambivalence in Cooper's Leatherstocking." *American Literature* 31 (Jan. 1960): 397–420.

The Pioneers: or The Sources of the Susquehanna: A Descriptive Tale (1823)

Contemporary Reviews

[Anonymous]. Review. *Port Folio* 15 (March 1823): 230–48. Excerpted in Dekker and McWilliams, *Fenimore Cooper: The Critical Heritage*. London: Routledge and Kegan Paul, 1973. 69–72.

[Anonymous]. "American Novels." *British Critic* 2 (July 1826): 437. Excerpted in Dekker and McWilliams. 73.

Criticism

Bower, Anne L. "Resisting Women: 'Feminist' Students and Cooper's *The Pioneers*, with a few Thoughts Concerning Pedagogical Approaches to *The Prairie*." *James Fenimore Cooper: His Country and His Art*. Papers from the 2001 Cooper Seminar (No. 13). Ed. Hugh C. MacDougall. The State University of New York College at Oneonta. Oneonta, New York. 17–20. 15 July 2005. <http://www.oneonta.edu/external/cooper/articles/suny/2001suny-bower.html>.

Jones, Daryl E. "Temple in the Promised Land: Old Testament Parallel in Cooper's *the Pioneers*." *American Literature* 57 (March 1985): 68–78.

Person, Leland S., Jr. "Cooper's *The Pioneers* and Leatherstocking's Historical Function." *ESQ* 25 (1979): 1–10.

Philbrick, Thomas. "Cooper's *The Pioneers*: Origins and Structure." *PMLA* 79 (1964): 579–93.

Pickering, James H. "Cooper's Otsego Heritage: The Sources of The Pioneers." *James Fenimore Cooper: His Country and His Art*. Papers from the 1979 Conference at State University College of New York, Oneonta and Cooperstown. Ed. George A. Test. 11–39. 19 May 2005. <http://www.oneonta.edu/external/cooper/articles/suny/1979suny-pickering.html>.

Robinson, E. Arthur. "Conservation in Cooper's *the Pioneers*." *PMLA* 82 (1967): 564–78.

Taylor, Alan. "Fenimore Cooper's America." *History Today*. 46.2 (1996): 21–27. 12 Feb. 2006. <http://www.historytoday.com>.

Thomas, Brook. "*The Pioneers*, or the Sources of American Legal History: A Critical Tale." *American Quarterly* 36 (1984): 86–111.

Valenti, Peter. "'The Ordering of God's Providence': Law and Landscape in *The Pioneers*." *Studies in American Fiction* 7 (1979): 191–207.

The Last of the Mohicans: A Narrative of 1757 (1826)

Contemporary Reviews

[Anonymous]. "The Last American Novel." *London Magazine* n.s. 16 (May 1826): 27–31. Excerpted in Dekker and McWilliams, *Fenimore Cooper: The Critical Heritage*, 83–88.

[Anonymous]. Review. *New-York Review and Athaneum* 2 (March 1826): 285–92. Excerpted in Dekker and McWilliams, *Fenimore Cooper: The Critical Heritage*, 89–96.

[Anonymous]. Review. *United States Literary Gazette* 4 (May 1826): 97–103. Excerpted in Dekker and McWilliams, *Fenimore Cooper: The Critical Heritage*, 89–96.

Gardiner, W. H. Review. *North American Review* 23 (July 1826): 150–97. Excerpted in Dekker and McWilliams, *Fenimore Cooper: The Critical Heritage*, 104–118.

Criticism

Allen, Dennis W. "By All the Truth of Signs: James Fenimore Cooper's The Last of the Mohicans." *Studies in American Fiction* 9.2 (1981): 159–79.

Alpern, Will J. "Indians, Sources, Critics." *James Fenimore Cooper: His Country and His Art*. Papers from the 1984 Conference at State University of New York College, Oneonta and Cooperstown. Ed. George A. Test. 1985. 25–33. 10 Oct. 2005. <http://www.oneonta.edu/~cooper/articles/suny/1984suny-alpern.html>.

Blakemore, Steven. "Strange Tongues: Cooper's Fiction of Language in The Last of the Mohicans." *Early American Literature* 19.1 (1984): 21–41.

———. "'Without a Cross': The Cultural Significance of the Sublime and Beautiful in Cooper's *The Last of the Mohicans*." *Nineteenth-Century Literature* 52.1 (1997): 27–58.

Butler, M. D. "Narrative Structure and Historical Process in *The Last of the Mohicans*." *American Literature* 48 (1976): 117–39.

Darnell, Donald. "Uncas as Hero: The Ubi Sunt Formula in The Last of the Mohicans." *American Literature* 37 (1965): 259–66.

"The Delaware." Access Genealogy Indian Tribal Records. 15 January 2006. <http://www.accessgenealogy.com/native/kansas/kansaskansans/page22.htm>.

Haberly, D. T. "Women and Indians: *The Last of the Mohicans* and the Captivity Tradition." *American Quarterly* 28 (1976): 431–43.

Martin, Terence. "From the Ruins of History: The Last of the Mohicans." *Novel: A Forum on Fiction* II (1969): 221–29.

McWilliams, John. *The Last of the Mohicans: Civil Savagery and Savage Civility.* New York: Twayne, 1995.

"Mohegan History." Revised 14 July 1997. *First Nations/First Peoples* Web page. Ed. Jordan Dill. 22 May 2006. <http://www.dickshovel.com/moh.html>.

Native American Myths: Creation by Women. 15 Jan. 2006. <http://www.crystalinks .com/namcreationwomen.html>.

Philbrick, Thomas. "The Sources of Cooper's Knowledge of Fort William Henry." *American Literature* 36 (1964): 209–214.

———. "*The Last of the Mohicans* and the Sounds of Discord." *American Literature* 43 (1971): 25–41.

Sundahl, Daniel J. "Details and Defects: Historical Peculiarities in *The Last of the Mohicans.*" *The Rackham Journal of the Arts and Humanities* (1986): 33–46.

Tompkins, Jane. "No Apologies for the Iroquois: A New Way to Read the Leatherstocking Novels." *Sensational Designs: The Cultural Work of American Fiction, 1790–1860.* New York: Oxford UP, 1985. 94–121.

Walker, Jeffrey. "Deconstructing an American Myth: Hollywood and The Last of the Mohicans." *James Fenimore Cooper: His Country and His Art* 10. 1 Oct 2005. Ed. Hugh C. MacDougall. State University of New York College at Oneonta. 77–84. <http://www.oneonta.edu/external/cooper/articles/ suny/1995suny-walker.html>.

The Prairie: A Tale (1827)

Contemporary Reviews

[Anonymous]. "Tales of Indian Life." *Colburn's New Monthly Magazine* 20 (1827): 79–82. Excerpted in Dekker and McWilliams, *Fenimore Cooper: The Critical Heritage*, 120–24.

Sealsfield, Charles. [Karl Postl]. "The Works of the Author of *The Spy.*" *New-York Mirror* 8 (1831): 252–54. Excerpted in Dekker and McWilliams, *Fenimore Cooper: The Critical Heritage*, 165–66.

Criticism

Brotherstone, Gordon. "*The Prairie* and Cooper's Invention of the West." *James Fenimore Cooper: New Critical Essays.* Ed. Robert Clark. London: Vision, 1985. 162–86.

Fields, Wayne. "Beyond Definition: A Reading of *The Prairie.*" *James Fenimore Cooper: A Collection of Critical Essays.* Ed. Fields. Englewood Cliffs, NJ: Prentice-Hall, 1979. 93–111.

Flanagan, John T. "The Authenticity of Cooper's *The Prairie.*" *Modern Language Quarterly* 2 (1941): 99–104.

Goetzmann, William H. "James Fenimore Cooper: *The Prairie.*" *Landmarks of American Writing.* Ed. Hennig Cohen. New York: Basic, 1969. 66–78.

Muszynska-Wallace, E. Soteris. "The Sources of *The Prairie*." *American Literature* 21 (1949): 191–200.

Ringe, Donald A. "Man and Nature in Cooper's *The Prairie*." *Nineteenth-Century Fiction* 15.4 (1961): 313–23.

Rucker, Mary E. "Natural, Tribal, and Civil Law in Cooper's *The Prairie*." *Western American Literature* 12 (1977): 215–22.

Sawaya, Francesca. "Between Revolution and Racism: Colonialism and the American Indian in *The Prairie*." James Fenimore Cooper: His Country and His Art. Papers from the Bicentennial Conference, July 1989, State University College of New York, Oneonta and Cooperstown. Ed. George A. Test. 1991. 126–34. 7 Nov. 2005. <http://www.oneonta.edu/~cooper/articles/suny/1989suny-sawaya.html>.

Vance, William L. "'Man and Beast': The Meaning of Cooper's *The Prairie*." *PMLA* 89.2 (1974): 323–31.

The Pathfinder: or, The Inland Sea (1840)

Contemporary Reviews

Belinsky, V. G. Review. *Notes of the Fatherland* 14 (1841): 8–9. Excerpted in Dekker and McWilliams, *Fenimore Cooper: The Critical Heritage*, 191–93.

———. "The Division of Poetry into Kinds and Genres." *Notes of the Fatherland* 15 (1841): 13–64. Excerpted in Dekker and McWilliams, *Fenimore Cooper: The Critical Heritage*, 193–95.

Balzac, Honore de. Review. *Paris Review* (25 July 1840). Trans. K. P. Wormeley, 1899. Excerpted in Dekker and McWilliams, *Fenimore Cooper: The Critical Heritage*, 196–200.

Criticism

Blakemore, Steven. "Language and World in *The Pathfinder*." *Modern Language Studies* 16 (1986): 237–46.

Bowden, Mary Weatherspoon. "Mabel and Dew-of-June: Female Friendship in *The Pathfinder*." *South Central Bulletin* 40 (1980): 136–37.

Bush, Sargent, Jr. "Charles Cap of *The Pathfinder*: A Foil to Cooper's Views on the American Character in the 1840's." *Nineteenth-Century Fiction* 20.3 (1965): 267–73.

DeFalco, Joseph M. "Burke's Ocean and Cooper's Forests: The Americanization of the Sublime." *Topic: A Journal of the Liberal Arts* 50 (2000): 48–58.

Owen, William. "In War as in Love: The Significance of Analogous Plots in Cooper's *The Pathfinder*." *English Studies in Canada* 10 (1984): 289–98.

Rosenzweig, Paul. "*The Pathfinder*: The Wilderness Initiation of Mabel Dunham." *Modern Language Quarterly* 44 (1983): 339–58.

Rust, Richard D. "On the Trail of a Craftsman: The Art of *The Pathfinder*." *James Fenimore Cooper: New Historical and Literary Contexts*. Ed. W. M. Verhoeven. Amsterdam: Rodopi, 1993. 177–84.

Swearingen, James E., and Joanna Cutting-Gray. "Cooper's *Pathfinder*: Revising Historical Understanding." *New Literary History* 23.2 (1992): 267–80.

The Deerslayer: or The First War-Path (1841)

Contemporary Reviews

[Anonymous]. Review. *New-York Mirror* 19 (September 1841): 295. Excerpted in Dekker and McWilliams, *Fenimore Cooper: The Critical Heritage*, 205–6.

Criticism

Darnell, Donald. "*The Deerslayer*: Cooper's Tragedy of Manners." *Studies in the Novel* 11.4 (1979): 406–15.

Liu, Celestine W. "Judith Hunter's Stunted Growth in James Fenimore Cooper's *The Deerslayer*." *Midwest Quarterly* 37.4 (1996): 422–33.

Nevins, Allan. Afterword. 1963. *The Deerslayer*. By James Fenimore Cooper. New York: Signet Classic, 1980. 535–41.

Person, Leland S., Jr. "Cooper's Queen of the Woods: Judith Hutter in *The Deerslayer*." *Studies in the Novel* 21.3 (1989): 253–67.

———. "The Historical Paradoxes of Manhood in Cooper's *The Deerslayer*." *Novel* 32.1 (1998): 76–99.

Sandy, Alan F., Jr. "The Voices of Cooper's *The Deerslayer*." *ESQ: A Journal of the American Renaissance* 60 (1970): 5–9.

Schachterle, Lance, and Kurt Ljungquist. "Fenimore Cooper's Literary Defenses: Twain and the Text of *The Deerslayer*." *Studies in the American Renaissance* (1998): 401–17. 1 Aug 2005. <http://www.oneonta.edu/external/cooper/articles/other/1988other-schachterle.html>.

Selley, April. "'I Have Been, and Ever Shall Be, Your Friend': *Star Trek, The Deerslayer* and the American Romance." *Journal of Popular Culture*. 20.1 (1986): 89–104.

Vanderbeets, Richard. "Cooper and the 'Semblance of Reality': A Source for *The Deerslayer*." *American Literature* 42.4 (1971): 544–46.

Additional Works Cited in this Companion

Bakhtin, M. M. *The Dialogic Imagination: Four Essays*. Ed. Michael Holquist. Trans. Caryl Emerson and Holquist. Austin: U of Texas P, 1981.

Barthes, Roland. "The Death of the Author." *Image, Music, Text*. Trans. Stephen Heath. New York: Hill and Wang, 1978. 142–48.

Burroughs, Edgar Rice. *A Princess of Mars*. 1912. New York: Del Rey / Ballantine, 1963.

Conrad, Joseph. "Tales of the Sea." *Outlook* (4 June 1898). In Dekker and McWilliams, *Fenimore Cooper: The Critical Heritage*, 287–88.

Cooper, Susan Fenimore. *Rural Hours*. 1850. Ed. Rochelle Johnson and Daniel Patterson. Athens: U of Georgia P, 1998.

"Cooperstown, New York: America's Village." 10 Jan. 2005. <http://www.baseballhalloffame.org/news/download/americas_village.PDF>.

Eliot, T. S. "Hamlet and his Problems." 1919. *The Sacred Wood: Essays on Poetry and Criticism*. By Eliot. London: Faber and Faber, 1922.

Foucault, Michel. "What is an Author?" *Language, Counter-Memory, Practice*. Trans. D. F. Bouchard and S. Simon. Ed. Bouchard. Ithaca, NY: Cornell UP, 1977.

Gibbeman, Susan. "Gene Roddenberry." *Museum of Broadcast Communications*. 20 May 2006. <http://www.museum.tv/archives/etv/R/htmlR/Roddenberry/Roddenberry.htm>.

Gilligan, Carol. *In a Different Voice: Psychological Theory and Women's Development*. Cambridge, MA: Harvard UP, 1982.

Glotfelty, Cheryl, and Harold Fromm. Introduction. *The Ecocriticism Reader: Landmarks in Literary Ecology*. Ed. Glotfelty and Fromm. Athens: U of Georgia P, 1996.

McCarthy, Mary. "Eugene O'Neill—Dry Ice." *A Bolt from the Blue and Other Essays*. Ed. A. O. Scott. New York: New York Review Books, 2002. 31–37.

Penn Library Exhibitions. "Robert Montgomery Bird: Writer and Artist." 15 Feb. 2005. <http://www.library.upenn.edu/exhibits/rbm/bird/case6.html>.

Poe, Edgar Allan. Review. *Graham's Magazine* 24 (November 1843): 261–64. Excerpted in Dekker and McWilliams, *Fenimore Cooper: The Critical Heritage*, 207–17.

Reagan, Ronald. Address to National Prayer Breakfast, 4 February 1982. "Ronald Reagan—Timeless Quotes." 15 Mar. 2005. <http://www.coralridge.org/specialdocs/RonaldReaganQuotes.htm>.

[Saint-Beuve]. F.A.S. "Paris *Globe* reviews Cooper." Excerpted in Dekker and McWilliams, *Fenimore Cooper: The Critical Heritage*, 125–38.

Sand, George. "George Sand on Cooper." Excerpted in Dekker and McWilliams, *Fenimore Cooper: The Critical Heritage*, 261–69.

See, Fred G. "'Writing so as not to die': Edgar Rice Burroughs and the West Beyond the West." *Melus* 11.4 (1984): 59–72.

Smith, Sidney. "Who Reads an American Book?" *Edinburgh Review* (January 1820). Legacy Preservation Library. 10 Jan. 2005. <http://www.usgennet.org/usa/topic/preservation/epochs/vol5/pg144.htm>.

Todorov, Tzvetan. *The Conquest of America: The Question of the Other*. 1982. Trans. Richard Howard. New York: Harper and Row, 1984.

Index

About the Author

CRAIG WHITE is an associate professor of literature at the University of Houston-Clear Lake, where he teaches classic and multicultural American and world literature. His articles on American literature, the history of science, and Native American literature have appeared in *Modern Language Quarterly*, *Prospects*, *Utopian Studies*, and *Early American Literature*.